Jazz Tales from Jazz Legends:
Oral Histories from the Fillius Jazz Archive at Hamilton College

By Monk Rowe
with Romy Britell

Foreword by Dan Morgenstern

Richard W. Couper Press
2015

Hamilton

Published by
Richard W. Couper Press
Hamilton College Library
Clinton, N.Y.

Copyright 2015 Trustees of Hamilton College

All rights reserved. No part of this book may be reproduced in any form or by any electronic or mechanical means, including information storage and retrieval systems, without permission in writing from the publisher, except by a reviewer, who may quote brief passages in a review.

Printed at Merlin International, Rochester, N.Y.

Cover designed by Marianita Peaslee

ISBN 978-1-937370-17-6

Contents

Foreword	9
Preface	11
Chapter 1. Basie's Number One Son	15
Chapter 2. Sidemen Stories	24
Chapter 3. Road Travails	55
Chapter 4. Arranging the Notes	68
Picture Gallery	87
Chapter 5. Inside the Studio	96
Chapter 6. The Color of Jazz	113
Chapter 7. Thoughts on Improvisation	126
Chapter 8. Motivation and Inspiration	144
Chapter 9. Potpourri	162
Notes	184
Glossary	191
Honorary Degree Recipients	194
Interviews by Category	195
Index	200
Acknowledgements	207
About the author	209

Foreword

When I first became seriously interested in jazz about seventy years ago, there was only a handful, literally, of books on the subject. Most dealt with recordings as the key to the still quite young music's history. Only two were in the words of musicians: Louis Armstrong's *Swing That Music* and Benny Goodman's *The Kingdom of Swing*. Though heavily ghosted, both included moments when the subjects' authentic voices could be heard. And in perhaps the best of the early books, *Jazzmen* (1939), the most touching pages were those quoting from letters written by Louis's mentor, King Oliver, in his declining years to friends and relatives.

A decade after my initiation, in 1955, two good friends first-named Nat—Hentoff and Shapiro—published *Hear Me Talkin' To Ya*, a title taken from one of the canonic Armstrong Hot Five and Seven recordings. Subtitled *The Story of Jazz as Told by the Men Who Made It*, the book was cleverly put together from direct quotes taken from a wide variety of printed sources. They add up to a most authentic history, a far better source than the mostly tendentious works favoring progressive or traditional views of the music.

At the time, what is now called oral history was still in its infancy, furthered by the rapidly improving technology of portable recording devices, which made for much higher standards for accurate reproduction of speech than even the best rapid note-taking. (Few students of jazz mastered stenography.) And eventually, a visual dimension was added, making it possible to create true portraits of the artists interviewed.

I vividly recall Monk Rowe's first visit to the Institute of Jazz Studies at Rutgers-Newark, armed with the first in what has become a wonderful series of interviews with jazz notables. This was with Joe Williams, not only a great singer but also a great human being, who, as Monk tells us in his Preface, was hands-on helpful in launching the Fillius Jazz Archive Oral History Collection. It was a terrific launch, and made me envious, since the Institute's earlier Jazz Oral History Project, sponsored by the National Endowment for the Arts' jazz program and focused on elder musicians, lacked a visual dimension, as do the Smithsonian Institution's additions.

Now numbering more than three hundred, the Fillius interviews are special, as the reader will soon discover. Having had the pleasure of visiting Hamilton and being honored with an interview, I can reveal that the secrets of the project's success include the relaxed atmosphere and the skill of the interviewer, himself a musician. This is of primary importance, for it ensures that the questions asked have a focus and relevance not always found in such interviews. And when the interviewer is not only a fellow musician but also a historian, it is no wonder that the results are of more than passing interest, and often entertaining as well as informative.

Considering the Joe Williams connection, it's no surprise that there is a large Basie contingent. The two Franks, Foster and Wess; trumpeters Sweets Edison, Joe Wilder, and Snooky Young; trombonists Al Grey, Benny Powell, and Bill Hughes; saxophonist John Williams; bassist Jimmy Lewis; and drummer Butch Miles cover quite a spectrum—and not one has a bad word to say about the Count.

Clark Terry of course has things to say about Duke Ellington, as do Louis Bellson and John Lamb, and on the subject of bandleaders, there is Lionel Hampton himself, and Jay McShann. Benny Goodman alumni include Eddie Bert and Jerry Jerome, and there are pianists galore: Dick Hyman, Derek Smith, Bill Charlap, Richard Wyands, Denny Zeitlin, and Marian McPartland among them; and speaking of distaff, the ladies include Ruth Brown, Maria Schneider, Iola Brubeck, Jean Bach, and Helen Dance—the latter two representative of the non-musicians included, as are producers Joel Dorn and Orrin Keepnews. This is just a partial listing of all those interviewed, so be prepared for some surprises.

This book is organized by topics, not instruments, which makes a great deal of sense. Much of interest is said about such matters as improvisation and arranging, as well as about being on the road and in the recording studio, which reflects the perspective of the musicians. The chapter called "The Color of Jazz" is, alas, still highly topical and includes a harrowing tale told by Clark Terry, in the inimitable way of that marvelously resilient and eternally optimistic man, who—like too many of the great people captured here—is no longer with us. But thanks to the Hamilton team, their voices and thoughts have been captured for posterity. And while unseen here, their visage as well.

We are most grateful to all involved for this invaluable gift.

Dan Morgenstern
Director Emeritus, The Institute of Jazz Studies at Rutgers-Newark
2007 National Endowment for the Arts Jazz Master

Preface

In May 1991, two jazz legends shared life stories over dinner in Clinton, New York. They reflected on memorable moments of their lengthy careers—the highs and the lows, the amusing and the life-changing events. Absorbing this jazz history was Milt Fillius Jr., Hamilton College life trustee, a member of the class of 1944. Milt Fillius was no stranger to these two musicians, and in fact had arranged for this dinner to occur. His longtime friend Joe Williams had received the first honorary degree bestowed upon a jazz musician from Hamilton College in May 1988, and Milt Hinton was the second musician to be so honored. Joe Williams showed his respect to both Milts by clearing his calendar for the weekend so he could take part in honoring "The Judge," as Milt Hinton was known.

Left to right: Milt Fillius Jr., Milt Hinton, Joe Williams. Hamilton College Commencement, May 19, 1991. (Fillius Jazz Archive)

Hamilton College is a small liberal arts school perched atop a hill in Clinton, New York. It is one of the oldest colleges in the country, celebrating its 200th anniversary in 2012. Over the years Hamilton has hosted numerous well-known jazz artists and sent out graduates into the world with refined taste in music and the arts. Milt Fillius Jr. was a member of what the college fondly calls "the crazy mixed-up years," consisting of young men whose college experience was interrupted by World War II. After serving as a submarine officer in the South Pacific, Milt returned to Hamilton to complete his undergraduate degree. The graduates of that generation shared a lifelong loyalty to the college.

As an amateur drummer and swing band fan, Milt Fillius became enamored of the musicians who played the music he loved. Milt was astute enough to recognize the limits of his own musical talents, and successfully made a living in the business world. He settled far away from Hamilton, in San Diego, but continued his close ties with the college. Milt was a faithful attendee at jazz parties across the country, and became a patron of the music in the old-fashioned sense of the word. He established the annual Fallcoming jazz event at the college in 1993, hosted in the building that bears his name, the Fillius Events Barn. Since Joe Williams and Milt Hinton, eleven other jazz musicians have been awarded honorary degrees from Hamilton, an initiative started by Mr. Fillius (see Appendix).

Most importantly, as he listened to Milt Hinton and Joe Williams trade stories about their experiences, Milt Fillius realized that this kind of conversation needed to be captured. He sensed an urgent need for such an effort, as he observed his favorite musicians passing on at an alarming rate. Such endeavors rarely happen in the timeframe desired, but with the assistance of the Joseph Drown Foundation of Los Angeles, the Jazz Oral History Project, now called the Fillius Jazz Archive at Hamilton College, was launched in 1995. Joe Williams lent his reputation and support to the effort, and conducted early interviews with Clark Terry, George Shearing, Milt Hinton, and Oscar Peterson.

At the time I was an adjunct instructor in saxophone in the Music Department at Hamilton and a working musician. My life changed when I was offered the opportunity to be the primary interviewer, and to make Milt's idea come to fruition. We met with our interviewees at jazz parties and festivals, and in major cities across the country. With the blessing of Joe Williams and his early participation in the interview process, our list of interviewees grew at a rapid rate, and to date we have conducted videotaped sessions with over 325 jazz personalities. While our concentration was first focused on Basie alums and associates of Joe Williams, our interviews did not carry a specific agenda. I feel that a musician's character and experiences are of equal importance to the music they produce, and this belief guided my questions. Specific themes and subjects that presented themselves during the interviews will be found in this book. The excerpts are presented with only minor edits for readability. No words or concepts were inserted or modified.

I grew up in an era when jazz was only beginning to be embraced by academia, and the bulk of my jazz education came through reading liner notes on my LPs. The path of sidemen through various big bands and the names of the rhythm section players who backed up my favorite soloists provided the education I desired. While I was challenged to memorize the Periodic Table of the Elements or algebraic equations, my retention of these liner notes would prove valuable during these interview sessions. Musicians can sense when an interviewer knows something about their accomplishments, and a meaningful dialogue is likely to ensue.

Certain interviewees have described the moment when their dream was realized—when their skill, experience, circumstance, and luck came together. My position as Jazz Archive director is a dream gig that has allowed me to vicariously experience the life stories of these jazz artists, both the famous and the unsung.

Our oral history project is ongoing, and all proceeds from the sale of this book will be used to support the mission of the Fillius Jazz Archive.

Monk Rowe
The Joe Williams Director of the Fillius Jazz Archive
Summer 2015

Chapter 1
Basie's Number One Son

Joe Williams and the Count Basie Orchestra, Wellin Hall, Hamilton College, September 7, 1996. (Fillius Jazz Archive)

Joe Williams and the Count Basie Orchestra performed to a standing room only audience at Hamilton College on September 7, 1996. As the cameras rolled, the Count Basie Orchestra swung into the intro to the Joe Williams signature song, "Every Day I Have the Blues." Joe Williams sat comfortably in the green room down the hall, waiting for his introduction by Basie band leader Grover Mitchell. This would be the highlight of the concert documentary *A Portrait in Song*,[1] a film on the life of Joe Williams commissioned by the Fillius Jazz Archive and under the creative control of filmmaker Burrill Crohn. Burrill and I had both agreed that capturing this moment was crucial.

Jazz Tales from Jazz Legends

I know this introduction well: six measures of piano set up four bars with the band, two 12-bar choruses from the full ensemble, and another eight bars of muted trumpet licks set up the first verse. This is the full 1:30 of introduction penned by saxophonist Ernie Wilkins for the 1955 LP "Count Basie Swings, Joe Williams Sings." It is the one song most associated with Joe Williams.

The first ten bars went by and Joe sat in the dressing room. The next twelve bars were ably played by this 1996 version of the Basie orchestra, and Joe continued to sit in the dressing room, as I paced. Did I need to remind Joe that the moment was coming up? The next twelve bars were now history, and I bit my tongue. Finally, a scant eight bars before his introduction ended, Joe rose from his seat and strode to the edge of the stage, and at the exact moment of Grover's introduction, made his dramatic entrance. Burrill and I both breathed the same sigh of relief. The concert was underway. But Joe was not done with the unexpected. After delivering the first two verses of "Every Day I Have the Blues," he introduced Chris Murrell, the then current Basie band singer. What could he be thinking? After all the logistics, the planning and the expense, Joe is welcoming a different singer in his signature song? He explained himself after the fact:

JW: Yes, things that are very, very good you should share, I think. I was very young, about sixteen or seventeen, and I was sitting in a night club and some people were performing. And I happened to be sitting with the guy that ran the place, and I said, "I can sing better than that." And he said to me, "You sit here and pay attention." And I vowed within myself then that if I ever found someone that wanted that microphone as badly as I wanted it then, I would share it with them. My manager, John Levy, used to give me hell about it. "Because," he says, "you share your space and your time with the musicians and everything. You'll have people say 'wow' and then you say 'put the spotlight on somebody else.'" He said, "Then you have to go back and grab them again." Well, I feel as though I can.[2]

A Portrait in Song became one of the highlights of our relationship with Joe Williams, and has been screened to great acclaim at jazz education conferences, colleges, and other arts venues.

It's safe to say that Joe Williams was larger than life. Not only was he tall and imposing, but he had an aura about him that was unmistakable and powerful. It made sense that he was a singer. It's hard to picture a man like him being in the background or in a supportive role, and even though he was a professional who constantly acknowledged his accompanists, there's no doubt he was the focal point when he performed.

Many of Joe's bandmates over the years spoke about him in respectful terms. They often said, "Oh, he's a musician," a high compliment for a singer. Singers likely bristle at making this distinction, for of course they think of themselves as musicians. So what makes a singer a "musician," and respected by instrumentalists? They respect a singer who has first done the basic homework, has their own songs prepared, knows the lyrics, know their keys, and are hip to the etiquette of performing with other musicians. They know that intros are usually eight bars, or could be the last A section of an A-A-B-A song, or they know when to listen for their cue. They are familiar with the format of singing a song one time through and being ready for soloists to take over. They know about reentering at the bridge and they can hear when the bridge is coming. They hear where they are in the song, even if they're not singing. The ability to scat helps move a singer into the musician category. Scatting requires another creative step, hearing the changes, finding new melodic lines and treating the voice like an instrument. Basie alums described Joe as a musician, like another instrument in the band.

Joe's tenure with the Basie orchestra lasted from 1954 until 1961, a small portion of his lengthy career. He had to distinguish himself from Basie's previous singer, "Mr. Five-By-Five," Jimmy Rushing, and did so by convincing the Count to let him try songs other than the standard blues fare.

JW: We went [to England] in 1957 and one of the critics stated, at the end of his obvious critique, that most of the applause was given to a young singer named Joe Williams, who is no Jimmy Rushing. I said, I certainly hope so. I wasn't trying to be Jimmy Rushing. That's why I fought Basie so hard. They asked me did I know anything of Jimmy Rushing and I told them no, I didn't. And I didn't really. It would have been simple for me to learn. I could learn his stuff in one night and perform it. But that was not the object of the exercise. I wasn't singing 1930s, 1940s, or even 1950 music. I was adding things that I wanted to present, and I'm glad it found favor not only with the musicians but with the audience as well. I had to fight to get [Basie] to do it, but I learned from it. He would sit, after we'd presented it and it was enthusiastically received by the public. Then he would look at me and he would nod approvingly. And I gleaned what he meant. If you believe in something strong enough, fight for it, even [with] those that are closest to you.[3]

Jazz Tales from Jazz Legends

Sidemen sometimes have ambivalent feelings about singers in the band, but trombonist Bill Hughes immediately recognized what Joe brought to the organization:

BH: I think when [Joe Williams] first joined this band he had performed with Basie's sextet somewhere before. Basie had heard him. I had never heard the guy until he came in, and when he came in I looked at him, pants were a little high, his wardrobe wasn't all that great, and I was saying I wonder why Basie's hiring this guy—until I heard him sing that night. Then I was saying I wonder what took him so long to hire this guy. Actually, I don't think the Basie band was about to survive as long as it has without Joe having been that catalyst back in 1954, especially after he recorded "Every Day" and "Alright, OK, You Win." Those were the two biggest, and then there was a ballad, "Teach Me Tonight." They were all hot tunes, man. I was young then, and I remember walking down the streets of New York and almost every record store you'd hear this sound coming out of it, and it would be Joe Williams singing these things. And I would be saying to myself wow, I'm part of this. The band was so hot, and Basie was so hot, and every night it was just a joy to go out and play this music.[4]

During our 2011 interview, Iola (Mrs. Dave) Brubeck recalled seeing Joe and the Basie band in 1956. The impression he made that day provided timely inspiration for what became "The Real Ambassadors," a Broadway version of a jazz show.

IB: I should have brought it up when we were talking about the idea for "The Real Ambassadors," because Joe Williams was a part of that. That summer I was in New York and I went to Central Park and Joe Williams was with the Basie band, and he was just so great. And the night before I had gone to a Broadway musical. And I said to myself Joe Williams said more and reached more emotionally with the Basie band that night than that big production I'd seen the night before. And that was one of the reasons why I started thinking in terms of a Broadway show.

MR: He was a big help to us getting this started.

IB: That's what I understand. Well, I loved Joe Williams. He was a wonderful, wonderful man. He was another example of a black man who, right at the height of the sort of division that was going on in jazz was not effected by that. And I can remember in Europe one time, Joe and some other musicians were sitting outside a hotel in the summertime, on a sort of patio, and our car pulled up and Dave and I got out of the van and Joe got up from where he was sitting with the other musicians and came over and they embraced, he gave Dave a hug and so forth. And it was just kind of a way of him saying "cool it, guys."[5]

Joe left the Basie family in 1961, just as Frank Sinatra had stepped off the Tommy Dorsey band bus. Trumpeter Sweets Edison provided an established small group that Joe joined, but soon he found that leading his own piano trio was the most effective setting for what he had to offer. Joe's wife Jillean spoke with Milt Fillius of the transition from Joe being a band singer to a solo act:

MF: Were there tough times when he broke loose on his own?
JW: Not professionally tough times, no. In fact I don't know any tough times. Basie saw him off. Basie came up and introduced him on his first single job, which was in Boston, and he went out for a while with Sweets in a group, Jerome Richardson and Sweets, and a wonderful group of musicians. And he always seemed to have work, we never had any bad years that I can remember. So I think he's done real well.[6]

Over the ensuing decades, his musicality, stage presence, and flexibility became part of his reputation. Norman Simmons, his longtime accompanist, described their relationship:

NS: Joe is the consummate professional, and I mean in consideration of the musicians and everything. Joe will cover for you if necessary, and Joe has his flexibility too. Whereas someone will request a song, and from the Club DeLisa thing, he's got that thing down. He don't mind. Just name a song and there's hardly a song he doesn't know, whatever it is. He'll turn around and say to me, "You know that song?" and I'll say, "What key do you do it in?" He'll say, "Whatever key you know it in." Joe's story is, hey, you go to a jam session, if you want to sing you sing in the key the musicians are playing in, and you don't go up there talking about here's my key, because you might not get a chance to sing. And Joe can find something to do wherever you put it. He's not uptight and he can hear very well, so he has the ability to cover for us at times. He also has a great gift of delivery to his people. When I first joined him, he would call a tune and could stand there and tell a story until I looked at the music and found out

Jazz Tales from Jazz Legends

Joe Williams promotional photo. (Fillius Jazz Archive, gift of Jillean Williams)

Basie's Number One Son

what it was. There would be no continuity loss in the show. He has a way of communicating that makes everyone feel like they're sitting in his living room when he's performing.[7]

Joe continued to hone his skills as a singer and entertainer in nightclubs, where jazz was still learned. In the winter of 1964, during a snowstorm in Providence, Rhode Island, Joe's work was caught on tape. This particular gig would become significant for the Fillius Jazz Archive.

Joe Williams passed away on March 29, 1999. A few months later, Milt Fillius and I were invited to his Las Vegas home by Joe's wife, Jillean. She graciously allowed us to take possession of some of Joe's memorabilia, music, and artifacts from his career. A drawer full of reel-to-reel tapes looked intriguing and proved to be a treasure of live gigs recorded over the years. I couldn't bear to think of this music remaining on a shelf, and eventually I found myself sitting with Joel Dorn and audio specialist Gene Paul, listening to selected tapes from the collection. I knew I had found the right producer in Joel when he leapt out of his seat and exclaimed, "Do you know what you've got here?" The music that most excited him was from that night in Providence, Rhode Island, in an almost-empty club in the middle of a snowstorm. Joe and his trio (pianist Junior Mance, bassist Bob Cranshaw, and drummer Mickey Roker) were surprised to be joined by none other than tenor saxophonist Ben Webster. How he happened to show up at Pio's in Providence that evening is a mystery, but a gift to us. Producer Joel Dorn explained what made him leap from his chair when this reel first rolled.

JD: Joe Williams and Ben Webster—no rehearsal, just playing. That's what it is. You don't plan magic. Magic happens. You capture magic.[8]

The ensuing CD, "Havin' a Good Time" was released on Joel Dorn's label, Hyena Records, in 2005. It captures a meeting of masters, created in the haze of nightclub smoke, with the accompaniment of clinking cocktail glasses and a smattering of applause. Fans of classic jazz gave the CD a thumbs up, and the upbeat reviews included these words from Nat Hentoff in the *Wall Street Journal*:

NH: Many of his recordings survive, but whenever I want to hear Joe again, this is the one I'll put on first.[9]

As Joe moved into the upper echelon of entertainers he found the business of music to be overwhelming. He was lucky to find a manager

Jazz Tales from Jazz Legends

who was a former musician. Bassist John Levy handled clients like Nancy Wilson and Cannonball Adderley, and spoke about Joe:

JL: He called me one day and said, "You know it's about time for you to take this telephone out of my ear." He said, "I'm tired of these people calling me. I don't know what they're talking about." He said, "You got it, whatever." And it's been that way ever since. And it's a family relationship. It's like we've been friends for years and I don't recall ever even having a contract with him. We just do it.[10]

Joe reunited frequently with the Count Basie Orchestra, even after Basie passed away in 1984. The band carried on with leadership by Thad Jones, Frank Foster, and Grover Mitchell, and Joe was always a welcome addition. Baritone saxophonist John Williams was a part of these reunions.

JW: It's a gas because it's like a big brother coming back home. It's not like a singer that you're accompanying just for a particular special concert. Because whenever Joe comes back to this band he's at home, and he is very unique because he immediately learns the names of the new guys and becomes a functional part of the family again. And that's easily understood because, you know, Basie referred to Joe as his number one son, and I think as long as Chief lived I strived to be the number two son. I loved him so much, so there was a little bit of envy when I heard him refer to Joe as the number one son. Joe was definitely the number one son of the family. In reference to being a singer, I always like to say that if Joe Williams isn't the greatest singer in the world, there's none greater. And in reference to being a human being, I think that one of the greatest attributes that a human being could have is good manners. And this is the one thing that I noticed about him that set him apart from many of the other performers with whom I've worked. Basie used to say, "God doesn't like ugly" in reference to people who are ill-mannered. And I could see why he was proud to call Joe his number one son, because Joe always, from the moment I met him, was a person who had very good manners. And it starts with self-respect. He had self-respect so it was very easy for him to show us respect. And I just didn't feel like a lowly baritone player who had very few solos to play, just an ensemble player, a guy making the front line sound good. I felt just as important in Joe's presence as one of the featured musicians. So good manners was the thing that really caught my attention.[11]

Basie's Number One Son

Despite the fickleness of audiences and the frequent changes in musical styles, Joe's career flourished right up until the time of his death. In 1995 he fulfilled a lifelong dream with the Gospel-inflected CD "Feel the Spirit," on which he stated: "I wanted to give thanks for the privilege of doing what I do." He would frequently cite Louis Armstrong and Ethel Waters as musical influences, but was equally inclined to note the sources of his character and integrity:

JW: Ellington started it. He was the one I thought expressed it better than anyone. He told a group once, "I'm not going to let you or anyone make me change my pretty ways." If you're happy with yourself and the way you live, let that reflection show others. I think that's the best way to do it. There was a man named Elbert Hubbard. He wrote a couple of things. One was a book of things that he enjoyed reading and the other was his own philosophy of life. He said, if I have a desire for myself at all it is that I be radiant. If I'm to help my fellow man at all, it would be by example and inference rather than by dictation. And when we went to church we used to hear songs like "We'll Understand it Better By and By" and "This Little Light of Mine." Someone may be lost and really think what am I going to do. Marian Anderson's mother told her, when she realized her daughter was an international celebrity, "Darlin' wherever you go and whatever you do, someone may be watching and would like to be like you. Please try not to disappoint them." And it behooves any of us as human beings. We owe it to the human race I think, to be as good as Marian Anderson's mother would have wanted her to be. We should sort of radiate.[12]

Joe Williams opened doors in the jazz community for us. The respect he received and the respect he showed his fellow artists served as a model as we embarked on our oral history effort.

Joe and all band singers were dependent on skilled sidemen, most of whom spent their careers in relative obscurity. Poignant memories from big band veterans are revealed in the next chapter.

Chapter 2
Sidemen Stories

At least half of the over three hundred individuals we've interviewed for the Fillius Jazz Archive experienced significant big band work during their careers. Some toiled with obscure bands before they found their way into the small group scene, studio work, or employment outside the music business. The most accomplished bands employed the most skilled sidemen and the music press followed their movements closely. It was the rare sideman who spent a whole career in one band. Most played musical chairs, seeking better pay and working conditions, or new musical challenges.

Ellington
A logical place to begin our sidemen stories is with Edward "Duke" Ellington. Ellington remains America's greatest jazz composer, an artist who was able to hold a band together for fifty years and who deservedly is a household name. Like most band leaders, Ellington usually made new hires based on the recommendations of his current band members. Bassist John Lamb was the recipient of good fortune provided by an avid Ellington fan. In 1964 John was living in Philadelphia making $48 a week as a mail boy in the office of the Acme Food Market chain. He was invited to play a "socialite gig," and he related the result of that engagement:

JL: One day I came home after a long day and I saw this telegram. It says, "Opportunity if interested give me a call." So a few days later I called and it was a woman who happened to be a member of a very prominent family in New Jersey. As a matter of fact at one time he was attorney general. His name was Walter Reed. And it was his wife, Mrs. Reed, had written the telegram, and she said, "I'm a friend of Duke Ellington's and maybe we could set you up with some kind of contact there. All you have to do is come over to the house and we'll have a little party and we'll have some Cornish hens, bring your family and your kids and I'll invite a few other people, and I'm going to invite some musicians to play along with you." And in the back of my mind I said she wants some free music for her party. And we set up a date and I piled my son in the back of the station wagon and my wife, and the bass, and we went over to Riverton, New Jersey.

Sidemen Stories

And we played and she stuck a tape recorder down there. I was aware that the tape recorder was there so what I decided to do was play in the style of Jimmy Blanton. So I was playing in the style of Jimmy Blanton, you know that very basic, driving beat. And so a few weeks later she shoved it in front of Duke when he came to the Steel Pier. I was living in a housing project by then and I was comfortable. I got this phone call, "Good evening, Mr. Lamb?" "Yes." "This is Duke Ellington." I said, "Who?" "Duke Ellington." I said, "Just a moment please." So I went back in there and told my wife, "That's Duke Ellington on the phone." She was very cool about that. So I walked back in and I says, "Yes, what can I do for you, Mr. Ellington?" And he says, "Well look here, Mr. Lamb, we'd like you to come up to New York and play some things with us." So okay, fine. We set up a date. He said, "We're up at a place called Freedom Land, why don't you try coming up there?" "Fine." "Bye." That was it. So I hopped on the train at North Station in Philly. Took my bass. This was before we had the wheel, and I carried it. Hopped on the train, went up to New York, got off the train, this was all on a Tuesday. Got off the train and got on another train and went up to the Bronx, and we ran out of subway. And so I had to take a taxi from there. So I took a taxi on over to Freedom Land, which at that time was sort of like a resort area or an entertainment place. And I walked in the place, back to the tents. I saw this guy walking around with his slippers on and I said that looks like Johnny Hodges. I'd seen his pictures, you know. And I walked back through there. "Where's the band?" I asked the guy. He says, "Oh, back there." So I went back into the tent, walked in and there was this guy sitting up with his blue outfit on, he had this blue bandana around his head. And the television was blasting, blaring, it was distorted. And he was fixed on that television set. Turns out that it was Duke. And I was approached by the band boy and he says, "Are you the new bass player?" I said, "Yeah." And he says, "Hey Duke, the bass player's here." And Duke stands up and he walks, very gracious, a very nice man. He was like a perfect six feet, a perfect mannequin so to speak, you know, so graceful. Even in that outfit that he had on. And he was very soft spoken and as a matter of fact I says, hmmm, I'm in the presence of something here, but I don't know what it is. And he says, "You want to take the next set? The second half of the show?" "Yeah." He said, "Okay." Then the band boy says, "Can he read?" "Yeah, I can read." So Peck Morrison was the bass player at the time, he was there for a short time. And so I went in and played the second show. The first tune we did was "Stompin' at the Savoy." I saw this blur, you know, he was kicking off the tune and I didn't—most band leaders will do something like this [gestures], you know. I didn't see none of that, he just did like that and the band started. I says, uh oh, this is a train. So I hopped on the train and we didn't quit until the end. It was in the key of D♭. "Stompin' at the Savoy." Okay, the next tune I did was one of the tunes from his "Far East Suite." He had written that. And I looked at the music and I says, this is written in fourths, I says, that's going to be very muddy, I can't play that that low, with a low A on the bottom. So I reversed everything and made it like this. And somebody says he had noticed that I was changing Duke's music. He said, "What's he doing?" So I changed the music around and played. It was a bass solo in the very beginning. As a matter of fact that same thing was recorded afterwards and it received an award. So we played that Far East thing and Cootie [Williams] says, "Uh huh, that's all." Everybody shook their head. So that was the end of that and the bass player came back out.

MR: Talk about trial by fire.

JL: Yeah, that's what it was. So I went in and did that and went on back to Philly. The next day another bass player was supposed to come by. But somebody was supposed to pick him up and the person didn't pick him up. And he didn't get the gig of course, he never showed up. He was depending upon somebody's word, whereas I took the train and lugged that thing up there and that probably made the difference. And the ability to play the bass notes. That's all it is is playing the bottom, whatever is required. And shortly after that I got another phone call back in Philly, it was from Mercer [Ellington]. Mercer says, "Hey John, Pop wants you to come up to New York in a couple of weeks." Well, I had to quit my job, you know, I had a day job. And so I said, "Okay I'll arrange that."

MR: What kind of salary did he offer you?

JL: Well, my being naïve about salaries, anything was better than what I was getting, $48 a week, and so they decided to start me off with [union] scale. They had to pay me the scale. It was about $60 a night. And the stars were getting all the money. I was just happy to get a gig. I had been making $48 a week at Acme Markets. So $60 a night was great. And so I worked my way up. Gradually it began to increase.[1]

Louie Bellson was one of Ellington's favorite drummers and was able to witness the mystical collaboration between Ellington and Billy Strayhorn.

Sidemen Stories

MR: Did you get a chance to see Ellington and Strayhorn, how they collaborated on their music? It seems like such a fascinating thing the way they pulled that off.

LB: Well, Strayhorn joined Ellington as a lyricist from what I hear, and Billy Strayhorn told me that he didn't think that Duke knew at first that he arranged. So Duke gave Strayhorn an assignment for lyrics, and he said, "I'll check you out when I get back, we've got to go to Europe." So when they came back from Europe, Billy said, "I write arrangements also." So Duke said, "Really?" He said, "Do you have one?" He said, "Yeah." And that was "Take the A Train." And Strayhorn told me that Duke put his arm around him and said, "You're with me forever." But you know that was a perfect match. Because nobody in that band, even the guys that had been there for years like Harry Carney, they couldn't tell the difference, whether Strayhorn wrote the composition or whether Duke did it. That's how close it was. They were an exceptional twosome. I would say they were both geniuses, really. Very superstitious. Don't ever whistle in the dressing room. Duke and Strayhorn never put a button, a finé, on an arrangement. They got down to letter S and then just let it fizzle out, then they worked it out at the rehearsal, but never really put like boom, the finale there.

MR: They didn't write it, you mean?

LB: They didn't write it. They worked it out at rehearsal, see? And [they] never wore a shirt with buttons all the way down, there was only maybe three buttons this way and then the slipover, and no color yellow, blue was the favorite color. And I made the mistake once of giving him a gift for his birthday, a pair of shoes. He says, "No, no, no, don't do that, don't do that. That means you're going to be walking out of my life." I said, "Oh really?" And so I exchanged those for a blue sweater. But they both had that great originality that you look for, that you strive for, and it came natural for them. You know Ellington never really went to school to learn how to write music. And Strayhorn may have had a little bit, but they had that God-given talent to be able to sit down and write music but it was strictly their style. They weren't getting it from somebody else. There it was. In the voicings in the reed section, the voicings in the brass section, being able to supply the soloists. He knew every soloist, what their range was, so when he wrote something for you, it was perfect, just like you getting a brand new set of clothes and they fit perfect. And he gave you the greatest introductions in the world. He really set you up you know. One thing, when I joined the band, Strayhorn and I roomed together for almost three weeks. And I made the mistake of telling Strayhorn one night, we were just talking and I said, "Strayhorn, how did Duke voice that 'Caravan' thing? Boy, man, I could really see the camels coming when they play that one part." And he went like this to me, "Unh unh unh." And I said, "Oh, excuse me, I'm invading your privacy." So I didn't say a word, and I guess Strayhorn had talked to Duke about me asking and so forth, and nothing happened for about three or four months, and all of a sudden we were doing a one-nighter and Duke got up on the piano, this was before the people came in, and he said, "Come here, sit down by the piano." He explained to me how he voiced "Caravan." What notes he gave to Johnny Hodges, what notes he gave to Procope, Carney, and so forth. "This is what I did." So I thought to myself man, here the great Duke Ellington is taking time out to show me some voicings.[2]

Trombonist Grover Mitchell spent time in both the Ellington and Basie bands, eventually leading the Basie Orchestra in 1995. Grover describes the discipline, or lack thereof, with a band that carried all the positives and negatives associated with a large family.

MR: I heard [Ellington] had his own method of discipline.
GM: Let me tell you, just to give you an anecdote. The first night, I lived in the San Francisco area. We had left the Monterey Jazz Festival. This was the second year, 1960 I guess it was. And we got to San Francisco in this club that we played that was owned by the DuPonts called The Neve. And the first night was just absolutely gorgeous. The band just roared. This was my first night with these people. And the second night, it seemed like everybody was late. There was a nucleus in this band that was always on time. You could always figure you would see Lawrence Brown, you know he was very dapper and he was sitting there and never late and all that stuff. And oh, Lou the trumpet player there, and the rhythm section pretty much would be there. And so some of the guys were out milling around in the audience and I mean here I am in what was my hometown then, trying to make this big impression and I was really embarrassed. So he had this funny old medley or something that he could play with two or three guys on the stand, and he would go through this act, you know, "Ladies and Gentlemen, we've been successful over the years," and he'd go into these unison-type things with maybe six people up there. So I told him I says, "Wow, Duke, man this is

terrible, this is embarrassing, all of my friends are here." And he says, "Look, I don't worry about these people. Number one, these people are not going to drive me crazy. I live for the night that this band is great. Tonight means nothing to me." I said, "Oh, how can you say that?" Because here are these guys milling around. And Jimmy Hamilton was sitting there, he was playing and I'm all upset, and I says, "Jimmy, look at all these people walking around out here, and we should be up on the bandstand playing." And he looks at me like I'm crazy and the waiter comes up to the bandstand and says, "Mr. Hamilton, your steak is ready." And right in the middle of the tune he steps over the rail and starts cutting on a steak. And so about a week later we were playing at an Air Force base outside of Sacramento called Mather Air Force Base now. So here's the band, and they've got to play. There's no place for these guys to fool around and you know, this whole military atmosphere, and so the band is just roaring, beautiful. And so I hear the piano player, Duke, saying dink-dink-dink-dink, dink-dink-dink-dink. And so I looked around, and he's over there and he says [whispers], "See what I mean?" So that's the way he was. Nothing bothered him.[3]

Life as a big band sideman was strenuous and occasionally exciting, but rarely financially rewarding. Salary issues played a role in the decision of moving from one band to another. Because of union regulations, loyalties, and simple good manners, leaving one band for a competitor had to be undertaken with delicacy. Trumpeter Clark Terry related to Joe Williams the story of his move from Basie to Ellington:

CT: I don't know if everybody knows about this, but when I left the Basie band to join Duke, well, we had kicked it around a little bit and he had sent his scouts around, and one time Joe Morgan said, "You want to join the band?" And I used to like his little hat that he used to wear. And he said, "I'll get you a hat like this if you'll join." So finally we talked about it long enough and I finally decided, well, I think I'd like to join Duke's band. This is when, at this time, Basie was down to a quintet. So we were working in Chicago —
JW: At the Brass Rail.
CT: At the Brass Rail, right. So Duke finally comes around and he says, "I'd like to discuss things with you." So he says, "Okay?" He says, "But we can't do it out in public, so later on I'll have to come to your hotel." So I says, "Okay, I'm at the Southway." He says, "All right, I'll come by and I'll call you when I get in the lobby and I'll

Jazz Tales from Jazz Legends

hurriedly get out of the lobby and meet you in your room." So I says, "Okay." So he comes to the hotel, and he calls up and I says, "Oh, all right." So he says, "I'll meet you on your floor and I'll meet you at the elevator and show me where it is." So Duke gets off the elevator about the same time I come out my door. And just as I walk out of my door Duke steps off the elevator, and next door to me is Freddie Green. Freddie Green opens his door and steps out. He says, "Whoa," and went back and slammed the door. So of course Duke and I went on with our business. But that night on the gig, I walked in and you know, Pep [Freddie Green] would look at you like this, he didn't even say hello. "If you don't you're a fool," he said. So the funny thing is, the conversation with me and Duke, he says, "Well, now we've agreed on the bread and everything," and for me it was a big bread in those days. 'Cause I was making with Basie $125 a week, and the last part of my stint with the Basie band I got a raise, $15 raise, so I'm making $140 a week. And Duke says, Duke would give me $225 a week. Oh, man, that was great big bread for me, you know, 'cause there was cats in there making three and four and five [hundred], but I didn't know it. But to me, that was big bread. So that day he says to me, "Well, it's just not proper protocol for a person to snatch somebody out of his buddy's band. So we'll have to strategically work this out." I said, "Okay, what do you suggest?" He said, "Well, I'll tell you what I think. I think you should maybe just get sick and tell Bill [Basie] that you're going to go home and recuperate and while you're home recuperating I'll put you on salary." Yeah? Wow man. Ain't no better deal than that. So I went back and told Bas' that I put my notice in. I said, "No Bas', I'm just not feeling good, I just need to go home and just get on." And he said, "Okay, well, when you get yourself together you can come on back, because this is always home for you." So I said, "Thanks, Bill, I appreciate it very much." So I went home, I'm on salary, and right away the first check, wham, before I get home, you know? So this went on and on until the band just happened to come through St. Louis, three months later, I'm on salary for three months, and they're coming through St. Louis playing the Kiel Auditorium on November 11th, Armistice Day. And I just happened to join the band. That was the Big Show with Sarah Vaughan, Peg Leg Bates, Patterson and Jackson and all them from the Big Show. I don't know if it was '51 or '52. But anyhow, I left and went with the band. I stayed with the band for almost ten years, you know? And years later, I went up to the Carnegie Hall when Basie was already sick and he had to take a little side elevator to ride up. And I went backstage to see him and I'm standing at the top and he's coming up and I said, "You know one thing?" I said, "I have a confession to make to you, something that's been bugging me for years and years." He said, "Yeah? What is it?" I said, "When I left the band, you know, I told you I was sick and going home." I said, "I wasn't really sick." He said, "Um humm." I said, "The reason I did that is because Duke had made me an offer I couldn't pass up." He said, "Um humm." He said, "Why do you think I took the raise back, you think I didn't know that?"[4]

Count Basie

For many fans of big band music, the Count Basie Orchestra was the epitome of what an eighteen-person ensemble should sound like. Throughout his five-decade career, Basie (a/k/a "The Chief") held tight to his inner compass of what and how his bands should play. Though he was a man of few words, he made his feelings and intentions known through subtle but forceful direction. The Fillius Jazz Archive oral history project focused first on Basie alums and we are blessed with a wealth of material about Count Basie and his career. Here Clark Terry focuses on why the Basie band sounded like it did:

CT: I'll tell you about this cat, Basie. Although Ellington was more endowed with harmony and theory and so forth, Basie was the king as far as tempo, and he taught us all the greatest lesson in the world and that is the utilization of space and time. They say he learned it through the medium of just socializing at Kansas City at the Cherry Blossom and the little places where you would have people sit, in a small room like this where you would have gingham tablecloths and he'd play a little bit with Jo Jones, and Walter Page, or Freddie [Green], and The Fiddler [Claude Williams], or whoever was there, and he'd go socializing. Bing-a-dink and he'd go over there socialize, "Yeah, baby, how you doing?" Bing-a-dink, go over there and have another taste over there and have two or three tastes. Meanwhile Jo Jones and "Big 'Un" [Walter Page] are still going [scats]. And he'd come in [scats]. So he was so endowed with rhythm and utilization of space and time, so he knew exactly the way a tune should be before you played it. Now the best example is when Neal Hefti was writing for the band, he brought in a tune and passed it out, and Basie played it and Basie shook his head. He said, "What's the matter, you don't like the arrangement, Chief?" He said, "No."

He said, "What's wrong with it?" He said, "The tempo." Well, the tune was about here [claps]. So he said, "Well, what do you think it should be?" "About here" [claps slowly]. Well, the tune was [scats]. He brought it in to be [scats slowly].
JW: That was "L'il Darling."
CT: He heard it. Right away he said, "Uh oh." And look at the result. If he'd a kept it up there it would have just been another also-ran tune. He was the king of space, time.[5]

Basie's band of the late 1930s was the loosest of his aggregations, operating more like a large combo. Much of the music they played was created on stage or in rehearsals and called "head arrangements," only to be written down later. Harry "Sweets" Edison talked of the challenge of finding his niche in a band that seemed to operate with a kind of musical magic:

MR: At the time you joined the Basie band, how much of the music was written out?
SE: We didn't have any music.
MR: Now how did that work? And how did you learn what to play when you first got in there?
SE: Well, that's an interesting question. Because when I first joined the band, everybody in the Count Basie band had played with Bennie Moten's band. So they all knew what they wanted to play. They all had notes to different—like "One O'clock Jump," "Swinging the Blues," "Out the Window." It was a head arrangement. The brass section would get together and they would set a riff behind a melody Basie would play on the piano. The saxophones would go in to another room and they would set a riff. And when we all came back to the rehearsal hall, we'd all have an arrangement, you know? So that went on with me for about a couple of years. And finally I told Basie I said, "I'm going to quit." He says, "Why? You sound good." I said, "Well, all these arrangements that you play every night—I can't find a note. I can't find a note to 'Swinging the Blues' and playing it fast." I haven't had a chance—I really was disgusted.
MR: Discouraged, huh?
SE: Yes. So I said, "I'd rather for you to take my notice." He said, "Well, if you find a note tonight that sounds good, play the same damn note every night." So that's what I did. He encouraged me to sit there. And it was very difficult. Because when they played a tune like "Out the Window" or of course "One O'clock Jump" wasn't too fast,

you could find a note, but "Jumpin' at the Woodside." Hell they're playing and you're trying to find a note to play, and it's passed, and they're finished before you can find a note.

MR: There's no rehearsal time to do that. You're playing every night, right?

SE: Sure. But he encouraged me, and I stayed there for twenty years in and out you know. And had it not been for Count Basie, I wouldn't be here with you because nobody would have never heard about me. He gave me a chance and I had so much fun I don't know why he kept me with the band because I was having a ball. You know every night was fun to me. Just absolutely—sitting next to Lester Young—gee whiz, what a thrill. Jo Jones. Walter Page. Freddie Green. Buck Clayton, sitting next to him—you know it wasn't but three trumpets, Buck Clayton, Ed Lewis, and myself; there was two trombones, and four saxophones. And four rhythm section. So I should have paid him to be in the band because I was having so much fun.[6]

One of the first things an aspiring big band musician had to learn was the difference between two-beat and four-beat—a subtle but profound change in the basic feel of swing. Trumpeters Snooky Young and Gerald Wilson were both Basie alums and often played a musical game of tag team in and out of various bands. They talked about that subtle swing difference, when they were interviewed together in Los Angeles:

GW: When I joined Count Basie, who do you think I was supposed to replace? Snooky Young. Snooky left the band, and Basie called me and he says, "Snooky there had to go back East, Gerald." So I went and played a couple of days at the Lincoln, and so Basie said, "Well look, Snooky had to go and he's going to rejoin us when we get to Chicago. You come on and go to Chicago with us and then Snooky will be back." I said, "Fine." So I left with the Count Basie band, which I loved. I mean let me tell you, that was another great day for me to be able to join a band like Count Basie, because I was going to get a chance as a writer to sit where swing had really started. And remember that there was the original rhythm section, which they called the "All American Rhythm Section," with Walter Page, Jo Jones, Count, and Freddie Green. So for me that was going to be another education deal. Because I'm going to sit here now as a writer, I can just observe really what's going on. And what's going on with this swing. Because you must remember the Count Basie band and that rhythm section, they're the ones that put the real meaning into swing. All bands had to change to that type of rhythm section. The Lunceford band would have had to change. Duke Ellington. Everybody. If you're not playing this type of rhythm, you're not into the newest form of rhythm that would finally take over the world. And because you must remember that bebop had no rhythm of their own. They had to use that same kind of rhythm in their first efforts. So it was a great day for me. But Basie had more in mind, by the way, because when we got to Chicago, Snooky didn't show up. And I said, I thought I was going to come back home. But he had other ideas. He also needed a writer at that time. And I was the man.

MR: That must have been a thrill. Is it possible to put into words what that rhythm section did?

GW: Well, you remember Jo Jones was an innovator in drumming. He had some things going that drummers had not been doing. Walter Page had been one of the first to start the walking bass rather than playing the root and the fifth. In other words Boom Boom BOOM Boom. In earlier days, they just played the one note. Boom Boom Boom Boom Boom Boom Boom Boom. So Page started walking on the chords more or less. And Freddie Green—nobody can play the rhythm guitar like Freddie Green. To this day.

SY: That's right.

GW: To this day. He never bothered about a solo.

SY: You know when I left Lunceford's band I went directly into Basie's band. And those two bands was night and day. I mean Lunceford's rhythm was a two-beat rhythm thing, you know. And it was great and all like that, but you'd come out of that and move into Basie's band, I almost felt like I didn't know how to read music. 'Cause everything was laying so different.

MR: Especially for a lead trumpet, right? Because you've got to be in sync.

SY: That's right. And I had to learn how to play with Basie's band because it's very difficult. You asked a question that kind of hit on that, and I left from one band and went directly into this band, this swing band what you're saying. And I noticed a difference. But Lunceford had great rhythm and everything, but it was a two-beat rhythm. And so most bands was playing two beats.

GW: Yeah, Lunceford had the two beats. But they had to get that, you know to play jazz, the ultimate jazz beat is when you're playing four-four. It's the ultimate rhythm. And they had this thing. Jo had it going here, and it was the thing that all bands needed, and still to this day, I mean the band you play with now, all bands, you've got to have this.[7]

Sidemen Stories

The early '50s were challenging years for big bands. Even the Basie band was struggling economically and the Count pared down to a seven-piece group for a number of years. Bassist Jimmy Lewis found that the Count's knack for creating intense swing could be applied to a small group as well as a big band:

MR: Is this when Basie had the small group?

JL: Yes, the small group. We had Wardell Gray, Clark Terry, Gus Johnson on drums, Freddie Green on guitar, me on bass and like we used Bud DeFranco. We worked the Brass Rail [Chicago] down at the Loop. We opened up one night and all the people were sitting at the table, and so Basie started off real soft. I thought I was playing louder than anybody, I mean I'm just playing it. Basie says, "Don't play so loud." He said, "They'll hear ya." So I cut down on the bass. And Basie set a tempo and then he'd watch the people's feet. He said, "Okay, everybody's starting to feel you over the conversation." He said, "Now Gus, pick up your sticks." Gus was playing with brushes. He said, "We've got 'em now." And by the time we opened up, everybody turned and you couldn't believe it. Buddy DeFranco walked out to the stand, and man, everybody would start to play. He and Clark Terry started doing tricks. Clark would take his horn, take the mouthpiece off and just put it in the end of a glass and blow you know, and make all kinds of funny sounds. And Gus Johnson. Then here comes Wardell Gray. He'd walk up and he'd just play something like Lester Young. And Freddie Green, boy, he was like a metronome sitting there. And you couldn't get away from him. The tempo might move up a little bit, I'd get excited, and Freddie would say, "Come back here. Right here." And boy that thing would take off. And Basie, he'd sit there and give signs. He had all kinds of signs. He'd do his face when he'd want you to play louder or softer you know. And when he'd get ready to close a number he'd double his fists. And like if he wanted some excitement, he'd stand up from the piano and look at you. And Gus was sitting on the drums and you'd hear this thing, it sounded like it was coming up out of the floor. And boy, the people just went crazy.[8]

The heyday of the big bands occurred well before the Civil Rights Era. While some swing bands made tentative moves towards integration after the Benny Goodman-Lionel Hampton-Teddy Wilson-Gene Krupa combination, there was an obvious distinction between black and white bands for many years. Grover Mitchell, a Basie trombonist and an eventual

Jazz Tales from Jazz Legends

leader of the band, reminds us why the Ellington and Basie orchestras were able to sound as they did:

MR: The Basie group that you played with had some marvelous players; one of the best ensembles he had. Who were your favorite bandmates?

GM: Well, we had some genius-level people you know. Ellington's band and Basie's band, the one thing that caused them in some way to be at the ability level that we were able to maintain was we, in the older days and prior to 1964, we couldn't get jobs in studios you know. We couldn't play at the networks and all that. And so Ellington and Basie had access to the greatest black musicians alive. In other words, that's what we had to aspire to. And you couldn't think of going to NBC or ABC or be in a Hollywood studio, which later I did, and quite successfully. But in those days they had access to the greatest black musicians available. The greatest. And so they had their choice. That's something.

MR: That's a really important statement. I haven't heard it put quite that way.

GM: I know, most people won't say it. They're afraid to say it. But I know it. Because we would sit there and our greatest competition was each other until Clark Terry and those guys in 1964 and '63 started getting into the networks and all that kind of stuff. There was a couple of guys here and there, you know. CBS was pretty good, they had a guy over there. And a New York contractor named Lou Shoobe, he was quite fair, and so some guys got jobs. But for the most part you couldn't even dream of getting a studio job, it was just unheard of in those days.[9]

Both Grover and Clark Terry spent time in Duke's and the Count's bands. This is tantamount to a classical musician touting the fact that they spent part of their career with the Philadelphia Orchestra under Eugene Ormandy, then moved on to the New York Philharmonic under Leonard Bernstein.

Tenor saxophonist Frank Foster is high on the list of important Basie figures. He was one half of the "Two Franks" tenor team of Frank Foster and Frank Wess, in the New Testament band. Foster became one of Basie's most dependable writers, but he was still subject to Basie's musical scrutiny.

MR: How about the first time you brought an arrangement to Basie?
FF: The first arrangement I brought to the Basie band was one I brought

from Korea with me that I had played with a band in Korea.
MR: No kidding.
FF: And the band needed a couple of Latin-flavored songs for the dancers that they were playing. And they only had one mambo. So this was a mambo.
MR: You wrote a mambo?
FF: Yeah. This was an original sort of thing based on a mambo groove, and it was very simple. And I brought it in to the band and we played it. And Basie encouraged me to continue writing. And the results of that encouragement were "Blues Backstage," and "Blues in Hoss' Flat," and eventually "Shiny Stockings." But it's not all peaches and cream or roses as it were. If you could count the arrangements that were rejected as stacked up against those that were accepted, the stacks would be pretty even.
MR: So you'd take it into a rehearsal and did it take him a long time to decide?
FF: No. It never took him a long time. If the arrangement played down the first time and nobody had to decipher it as though it were hieroglyphics and it swung, it was in. Generally if it took too long and people had to labor over phrases and how does this go and what does this mean, and if it sounded like too much dissonance, or too many "pregnant nineteenths" as Basie used to say.
MR: Did he say that?
FF: Yeah he said, "Son, when you write an arrangement, don't put too many pregnant nineteenths in there." So I knew what he meant by "pregnant nineteenths." And if it was too busy, too overloaded, every time it got rejected. Which brings me to the story of "Shiny Stockings." We were playing a place in Philadelphia called Pep's Bar. And we'd just arrived in town that morning and we had to rehearse that day because it was customary to rehearse on the opening day of each nightclub engagement. But we had arrived late and checked in late at the hotel, a long trip from somewhere. Everybody is tired, ill-tempered, hungry, and no one felt like rehearsing. You know we'd rather have done anything than rehearse. And I brought "Shiny Stockings" in. And the first rehearsal of "Shiny Stockings," it just sounded like a forty-three-car pile-up on the New York Thruway. Everybody ran into everybody. I said oh my, he'll never play this song and I put so much into it. Well, Mr. Basie must have heard something, because with that horrible rehearsal, he must have understood how tired everyone was and how unwilling we were to rehearse and that was the result of our attitudes. He must have

heard something because we played it and played it and played it and I guess you could say the rest is history. But many other songs that sounded like that in rehearsal never got played. And we had an expression, if we were rehearsing something and it wasn't going well, either because it was too busy or the harmonies weren't right or it sounded amateurish, we had an expression, "Pasadena," which meant pass it in. And after we worked on that chart for about ten, fifteen minutes, Marshall Royal, who was the straw boss, he'd say, "Pasadena." And I guess this was sort of code terminology so that if the arranger was somebody outside the band, he wouldn't know what we were talking about, but you'd see all this music converging on one spot, and it was being passed in. Years after, this must have been in the early '60s now—"Shiny Stockings" was introduced to the book in 1955—Basie pulled me over in the corner and he said, "Kid, you know you wrote that 'Shiny Stockings?'" I said, "Yeah." He said, "You really put one down that time, boy."

MR: He was a man of few words most of the time?
FF: Definitely. But every word meant something.
MR: Just like his playing?
FF: Right, exactly. Like his playing.[10]

Almost without exception, Basie alums talk about the skill that the Count displayed in leading his band. His approach to hiring and maintaining his band with the members he wanted was as unique as his playing. Trombonist Benny Powell joined the newly-formed Basie band after the small group experiment, and addressed Basie's leadership personality:

BP: I joined [Basie's] band when I was twenty-one. I'll tell you the essence of my experience with Basie. I was at the Apollo Theater working for a week in Joe Thomas's band. Also in the band was Charlie Fowlkes, who had been with Basie. Basie was on a hiatus and he was about to form another band. So Charlie Fowlkes invited me to the rehearsal. So I went, and it was nice. Pretty uneventful. I can't remember—at this particular time there were a couple of jobs I wanted. The job with Charlie Ventura, then I was waiting to hear from Illinois Jacquet also. In the meantime, the Basie thing comes up, I make the rehearsal and that's fine. Charlie Fowlkes tells me when the next rehearsal is. And I come back and I make that also. I don't know how many rehearsals we did, but pretty soon we started working, and the first date I played with Basie was October 31st, I think, 1951. So at this time we would go out of town for maybe one night or two nights a weekend, and come back in town. Well, this went on for just a little while, a couple of weeks. In the meantime, from Basie I'm trying to find out if I'm hired, if I have a job or shall I tell Illinois Jacquet no. But there was a strange quirk about Basie. If he had something that you wanted, he would sort of play a cat and mouse, you know, dangle it in front of you. Anyway, he knew I wanted him to say yes, Benny, you're hired. I was sort of in awe of him anyway. I think I was all of twenty-one and he was the world famous Count Basie, so I would sort of find myself next to him by my own design, and I would say, "Mr. Basie, how do you like the trombone section?" He'd say, "It sounds all right." And that's all I got out of that conversation. So maybe the next weekend I got brave enough to say, "Mr. Basie, are you satisfied with the trombones?" He said, "Yeah, it sounds pretty good." That's all I got out of that one. Each time I would disguise it. But finally I said, "Mr. Basie, what I'm trying to find out is, you know, am I hired? Am I with the band?" He said, "You're here aren't you kid?" And every time after that for about four or five times, that's what I'd get. "You're here aren't you, kid?" So finally I stopped asking him. And during the twelve years, I don't think he ever said, "Yes, Benny, you've got a job. You're hired." But he was a wonderful man. I loved him. I was always in awe of older musicians.[11]

The "old" Count Basie would have been forty-seven when Benny joined the band in 1951. His best-known Basie moment is his 8-bar bridge solo on the classic "April in Paris" recording.

I heard the thrill in Benny's voice when he spoke of the 1961 convergence of the Ellington and Basie bands. The making of the LP, "First Time: The Count Meets the Duke," resulted in an experience Benny never forgot.

BP: It was called "Battle Royal." I was like a kid in a candy store because where I was seated I was in eyeshot of both Basie and Duke Ellington, and I kept pinching myself. I said you're not here, you're going to wake up any minute. I think it ended up with Basie playing a solo on "Take the A Train," and Duke playing a solo on "One O'Clock Jump." Those guys were such statesmen, they'd say, "Well, Mr. Basie, this number just demands your presence." "But no, Maestro, I wouldn't dare." Oh man those guys were cool. And I was a little kid, and I'm looking at these guys and I don't believe it. But also I remember one of the biggest sensual thrills I've ever gotten, on the end there's both of these bands playing huge power chords in Sonny Payne's solo. The drum is playing through all of that. Oh man, if you were in the room, it rearranged your cells.[12]

The Basie mode of leadership provides a lesson about how to be a boss. Drummer Butch Miles talked about his way of silent but positive reinforcement, and it reminds us that although the Count was a man of few words, he was not someone to be disrespected:

BM: Oh, he [Basie] was wonderful. He was a wonderful boss because he never told you what to do or what to play. I asked our band manager at that time—it was Sonny Cohn—and Cup [Cohn] sat right in front of me on the band bus, and after I'd been with the band about maybe two weeks I said, "Sonny, Basie hasn't said anything to me about whether he wants it this way, or he doesn't want it that way." Because I'd worked with a number of other people who'd made it quite clear what they wanted and the way that they wanted it. And Basie didn't say a word. And so Cup just looked at me, he says, "Well, if it's wrong, he'll tell you, and if it's not, he'll just let you go." And that was why he had great professionals in the band who took care of the business so well, because they were professionals. Basie didn't hire somebody that just turned sixteen with an incredible reputation but couldn't play. So one time we had a trumpet problem and somebody recommended a young trumpet player from Chicago. He flew in to New York, and there was no rehearsal or audition, it was kind of like a closed shop. You got in on a recommendation or if Basie had heard you play himself and wanted you to come in with the band. And I can't remember the young man's name but he came in and he was all full of fire and brimstone. He was ready to show the world that he was like the greatest trumpet player in the world, probably like in his early twenties. And the night of his first gig with the band he made the absolute mistake of thinking that Basie was a real cream puff and he lipped off to him. He said something sassy or nasty, right before the job. I never saw this happen before. Basie fired him, right then.

MR: The guy didn't play a note?

BM: Not with the band. Basie fired him, right then, gave him his ticket home and told him good-bye. He never did play a note, not with the band. He came in all hot, you know had his hat over to the side. It didn't work like that. The band was a very well-oiled machine. It was a big band, it was a full ensemble. Basie played the band like he played the piano. And it had to work like that. You couldn't have eighteen or nineteen superstars up there 'cause it never works. So the band was a unit. And it had to be that way. Oh we had stars. We had Jimmy Forrest, we had Al Grey, we had Curtis Fuller at one point, we had Bobby Plater, Charlie Fowlkes, a great baritone saxophonist, you know, various people that passed through the band from time to time over the years. But you didn't have anybody that ran roughshod through the band. Basie wouldn't stand for that. He just would not. And I never saw him get mad at anybody in the band except that one time. He was a very affable, easy going, wonderful man and just marvelous to work for, but you did not sass him.[13]

Trombonist Al Grey was nicknamed "Fab" and was thrilled to become a Basie member, but quickly became frustrated when, as the new guy, he could not get in the queue for solo space. Al spoke to my colleague Michael Woods and related a story of one of the few times that Basie stepped out of his silent mode with a fatherly gesture:

AG: You must also remember that when I joined the band, Count Basie's personnel had been the same for like twelve, fourteen years. So when I joined the band, I didn't have no name at all. I was called the "new boy" and I didn't used to like that. And that was on me for a whole year, until the next person came into the band, and this is when I got my name. "Fab." That comes from Count Basie who started calling me fabulous because I could go out and get standing ovations every night. Now I come in to Count Basie's band, and there's no music written for me. Now I want to solo so bad, 'cause Joe Newman just went out there and he just performed like ever. And here's Sonny Payne and Frank Wess and me, and Henry Coker who was a trombone player, and Benny Powell. Now I get no chance to play. Nothing.

MW: Was there any etiquette by which you could kind of go to Basie and say, hey, you know, I want you to throw me a solo here?

AG: Well, it boiled down to where I felt as though that coming from Dizzy [Gillespie] I should get a few bars. So one day we were in line, this is when you had to jump off the bus and run in and get in line because you know that the bath is going to run out. So this particular day I jumped off and run in and I get in line and here I am the new boy, and everybody was always jumping in front of me because I was the new boy. So you're the new boy and you'd better recognize it and accept it if you're going to stay in that band. And so this day I was getting ready to sign in for this bath, and Marshall Royal ran in and said "Royal" and, he was the straw boss, and they gave him this last bath. And I just went off in the lobby of this hotel. I just went to hollering and screaming and cussing and going on. And of course you know this is a no-no, you know you're not supposed to do like that in the Queen Hotel, and because I was completely so uptight from not playing any solos. And you'd pick up the paper the next day and they're talking about Marshall and Snooky and all these guys that did all this last night, and you don't see your name or anything like that because you hadn't did anything, see? And so he got this last bath and I just went off because I was so upset from not playing. But Count Basie was sitting in the corner over there. He would always wait until last because you know he had his suite coming and everything like that. And he finally got my attention and he beckoned me and he says, "Come over here." And I says, "I was in line and I was correct to get my bath and he just stepped in front of me." And Basie said, "Well, he's straw boss. You know how they are." And he tried to calm me down. But I went into saying, "Well look, I don't know why you hired me because I come over here and you won't let me play anything." And this is when he came up and I had never heard him cuss or anything like that but he came up with a cuss word, and said, "One minute—you just got here. Now when we get back to New York, we're going to fix up music and everything for you, but you just got here and so we can't do nothing about it and this is not an old jam band and so we're not going to have no jam session." And he says, "But you know I like you, and I'll tell you what I'm going to do. I'm going to let you come down and have a bath in my room and there's an extra room over here, the suite, and you can stay there tonight." And this is like he became like my father. Because then I would listen to everything he had to say.[14]

Benny Goodman

Basie and Ellington are widely considered to be the epitome of big band jazz, but a number of white groups surpassed them in drawing power and record sales. Benny Goodman was credited with ushering in the swing era in 1935, earning him the title the "King of Swing." Stories about Benny's quirky personality abound and we call on Sonny Igoe for a big band memory:

SI: I can remember when I started with Benny Goodman's band, now

Sidemen Stories

we're talking nineteen—what would that be 1948 and '49. That's right. And there's a long story concerned with this. You can't do anything alone. Somebody's got to help you. So I had come off the road playing with three what we would call back in those days "B bands." They weren't like the Benny Goodman or that sort of thing. They were Tommy Reed, and Les Elgart, and a lady bandleader named Ina Ray Hutton. So those bands, Tommy Reed, Ina Ray Hutton, and Les Elgart, were ninety-dollar bands. That's a week on the road with hotels and meals you had to pay your own. And you wonder, ninety bucks, how did I ever do that? So okay now I know that Benny Goodman is rehearsing a new band. I had also heard that he was getting a drummer every day. He didn't like anybody. So guys were telling me—there used to be a hangout in New York called Charlie's Tavern, where everybody used to go because beers were a nickel and we could hang around there, drink beer, lie, you know tell a lot of lies. So anyway, this guy goes, "Hey Sonny, you ought to go up to Benny's rehearsal." He said, "He's having trouble finding somebody he likes." I said, "He'll probably hire Shelly Manne or somebody like that." But I thought about it and it came to me that I had the acquaintance of a man who was an insurance executive who was a friend of Benny Goodman's. He loved musicians. So I asked him. His name was Eddie Furst. And I said, "Ed, do you think you could introduce me to Benny Goodman so I could audition?" He said, "I don't know why I didn't think of that, I'll call him." So he called me the next day and said, "We're going up Thursday at eleven o'clock." So he takes me and we go up there and he's rehearsing at MCA in New York. And I had a very good ear. I memorize very quickly, luckily. It's another lucky thing, you can't teach it. So anyway we go up there and the band is playing and they were rehearsing this one tune three or four times through, five or six times through, whatever. And I'm listening to it. And I'm getting that down pretty good already, and I'll see if I can play that tune. But you never know, you might have to go up there and sight read. But anyway they take a break. And so Benny said, "Eddie, how are you?" And he comes over and shakes his hand. And he says, "This is the young man I was telling you about, Benny." And he said, "Oh, nice to meet you Sonny." He says, "We'll take a ten minute break. You play the next set." The drummer was from Philadelphia and he was very inexperienced. Scared to death. Not that I wasn't nervous. Benny Goodman, my God, this was a whole new strata for me. And this kid, I don't think he played with anybody. But anyway he was so accommodating. I said,

Jazz Tales from Jazz Legends

"Do you mind if I use your drums to play the next set" or something. He said, "Oh please." And we introduced ourselves and all that kind of stuff. So I sit in. And they play that tune that I had sat through five or six times. And I had the part up, like I pretend I'm reading it. I didn't have to really read much of it, it wasn't that complex, but there was a couple of starts and stops and a few things in it. And I went through it [claps] just like that. So Benny looked up like this. And he said, "Stay up there, Pops."

MR: He called you Pops already.

SI: Everybody. Yeah, he called everybody Pops. So I stayed up there and I played a few more tunes I got lucky enough to get through. And then he said, "Okay, everybody's through, we'll play with the quartet." So he said, "Stay up there, Pops." So Buddy Greco was the piano player and Benny, and bass player was a fellow named Clyde Lombardi. So we played with just a small group for about an hour, then he packed up and walked out. He didn't say a word to me, that was it. Oh he did say, "Come back tomorrow, bring your own drums in." Something like that. So I go back tomorrow, and then I played the whole rehearsal. And then again at the end he goes through the small band, because he loved playing with the small group too. And so it's going on three weeks now. And I get a call from another clarinet player, a guy named Jerry Wald. He was going into the Paramount Theater. And he asked me if I'd be interested in doing the Paramount with him. And I said, "I'm rehearsing with Benny." He said, "Well, did he hire you yet?" I said, "I've been doing it for three weeks he hasn't said a word." He says, "Well listen, I can give you another couple of days and then I'll have to get somebody else." He says, "But the job is yours if you want it." And I said, "Okay, thank you, very nice of you." So the next day I'm at rehearsal with Benny, right? Now Benny used to walk around as I call tooteling all the time. And he comes up to me and gives me a nudge, and he's tooteling. He says, "Get your suit yet, Pops?" And I said, "What do you mean get my suit yet?" He says, "You know, your uniform." Because the band was going to Saks Fifth Avenue for tuxedo coats. So I said no. He said, "Why don't you get your uniform?" I said, "Nobody told me I was hired." He said, "Nobody told you you were hired? You were hired the first day." He said, "Nobody said anything?" I said, "No, you never said anything." He said, "He's supposed to—where's what's his name—" the manager. "Come up here. Talk to him." So okay. Now the big decision of my life comes up, right? So the guy says, "Oh Sonny, it was my fault," he says. "I apologize." He said,

Sidemen Stories

"You got the job," and he said, "You've got to get your uniform." And he said, "Now how much money do you want?" Nobody ever asked me that before. Right? I can remember Gene Krupa saying, "If you ever play with Benny Goodman he respects you if you ask for a lot of money." But I didn't feel as though I was that secure [because] I had come from these ninety-dollar bands. Never made more than ninety bucks a week. So I kind of haltingly said, "How about 125?" He says, "Well, I think we can make that." And I could almost hear him going chuckle-chuckle-chuckle. So that's the way that went. I was the lowest paid guy in the band. I would have swept out the bus, I don't care. But I spent a year with Benny until he broke up the band. And I really felt as though I learned a lot. I came a long way experience-wise and how to really play in a band, and gee, to have somebody as good as him. A lot of guys said he used to be very bad on a lot of people. But he never once said anything to me about my playing. He never said you're playing too loud, you're rushing, you're dragging, you're doing this, you're doing that. So that put me over the top from the standpoint of having to audition with other bands. I went from Benny Goodman to Woody Herman. That was my next step. But it was funny in those days the way everybody said, "Boy you're working for Benny—did you get 'the ray' yet?" I have a story about "the ray" if you're interested. He said to us one night at the Palladium in Hollywood, "You've heard a lot about the ray. I'm not really mad at anybody. Sometimes I daydream and my mind wanders and I just happen to be looking in somebody's direction. I'm not trying to stare them down or anything like that." So now we're in Canada doing a whole string of one-nighters in the hockey rinks. They used to put the boards down on the ice so people could dance, and then they would build this tremendous movie set for the band. They'd have the saxes down here and each section up. The drums were way up at the top. You couldn't hear the band, you were so far away. And Benny's down there. So we play the first set and Benny, he's looking around and puzzled. And he looks up at me, and I had another small set down in front for the small group. So he looked up at me and he goes—you know what that means. You come on down here and play down here. So not a word was said. So I pick up my sticks and brushes and go down to the other set. And I played a set down there and I'm in seventh heaven because the whole band is right here in my ear. Oh what a feeling that is when you have the brilliance of the brass and the saxophones right, oh man, it's the original hi-fi. So we take a break. Now we're coming back up and I'm down front now and I got a little closer and got myself comfortable. And Benny's right over my music stand like this, eye level. I'm kind of kitty corner to him. If I look there, there he is. Now he had the habit of having his clarinet under his arm. So he was in that pose looking right at me. And I could hear some murmurs in the background, guys in the sax section saying, "Uh-oh, look's like it's Sonny's turn in the barrel tonight" or something like that. So he's just looking at me over the top of my stand. Just staring at me. And geez I'd had enough. So I stood up, and this is true, I stood up and I went like [waves] this in front of his eyes. He never budged. And the band, everybody's having hysterics. They thought I'd get canned right then. He said, "Sit down kid, what are you doing?" He never knew I did it. So he says, "Okay let's go." And we went on to the next number. That story got around town in New York even. "Geez I heard what you did to Benny." It was funny. He never even acknowledged it. But I did see him ride some guys sometimes and I felt sorry for them. I think it was one of those things that every once in a while if he got in that mood, if he knew he could ride you he'd ride you.[15]

Glenn Miller

The Glenn Miller Orchestra is the Swing Era group that evokes the most vivid memories with today's senior citizens. In Hollywood's version, Jimmy Stewart presented a more likable character than Glenn in real life, but the plot line about capturing "the sound" rang true. There was fierce competition between swing orchestras, and finding something unique was the goal of every band leader.

In 1964, as a fourteen-year-old aspiring saxophonist, my parents took me to see the Glenn Miller Orchestra under the direction of Ray McKinley in a Rochester, N.Y., auditorium. The band sounded much like the records I had come to know. I stood at the front of the stage staring up at the saxmen in their matching blue sport coats, picturing myself as a member. It didn't occur to me that I was born too late and had missed the era where such gigs were prevalent.

Saxophonist Jerry Jerome was with Glenn's first band in 1937, a short-lived group that broke up and then reformed without Jerry. He never enjoyed the hits and the popularity of the second Miller band, but had no regrets:

JJ: George Simon had given me an A-minus rating in the band [the Cliquot Club Eskimos]. He said, "George Seravo and Jerry Jerome would be the outstanding players in the band."

MR: You mean in print he had done this?

JJ: Yeah. He was the editor of *Metronome* magazine. So Glenn came over and said he liked my playing and would I like to join the band. I said, "Glenn, what does it pay?" Because I was still interested in going back to medical school. He says, "$45 a week." I said, "That's what I'm getting with Harry Reiser." And I couldn't see any advancement that way. He says, "Yeah, we're going to grow and I'm recording next week at Decca." "Oh, that sounds pretty good to me." So I made my decision, I left Harry and went with Glenn. And this is a cute story, Monk. I went into the studio to record the first thing with Glenn. And I got to recognize some of the musicians: Manny Klein, Charlie Spivak, Will Bradley. This is the kind of players. I says, "Oh my God, what am I doing here?" And Glenn says, "Now Jerry, in 'I Got Rhythm' would you take thirty-two bars?" "Wow. I'm playing jazz? Hey, this is it. It's worth the forty-five bucks." And I played my first record with Glenn with "I Got Rhythm," with Hal MacIntyre. We were the only two people that had been with the new group that Glenn had gotten up, and I couldn't figure what I was doing with this band, until I got up to the Raymour Ballroom to rehearse and there wasn't any of these guys, just Hal and myself, and all new players. I said to Glenn, "What happened to Charlie Spivak and Manny Klein?" "Oh," he says "they're buddies of mine, and I wanted to make a real good record for my first big band record." So he said they came in.

MR: He got the ringers.

JJ: I didn't know. And then we went to work. And it was work.

MR: He was a task master?

JJ: Oh, unbelievable. I didn't mind, you know it was all new for me. He was a task master but he wanted perfection. And he was also struggling for an identity. You know in those days band leaders had identity, a hook.

MR: A sound.

JJ: A sound, something. Even a guy like Kay Kyser, his sound was his personality. Just introducing the band, "Here comes sassy Sully Mason to sing a tune." But that was how you could identify him. Or Shep Fields blowing water through a straw, you know a bubbling rhythm. Whatever pleases. And Glenn had trouble. He was not a trombone player like Tommy Dorsey. In fact he was rather pedestrian, I thought. You know I didn't think his jazz amounted to very much. And proof is, he never really fronted with his trombone, playing. He would lead the band up front and go back and play with the section.

And so he had to use his arranging acumen.

MR: Because he wasn't a really outgoing-type personality, right? So he couldn't push that part of it.

JJ: Oh, not at all. But Glenn was a great learning experience. I learned what playing notes properly is and how to really play by the mark. Glenn would say, "Crescendo—diminuendo," and he says, "Keep it under—keep it above." But one thing that comes to mind that's so cute, when I played my solo for "I Got Rhythm" with Glenn, I listened to it and it's a chorus and you know you can do a thousand of those on a recording, you never do the same thing, you're improvising. So we went out on our first one-nighter after we did our recording somewhere along the line, I got out and played a totally different chorus, which is a soloist's preference I would think. Glenn came over to me and he said, "Jerry, when you stand up and play your solo, I wish you'd play the one that's on the record." I said, "Why?" "Well," he says, "I consider that part of the arrangement. People expect it. They buy the record and they expect to hear that." Oh, wow.

MR: I sometimes wonder, those classic trumpet solos in some of the Miller arrangements, were they improvised first and then someone actually wrote them out? You know like in "String of Pearls?" Even though it might have been improvised first, it became a part of the arrangements.

JJ: Without question. There have been a lot of Miller bands that have come along the line and I notice that most of them that stand up, play the solos that are on the record. And I think that's for identity. It makes it sound more like the Miller band. So he had a point. But the Part B of that statement is when I joined Benny Goodman, and I got up and stood up and played "Undecided" on a one-nighter, and I played what I'd played on the record, and Benny came over to me and he said, "Did you like what you played on the record?" "Oh," I said. "Thank you, Benny." Yeah. See that's the difference.

MR: Glenn Miller was not a jazz band per se, it was more of a dance—

JJ: Yeah. And the best. Really he was great. His tempos were great, and he strove for an audience reaction too. What do you like? What can I play for you?[16]

Glenn's first band was short-lived and Jerry declined the invitation to join the second iteration. He was the first to admit that his replacement, Tex Beneke, was the right guy for the band.

Sidemen Stories

Les Brown

When I interviewed saxophonist and arranger Dave Pell in 1996 I could tell that he was a bit of a cut-up, a man who never lacked in confidence or the willingness to take a chance. Much of his early career was spent with a lower tier of big bands, but the sidemen always wanted them to sound as polished as possible. Their efforts to ensure this could even include upstaging the leader.

DP: Oh, it was fun. I was in Bobby Sherwood's band and I took Zoot Sims's place. He moved to first alto and I played his tenor chair. Well, I'm sitting next to Zoot all night. I mean what could be bad about that? We're both kids you know. This was in the '40s. And I quit the band I was with in the '40s and stayed on the West Coast and got the job in the relief band. And Stan Getz, myself, great players were sitting in the relief band, a Latin band. And we're having a great time. Stan was the greatest dressing room player that ever lived. He'd get out front and he'd choke. He was terrible. He was so insecure and such an introvert that he couldn't get up like me, no. I don't give a damn, I'm going to get up and play you know.

MR: Can you explain relief band?

DP: A relief band is—the main attraction has got to get a twenty-minute break, and you had to have a live band on stage. And usually a different kind of band so that you could do the rumba, like we had a Latin band playing a Four Brothers-type tenor book. And then we'd play Freddie Martin style.

MR: And then you went with Tony Pastor later on?

DP: The story about Tony Pastor, I get to California and I say, "Gee Tony, this is great. Good-bye. I'm quitting." He says, "You can't leave me in L.A., this is wilderness. There's no guys." I said, "Good-bye." And so he says, "Well, stay with me until we leave California and then you can quit. So six weeks later I left the band. But I had fun with Tony because I'd run out to the microphone to beat him to his own solos. Because he didn't really like to play. But the only way I could get to play was to be a cocky kid and run up to the mic when he's ready to play and I'm up there playing already. "Sorry, Tony."

MR: Sounds like you didn't lack for self confidence.

DP: Oh, no, I was a smart ass, it was just terrible. But that's kind of a thing that you have to do. The sidemen on the band, they keep watching the leader, and watching all the mistakes he makes and all the wrong things he does. Because in the back of his mind, I'm going to be a leader some day. I mean Les Brown, I had a great time with

Lester's band and played on every tune, you know I had a great book to play, and we had [Don] Fagerquist and all the good players. And I remember as I went out every time to play a solo, we just didn't stand up, we'd go out front—show biz. I remember kicking over Les's horn at least once a night. "Oh, I tripped, ohhh, I'm so sorry, oh, Les I'll fix it later." Well, he didn't play too well. And we didn't like him playing in the band with us, because the saxes sounded so good. But when he played he played awful. And so if his horn didn't work, he wouldn't play. And after years and years he finally figured out I was doing it on purpose. You know, "I'm so clumsy, Les, I'm sorry." But I was kicking over his horn so he wouldn't play. Terrible, terrible. But I always wanted to be a leader and you want to be able to, so "No, no, my tempo." And then the drummer in the back says, "No, Dave, that's the wrong tempo, you've got to kick it up here."[17]

Stan Kenton

An elderly gentleman who often comes to my gigs goes into his own bit of heaven when I fill his request for Stan Kenton's "Intermission Riff." He never fails to tell anybody around him that Kenton was a genius. The Stan Kenton Orchestra was the most controversial of all big bands. Stan's idea of what a big band should sound like didn't include the basic parameters that were normally expected. Trombonist Eddie Bert spent time with Kenton and was shocked to learn what Stan wanted and didn't want from his band:

EB: [Stan Kenton] featured trombones. That's why I wanted to go with that band. And he was very popular. I mean guys were poll winners in the band, like Shelly Manne and Art Pepper. Because Kai [Winding] had done great on the band and Kai and I were friends. So I went with the band. And it was like a family that band. He was a great guy to work for.

MR: Some people didn't think he swung very good.

EB: No. That he didn't. One night we played in Mankato, Minnesota. Mankato Ballroom. And generally Stan would like spread out. But this night the bandstand was small. So we were like this. And the band started swinging. And of course we all wanted to swing. So the band was swinging and he stopped it. He said, "This is not Basie. This is Stan Kenton." So we were looking at each other like—damn.

MR: That's really curious.

EB: Yeah I don't know, he just didn't understand swinging. We all looked at each other like what is he talking about. I mean Shelly is a swinger.

You know, Shelly Manne. Well, we always used to go out after the gig and go blow somewhere, wherever we were. But when you get on the bandstand it was Stan Kenton.

MR: But people who came to Kenton expecting to dance, was that a problem?

EB: We used to play the "Concerto to End All Concertos" and that was like all different tempos. And I swear I'd see people dancing. I don't know what they were doing but they were dancing. You'd have the crowd in the front they were all standing there, and in the back would be people dancing. Well, maybe they caught the changes, I don't know. But his band was very popular. He had like a machine. In other words, he had a guy that would go out a month in advance and set everything up, have pictures in all the music stores, have the records. Then Stan would leave after the gig, wherever we were, he'd have his car, and he'd leave and do interviews and be on the radio in whatever city we were in, and it was like a machine. So it all kept rolling like that.[18]

Doc Severinsen's *Tonight Show* Band

Big bands eventually passed from consistent national exposure with the exception of the *Tonight Show* band. Johnny Carson was an amateur drummer, and held enough sway with NBC to insist that this big band would remain intact throughout his tenure. It was led by Skitch Henderson in New York, then by the fashionable trumpeter Doc Severinsen in Los Angeles. Several members of the West Coast *Tonight Show* band were interviewed, and all spoke fondly of their experience. Trumpeter Conte Candoli:

MR: I can recall Johnny looking over there, and saying your name. He knew all the guys in the band.

CC: Yeah. He was great. I'll tell you what, he was a very personal, private person. But when it come to the band, he was very protective of us, man. He would always come and listen to us rehearse, and he knew every one of us, and always went out of his way to be good to us. You know very few people ever got to see his home, and where he lives. The band did. Absolutely.

CC: Doc and the band, we go out and tour twice a year, with the ex-*Tonight Show* band. It's nice to see the cats and get together. On Carson's seventieth birthday, we were on tour. We happened to be in Kansas City. And Doc called Carson's wife and arranged for the band, we were at a rehearsal, to get Johnny on the phone. And when he came to the phone, we played "Happy Birthday" to him. And he says "Where are you guys?" And Doc says, "Well, we're in Kansas City." He was on a speaker phone. He says, "You mean everybody's there—Snooky, Conte, and Shaughnessy and all the cats are all there?" He says, "Yeah, we're all here, man. Happy seventieth, Chief."

MR: That's terrific.

CC: When Buddy Rich died, we were rehearsing the show and Johnny got word that Buddy died. Bam, he canceled the show immediately. They put a rerun on that night because Buddy was one of Carson's favorite people, not just musician. He was tremendous. I don't know if you ever caught any of the shows that Buddy did, but he was great at the panel with Johnny. He was just slick as they come. And they would always try to fool him. Like they put a breakaway cymbal on there. You know and he'd hit it and it would break and fall apart. And it wouldn't stop him.

MR: He wouldn't miss a beat, right?

CC: He'd start tapping on something else man. Once they tied his foot pedal, where he couldn't use his foot pedal. So he just worked with his hi-hat the whole time man. Oh, talk about genius man, this guy was great.

MR: Yeah, he used to do air solos?

CC: Yeah. And never rehearse. They'd always have his drums set up. And he knew that they were going to try to trick him some way, like his snare drum, they put a breakaway skin head on that, the first time he hit in, choom, it went right through. Bass drum, one time they put the same thing on the bass drum, pow the pedal went right through man. It didn't make any difference. The way he would do it.[19]

Saxophonist Tommy Newsom was interviewed with pianist Ross Tompkins, and related that because of on-air time constraints, the band rarely played to the end of a chart:

MR: Some of your music, the TV audience must have heard the first ten seconds and the last five seconds. That always bugged me.

RT: Well, if you were in the studio, you heard a lot of music. You can tell it by how many commercials, because we played through all the commercials. Unfortunately, out over the air it only came the last ten or fifteen seconds.

RT: We used to be on the air for a minute at midnight every night, and then they took that away and filled that up with commercials.

TN: Yeah. In fact, you know what happened? We played a gig at Dante's in L.A. one time. It was a jazz joint. And it was the whole *Tonight Show* band and I was in front. And we were playing the same arrangements, but when we were playing the jobs we'd get to the third page, which we never had got to that.
RT: Some guys never saw that page.
TN: That's where it disintegrated. I don't know whether it was that they couldn't read, or I think it was the shock of the thing, you know?
MR: That's funny. You expect someone to say "Okay, cut."
TN: That's right. Nobody to save you.[20]

Ed Shaughnessy played the classic drum lick that launched the *Tonight Show* theme. He cited the high standards that Doc Severinsen demonstrated and demanded of his sidemen:

MR: Give me one thing about the *Tonight Show*, good or bad.
ES: I'll give you something good. I'd say that Doc Severinsen tried to maintain a standard with that band, just as high from the first week he became the leader, to the very last week. And it never slacked off, ever, ever. And I think he deserves a lot of credit for that because everything comes from the leader. Shoddy playing comes from a leader that doesn't care. Playing that is really there and popping and good energy and good spirit comes because you've got a leader who insists on it. And even though I think you should always play like that, I give Doc full credit for the fact that he made sure sixteen people always were like that. Now I don't mean to paint him like a pain. He wasn't a pain. He just wanted a high class standard of performance. And because he practices two to three hours a day, and because he's always there, there's not one guy in the band that could say, "Yeah, but you don't really work at it." Because probably nobody in the band works as hard as he does at his horn, see? So I give him a lot of credit for that, and I think it's why people are constantly coming up, including today, and telling me how much they miss the band on TV. I think it really locked in an image of a high class, great, powerhouse big band. And I'm glad we did because we were the only thing a lot of people could listen to other than the rock & roll kind of combos that are on most of the other shows. It was a wonderful band to play with, mostly because Doc kept a high standard. And I always have gotten along good with Doc because of that, because I think that's the way you're supposed to play. You know, our saying was you're either going to play good or get the hell out and don't be here.[21]

Jazz Tales from Jazz Legends

Jazz has progressed through stylistic changes at a frantic pace, and big band swing was no exception. Changes in popular tastes and travel restrictions during the World War II years contributed to the decline of the big bands. The limited solo space frustrated the more talented sidemen who then embraced the challenge of bebop. Jazz became music for listeners, soon to be accepted as an art form worthy of an academic focus. Big band nostalgia remains healthy, and swing era hits like "In the Mood," "Take the A Train," and "Sing Sing Sing" still touch a nerve in our consciousness. A short-lived swing revival occurred in the early 1990s with groups like the Squirrel Nut Zippers and the Cherry Poppin' Daddies offering a swinging brand of jump blues.

The most significant legacy passed down from big band sidemen can be found in scholastic jazz ensembles. A dwindling number of Swing Era musicians have lived long enough to hear their great-grandchildren playing in big bands, this time on the concert stage at schools. These young players won't live through the joys and trials shared by Basie, Ellington, and Miller veterans, but they can still experience the original hi-fidelity of saxophones, brass, and rhythm described by Sonny Igoe.

Chapter 3
Road Travails

One reality of the music business is that you have to go where the gigs are. Bands have to venture out from their home base to appeal to new audiences and potential record buyers. Traveling has changed dramatically for musicians in the past five decades and artists are now more likely to have complaints about delayed flights, congested traffic, and problems with airlines transporting valuable instruments.

During my 1980s stint with the progressive rock group Mr. Edd, my bandmates and I shared more travel nightmares than I can remember. A Ford Econoline panel van with no heat and a finicky carburetor played a major role in most of our road stories. The majority of gigs entailed leaving home in the late afternoon and watching the sun come up upon our return. It's a young man's game and not something I would choose to do again, but my experiences pale in comparison to the stories I heard while gathering interviews for the Fillius Jazz Archive.

Of all the musical styles under the jazz umbrella, swing was by far the most commercially successful. Well-crafted arrangements, danceable tempos, and the inclusion of a "boy" and/or "girl" singer inspired young fans to flock to theaters and dance halls. *Down Beat* and other music magazines fueled rivalries between the top bands, and headlines would dramatically announce the raiding of one band's star players by another. For almost fifteen years, starting in the mid-1930s, bands of varying talent and reputation crisscrossed the country, well before the era of thruways and interstates. Buses or a convoy of cars were required to transport these ensembles, and musicians had to deal with the realities of the road.

Once again we hear from trombonist Eddie Bert, about a common practice among road musicians, "ghosting":

EB: When I went with Benny Goodman, he was going to stay out there [in California] for six months, he told us. He stayed for six weeks and then started coming back. So that was kind of a drag.
MR: What was it like to be on the road at that time? Was it a tough life?
EB: Yeah. I mean you don't eat right and all that. You're traveling by bus mostly. And when you stop you stop. You're liable to stop in some place that don't have that good food and stuff like that. So it's kind

of a scuffle.

MR: And a typical day, would the bus leave after you're done playing?

EB: It depends how far the trip is. If it's three hundred miles or five hundred miles, you've got to leave after the gig. And you had to pay for your own hotel in those days. So a lot of guys ghosted. In other words, you had two in a room instead of one. Or three. Whatever you can get away with.

MR: And what was the [weekly] salary like?

EB: From a bill and a half to two bills [$150 to $200]. But your expenses had to come out of that. So it wasn't like today. Today they put you up. It's different.[1]

In our Mr. Edd travels we did a lot of ghosting, often three or four people to a room. Since I owned the van I occasionally opted to sleep in it.

The hours of monotony that musicians experienced during tours often contributed to unhealthy habits. Drummer Sonny Igoe shared a vivid memory from a Woody Herman road trip:

SI: I was always a Boy Scout. I could have more fun with the guys—they were smoking a joint or something like that they'd say, "Come on, Sonny, you never tried it." I said, "All right I'll try it." So I tried it. Nothing happened. I said, "I can have more fun on a bottle of beer. I don't need that." And so anyway I never got involved with that. And a lot of the fellas got involved with that pretty heavily and then they went into some other things pretty heavily, like heroin, cocaine, and stuff like that. And several guys actually, lives [were] ruined completely with that stuff, because they could never kick it. And I won't mention any names, but some very good friends of mine, guys I admired as players, got screwed up badly with that stuff, really bad. Are you ready for another story? We were on one-nighters with Woody Herman's band when I joined. In 1950 he was fighting big debts, you know IRS and GMAC, his booking agency, I think he was into them for about $90,000 or something like that. And he owed over $100,000 to the IRS, that's from the manager who screwed him up. And he had this guy Abe Turchin as manager, who got him out of debt and then he screwed him up. He died broke because of him. But anyway we were on the bus and this dear friend of mine, marvelous trumpet player—I won't mention his name—could play anything on the trumpet, played high screeching, beautiful soft ballads, fast bebop, any style—Dixieland, swing, bebop, anything. World class. And he was a junkie. And when they would run out of junk they'd drink whiskey like it was coming out of a water faucet, to try to help get over it. Well, we were in an un-air-conditioned bus, we were down in Kentucky or South Carolina, someplace, I don't know, Georgia, in that kind of country. All rural, all hot. And we each had a double seat because there was a lot of seats on the bus and there was fifteen guys or whatever. So right across from me is this guy who is a dear friend. And I'm finally falling asleep and I said, "Go to sleep, go to sleep." So anyway I'm falling asleep [sniffs]. I smell burning flesh, okay? And I look over and here's this guy, he had a cigarette with his hand, he was unconscious practically. He has a cigarette and it had burned down between his two fingers and was burning his flesh and smoking. It was actually smoking. So I go like this across the aisle, knock it off, naturally wake him up. And he started in on me like—I can't mention the words he used and how dumb I was and what's the idea and blah-blah-blah. And I tried to explain to him. The next day he saw it, it didn't bother him at all. He played like it never happened. But that's how, unfortunately, some of those guys ruined their lives with that stuff. I was a square.[2]

Sonny bequeathed his musical genes to his son, Tommy, who now leads the high-powered Birdland Big Band from his drum stool.

Bucky Pizzarelli has played guitar in every conceivable situation. Coming from a long line of musicians, the idea of traveling to gigs was not cause for parental concern. He received his first significant travel lesson with the Vaughn Monroe Orchestra:

MR: The transition from high school into Vaughan Monroe, your parents were supportive of that?

BP: Well, they were in a way because my mother's brothers were on the road—a brother was on the road—with a lot of different bands, Clyde McCoy, Buddy Rodgers, Raymond Scott, Teddy Powell, played with all the bands, played just rhythm [guitar] but he was very good at it. Bob Chester. And I was on Christmas vacation, I was just about to graduate from my school and a lot of the big bands were losing men to the draft. And Vaughan Monroe almost gave up the band thinking that he was going to be drafted, but he didn't. So he said let's get the band back together again. And there were a lot—about seven or eight chairs open for anybody. So my trumpet friend called me and says, "Come on, come with the band." So I jumped on a bus and played Scranton, Binghamton, and Rochester, and went back to school the following Monday. But the funny thing

Jazz Tales from Jazz Legends

was my father gave me fifteen bucks out of the cash register, and I came back with change.

MR: And you were buying meals and the whole thing?

BP: Well, that was the era of the dime tip and the blue plate special you know. You couldn't spend any money. Everything was a buck.

MR: But do you recall thinking of that as really inexpensive?

BP: No, I didn't.

MR: Because everything was relative.

BP: Fifteen dollars was a lot of money. Three five-dollar bills. Then I came home with change, and a steady job. So I graduated the week after, and I went on the road with Vaughan, and we played about ten weeks of theaters, just a week at a time—Cleveland, Baltimore, Boston. Places like that. Pittsburgh. And I got a geography lesson at the same time. And it was very thrilling for me.

MR: In the book that I was reading about you there is a short bit about a fire on your bus. How did that come about?

BP: Well, you know we had the brakes fixed on the bus. And somehow in hot weather, if you used them too soon they expand. And we were in West Virginia and we were going up and down and up again and all of a sudden one of the trumpet players in the back said, "Hey, there's flames coming out of the back." The bus driver said, "You're crazy." "No," he says. We stopped the bus and sure enough. We were playing cards. We all jumped off the bus in our tee shirts. And the bus burned down in about fifteen minutes, right down to just the four wheels. And we had a gig that day. So we waited for a Greyhound to come in, jumped on the Greyhound and went to the theater in some little town. And they had no backstage. The band had to go right down the center aisle, the way we looked. No uniforms—the uniforms were gone. Luckily the instruments were saved. They went in another truck.

MR: When you say we played a theater, what exactly does that mean?

BP: Well, the bands used to play theaters. Like similar to the Paramount, for instance. Now they'd play an opening number and they'd bring out the singer, then they'd bring out a juggler or a comedian. And we'd play a couple more numbers, then they'd put the picture on. But you'd do that four or five times a day.

MR: Did they have a screen that came down?

BP: No, the band came out of the pit. First they would show a newsreel. And that's when the band would assemble in the pit. As the newsreel was finishing the pit would come up and you'd see the newsreel and the band briefly. And they'd go through their act. Sometimes we'd

Road Travails

       play for a big singer, like Dinah Shore, Frank Sinatra.
MR: Okay. Someone that wasn't in the band but you would play their charts.
BP: Yeah. And we had an animal act too. It was funny, a funny situation. A juggler.
MR: You learned to do just about everything.
BP: Yeah, you had to play that show. But when you do that for ten weeks, it gets a little crazy.
MR: Did you ever have any train wrecks?
BP: Oh yeah. Once we were playing a monkey act and the monkey came out on one skate. "Due to gas rationing my partner was a little late," so all he did was sit there in a chair while he did an act with a little dog that did all the tricks. But the act was that the owner would turn around and yell out "Frank Buck" and the monkey would go [motion, flails his arms]. Frank Buck was the guy that brought all the animals over from Africa.
MR: Oh my God. I see.
BP: That was a no-no. And once down in Philadelphia when he came out on one skate, there was a cat came up from the pit, see? And he saw the cat and he chased the cat right down the center aisle. He didn't care about the act or nothing. Then during that one tour with this chimp, the saxophone players would put candy on a string so as he came out he would scoop it up and eat it. Then when they had the string they pulled it and he wouldn't get it see? He'd miss it. And he jumped on the whole sax section trying to get that candy.[3]

    Bucky's story makes it clear that swing musicians were obliged to play an eclectic mix of music and act as accompanists for whoever or whatever was on the bill that night. Like Sonny Igoe, Bucky has passed his musical genes on to his sons, John and Martin.
    Jay McShann made his reputation as a consummate blues pianist with an astute eye for talent. His hires included saxophonist Charlie Parker and singer Walter Brown. During our conversation he spoke of the relationship between dance halls and traveling bands. His recollections offered a fascinating look into the day-to-day life of a traveling musician in the '40s, and an issue specific to pianists:

MR: You had some pretty good records with Walter Brown.
JM: Yes, yes, yes. We were lucky to have Walter Brown.
MR: And you toured around the country?
JM: Sure did.

Jazz Tales from Jazz Legends

MR: What kind of places were you playing at the time. They were dance halls?

JM: Well, we were just playing dances. A lot of parts of states at that time were hungering for dance, hungry for music, hungry for hearing something different, and so quite naturally a lot of bands, road bands, were traveling. And you could get into Texas for two weeks, because you had all those towns and all those dance towns. See what I mean? Start at Dallas, Fort Worth Sunday night, Austin Wednesday, Houston Thursday, Galveston Friday. And just town after town like that. And that's the way they could book 'em.

MR: Were you playing for segregated audiences at that time?

JM: Yes. In some places we played I mean whites on this side and blacks on that side.

MR: How did they keep them apart?

JM: Well, they might have a rope coming down.

MR: No kidding. I bet you played some bad pianos over the years.

JM: Oh, we've had some awful pianos. I know I used to—sometimes we'd get pianos and the pianos would be so bad I'd get drunk. Yeah I'd get in front of that mess you know, and say, "Well now, we ain't going to have no piano tonight." I says, "Brown, there ain't going to be no piano tonight, you'll have to sing with the horns." And some of the pianos you'd have to tune, like we used to tune up with A. Sometimes you might be tuning up with C above A. Or maybe F below A. Now that's how far they were out of tune some of them. And a lot of times if the band was playing in A♭ I'd probably be playing in B♭ or B♮. That made us have to go get drunk on that night. I had my excuse already made out. I'd get in front of that mess, cut out and go back to the hotel about eleven.[4]

Big bands rarely traveled by air. Even lengthy cross country jaunts were made by train. Bassist Jimmy Lewis experienced an exception, much to his chagrin. Jimmy was a member of the Count Basie band in the early '50s, and a series of gigs for the U.S. military resulted in a rare but memorable plane ride:

MR: I was glancing at your notes and you had a story about flying with Basie?

JL: Yeah, you know we had some Army camps to do. We had to ride in the Army planes, the ones with two tails, and that big thing in the middle. So one day we got on this thing going to one of the camps, and it was noisy. This thing was so noisy you couldn't hear. Now Billy

Eckstine and all those guys were used to riding. But me, I was scared to death. We all had parachutes. Basie had on a parachute over by the door. So we were going to Corpus Christi, Texas. So the plane took off, but before we got there, something happened just before we got ready to land. They couldn't get the landing gear down. So the guy kept punching it in back, there was some long pole they couldn't get it down. So the man said, "We're going to have to circle around and go further, and come back around again." So they went around, and started back to see if we could land, and still couldn't get it open. So one of the guys, the one who was right by the back door here, pulled that big door open. Now we were flying. So I said, "What's this? What are you doing?" The guy said, "Well see, we're trying to get a little more air in the plane." I said, "Air in the plane!" I said, "Man, we don't need no more air." So he said, "Well, I'll tell you, we're having a problem with the landing gear." And he said, "You might have to bail out." And Basie looked at me. He said, "What do you mean bail out?" And so he asked the pilot, he said, "Look, are you going to bail out too?" The pilot said, "No, I've got to stay with the plane." He said, "Well, I'm going to stay with you." "Because," he said, "if I jump out and I pull this string and the 'chute don't open up," he said, "man, I can't fly. I don't have no wings." Well, everybody was laughing. And so Billy teased me, he said, "Man," he said, "we're going to crash"—oh baby, I don't know what to do. And I'm running back and forth. It's funny. I'd never been in a plane before anyway.

MR: Something finally happened because you're here with us.

JL: So we get to Corpus Christi, Texas. So finally we land. Everybody set there about fifteen minutes before they got out of the plane. It was quiet. Boy, you could hear a mouse. So everybody started getting out one by one, taking off the parachute, taking their instruments and go outside. We got outside, and we had to play under some trees. We get out there, and set up under these trees out there, in the hot summertime. Oh, man, it looked like a big field. And people, as far as you could see. And they had all these big speakers. So they set the bandstand up, all the stands, they put the music, the fella, he'd take care of all that. And so then Basie went up to test the piano to see if it was in tune. So then he called us, his band. We got up there and Basie was telling about this trip, how much trouble we had with the plane and all that. So the people settled down and we started playing. As soon as we started playing, all these little chrysalis come out of the tree and started falling on the bandstand. And it's falling in the bell of the horn, and the guy'd dump it out and keep playing. I got me some string, tying it all around my pants legs you know, in case they would crawl up my leg. And so when we finished the job, now we've got to take this same plane and go to California. So me and [trumpeter] Wendell Culley walked out to the plane and looked in, and we see all these parachutes on the seats, and Culley said, "They look like dead people, man." He said, "We can't take this thing, can we?" I said no. So I said, "Well, let's go tell Basie we don't think we're going to go on this." So we went and told Basie and he said, "I don't blame you." But he said, "I've got to stay with the band and so you go ahead and see if you can get a train out, and meet us in California." So we did. We got a train. We got to California three days later. And I think we missed one gig. But we got to the gig and we played and everything. So we asked Basie, "How was the trip?" He said, "Man, that was the worst trip I ever had." He said, "Good thing you didn't come, because somebody would have died."[5]

Jimmy survived this ordeal and in subsequent years found work in New York recording studios. His distinctive bass lines were a major contribution to the success of the 1968 Broadway musical *Hair*.

By the early 1950s the big bands had been mostly replaced by vocalists supported by small groups. A few big bands managed to put together tours, and clarinetist Kenny Davern signed up with the Ralph Flanagan band while still in high school. In his inimitable style, Kenny offers a reality check on what was then still a young musician's dream:

KD: We did sixty one-nighters in ninety days. We made the most amount of money any band had ever made on the road, whatever it was. I don't want to quote any figure I'm not sure of. And all the guys came up to me and said, "Oooh, wow, you're the big time." "Big time my ass," I said. Horrible. It was awful out there.

MR: Why it was awful?

KD: Well first, maybe you're driving through Keokuk, Iowa, on the way to Ames. Or maybe it was Ames on the way to Keokuk. Anyway, the most you might see was a Stewart Drive-In, root beer and hot dogs. You know you'd have that and an ice cream. Back in the car, some more traveling. You get to this place, you're in your jeans and sort of like a man dressed in hell. Well, it was hot. The cars didn't even have air conditioners in 1953. Some did but ours never did. And you'd get there at maybe five, six o'clock, and you're right at the gig, at the ballroom. And there's the ballroom. The ballroom is

Road Travails

like on Highway 483 midway between Chicago and Detroit. And to shave you had to plug in, there was one outlet by the bandstand. You'd plug that in, each guy would take a turn with his electric shaver shaving. Next. And then there was like one sink in back of the bandstand with cold water only and a naked light bulb hanging down, and a cracked piece of a mirror. And that's where you washed up. And you put on a shirt. Nylon shirts had just come out. Short sleeve nylon shirts. And it was the summertime. Because you needed something you could wash out right away and hang up and dry and cotton shirts just weren't in then. I mean you could do that but it wasn't really practical. And so these shirts were hot, I'm telling you, you closed up that collar and you put on a black bow tie, which you had to make yourself in those days. And then you put a wool jacket on and your tuxedo pants. You were roasting. And you did four sets, four hour sets, and then you packed up the horn and folded up the book and put it on the pile and packed up your horns and they put them on the truck and you got in the car and you rode, let's say maybe 350 more miles, and you'd go through the towns at that time, obeying the speed limit because they were all speed traps, and if you'd go one mile over they grabbed you and you had to pay off. So all the drivers were aware of this. And a lot of times you almost got killed speeding on a three lane. The middle lane was for passing in either direction going through.

MR: So it wasn't like thruways and all that.

KD: No, there were no thruways. So I'll finish with this road travail. And what the hell, you ever doze and try to fall asleep in the back seat of a 1953 Buick? What do they call it, where the hump is?

MR: The drive shaft?

KD: The drive shaft. Well, the drive shaft was like two feet up, so you had your knees in your chin. And two guys on each side of you. And two guys up front. Well, I mean you're zooming along and all of a sudden you hear, "Hold on to your hats, fellas," and you look up and you see two eighteen-wheelers, one on each side of you, one going this way and the other one going that way, and you're in the center of the two of these guys. Very frightening. And a lot of guys got killed in those kind of precarious road driving things at the end. And then you get into the town where you're going to go, you know you left at about eleven-thirty, twelve [at night] let's say. Maybe about six-thirty, seven in the morning you've rolled into the other great town which boasted a Milner Hotel at $3.75 or $2.75 a night, I forget which, and you couldn't check in, you see. So the bell captain would take your luggage. And these were very cheap hotels. And then you'd walk around town. You'd have breakfast in one of those Dew Drop Inn places, maybe visit the local music store to see what kind of instruments they have, because good horns were still relatively easy to find, premium horns. Of course none of us had any money, but if we needed it we would borrow or whatever. And then when you checked in maybe at eleven, twelve, or one o'clock, you may have gotten a haircut, whatever. Anything to kill some time. And you slept 'til about five o'clock, and that's when you had your wake-up call, you got dressed, you shaved and showered and you went down to the local buffet, cafeteria style. And you had spaghetti or whatever, depending on what part of the world you're in. And then you went to the gig and that night you were able to stay over but you left at nine the next day because again, you had 350 miles to go. So you know you do that —

MR: Day after day.

KD: Yeah. It was really quite hard. But you know as a kid you don't care about that. I think I made $125 a week, and I cleared $117.50. You could save money, believe it or not, in 1953.

MR: Because the rooms and the meals weren't that expensive.

KD: Right. Every other night it was $2.75 or maybe $3.00.

MR: Well, that experience may have put some perspective on things for you.

KD: I expected much more. From then on I just got very—like I said when I came home, "Oh boy," they all said, you know, starry eyed, and thought I'd be stage struck. "How was it?" "It was the f---ing worst," I said. Plain and simple. Ohhhh, they all wanted to do that. And I had done it. So I didn't see any romance to that whatsoever.[6]

Kenny spent the rest of his career playing with small groups, where he was less likely to be stuck with the driveshaft. He performed numerous times at Hamilton College and consistently delighted me with his musicality.

By the 1960s dancers had embraced rock & roll and the few remaining big bands were booked in concert settings or jazz clubs. Ellington, Basie, and Woody Herman survived and were joined by high-powered groups led by Buddy Rich and Maynard Ferguson. Alto saxophonist Lanny Morgan shared a story illustrating that the travel ordeal could remain the same even as the music progressed:

MR: What was the travel situation like [with Maynard Ferguson]? Was it a tough grind in those days?

Road Travails

LM: Yes. Looking back at it you forget all those things. It was a wonderful experience but I wouldn't want to do it again. Yeah, because we didn't have a bus, we had station wagons. And starting salary on that band was $120 a week. I made $135 because I was not only the lead alto player but played a lot of jazz too and because he'd known me. And so $135 a week and he had two station wagons and then he drove himself. I wound up driving one of the station wagons. And well you can imagine, if you have a one-nighter in Chicago, I just found a pay receipt for this the other night, it was for $23.65, a one-nighter in Chicago. Now out of that tax was taken, so you get about $19.00. Out of that you have to pay for your own lodging and for food, so we used to stay at the Croyden Hotel in Chicago, that was like $2.50 a night, another 50¢ if you wanted a black & white TV. And say another $6.00 for food maybe. So in other words you're coming home with $11.00, $11.50. So I took the driving job because we got one cent a mile. Well now, Chicago is 960 miles, so I would come home with an extra $18.00, or a little over $19.00, plus my $11.00, would be thirty bucks I would have.

MR: That was like an extra night of work.

LM: That's right. When I joined that band we rehearsed the day I got there, and the next day we opened at Birdland. It seems like we played there for three weeks. A good band. And then we had one day off and we went to the Brooklyn Paramount and we played there opposite the newly-formed Jazztet. That was for ten days. And then we had about four gigs on the road—Pennsylvania, around Philly, in that area. And then I thought, this is wonderful. What is that, like 135 times 5 almost. I'm rolling. I was paying $155 a week for a place at 85th and Broadway in Manhattan and I thought I'd died and gone to heaven. Then we didn't work for a month and a half, see, and nobody was on retainer. Everything was pro-rated when we did work. So the reality set in there. Because then I really went from wealthy to poor in about five weeks. But the driving was terrible. I'd set out like at eight at night from Junior's or Charlie's Tavern at 52nd and Broadway, to go to Chicago or even Pittsburgh or some place, and it would be snowing so hard you couldn't see somebody standing as close to me as you are, and have to drive all that way, and usually we'd leave late so we could catch the day sheet, which meant you'd check in about six in the morning and you'd grab a few hours' sleep, and then you'd leave right after the gig and come back to New York to save money.

MR: The day sheet?

Jazz Tales from Jazz Legends

LM: Well, the day sheet begins usually at six or seven in the morning. In other words that's that day.

MR: Are you talking about a hotel?

LM: A hotel. Their sheet for new people checking in begins at probably seven or eight in the morning, if they have any rooms available then. So we would try and catch that and get a good day's sleep and then leave after the job and drive all the way back to New York which was difficult.

MR: You mean you drove to Chicago [from New York] for a one-nighter?

LM: Oh yeah. Several times.

MR: Boy, I thought the rock & roll business was something.

LM: No, we did that quite a few times.

MR: And the thruway system, the roads were a long way from where they are now?

LM: The thruways and the turnpikes were finished, but the interstates were not. And of course although we got reimbursed for tolls, it took time to stop and go through the toll booths all the time. And when you're on a roll, you know I couldn't drink during that period. I had to stay sober. Because driving through a blizzard with these guys—but you just get on a roll and you want to go. It's kind of hypnotic, and I really shouldn't have done that. But we would try these new interstates and they were a drag because you'd take an interstate for a hundred miles and you'd think, oh this is wonderful, and they were brand new roads and so forth. And then it would say "END." End of interstate. Merge into one lane. So you'd come into one lane and then it would take you probably an hour and a half to get back to a decent road. So that part of it was a drag, and there were some places like Cincinnati that it was almost impossible to get to. There were a lot of two-lane highways, backwoods gas stations where you were almost afraid to stop. We had a couple of carloads of kids follow us into a gas station in West Virginia once and they had chains. You know they were going to get us good. Fortunately our car was newer and we got out of there fast. But there was a lot of that really. It was not completely safe to be traveling, even with six guys in the car.[7]

These travel experiences are part of paying dues and cannot be taught in the classroom. Phil Woods offered one possible way to give aspiring music performers a taste of the road:

PW: Get some ill-fitting uniforms, you know, very uncomfortable. The lightweight in winter, the heavyweight in the summer. A bus whose windows don't open and no air conditioning, no Walkmans allowed. Everybody's got to double. All the saxophones have got to have at least four or five cases to carry, and a big thick book of about four hundred charts. Put everybody on the bus and just drive around in circles on the campus for about twelve, fifteen hours. Then get off the bus, everybody put on these terrible uniforms, call out a set, and the book is never in order. It's like [saxophonist] Gene Quill style, you know, 1, 2, 47, 93, 207, 5. Call out the set real quick—everybody gets all their instruments out. Okay, put the instruments back. Put the music back. Put your book in order. Hang up your suit. Get back on the bus. Drive around for another twelve or fifteen hours. Do it once again. And I think you might cut the wheat from the chaff. Who wants to do this? I mean it's an exaggeration on all points, because there are no more big bands where you could even do this. But that's the way it used to be. I don't think it has to be that way. But nevertheless the hardest part of the music business is the traveling, whether it's a bus or a plane, or just the idea of existing. I mean it ain't about playing. The playing is easy. It's all the nonsense you go through to bring your horn up to the bandstand. That's the altar. That's the safe place.[8]

I can imagine an ad in the Help Wanted Section. *Wanted: Musicians to perform four hours of music nightly, may or may not be to your liking. Extensive travel required (tedious and potentially dangerous). Weekly salary minimal. You pay for food and accommodations. Benefits not included.*

So why did they do it? What was the reward that justified these road travails? Tenor saxophone player Billy Mitchell referred to it as "a calling,"[9] and alto saxophonist Jerry Dodgion declared, "It's why I'm alive."[10]

Musicians share a curious trait with inveterate gamblers: every win erases all previous losses. They do it for that winning night on the bandstand where everything is in sync. The ensemble is playing as one, the rhythm section is in the pocket, the soloists are playing above their own individual abilities, and the audience becomes a participant in the joy. They can celebrate—even if briefly—getting paid to do something special that only a chosen few can do. For a while they can set aside the tedium and trials that brought them to that moment, and revel in a feeling that can't truly be articulated.

Chapter 4
Arranging the Notes

I recently watched *The Glenn Miller Story*[1] yet again. Thanks to my parents' LP collection, Miller's recordings provided my first exposure to jazz-related music. I love the part in the film where Glenn (Jimmy Stewart) describes his obsession with achieving a unified sound from a variety of instruments and musicians. I have this arranging bug. I'm not happy unless I am arranging something: a tune for a saxophone quartet, a full big band score, or a duet for two flutes.

In the early twentieth century, jazz was mostly a small group affair, with instrumentalists making up their parts and predominantly playing by ear. As bands grew larger, this improvisatory approach became untenable, and the role of the arranger increased in importance. All the successful band leaders depended on arrangers unless they wrote the music themselves. Many top arrangers remained in obscurity, known only to fellow musicians or the most ardent fans.

Arranging work can encompass a wide variety of situations, from writing a chart for the Count Basie Orchestra to scoring a grade C horror film. Almost every piece of music we hear that involves more than a four-piece band requires input from these specialists.

For Dick Hyman, playing piano in a variety of musical settings provided an effective tutorial for his expansion into arranging:

MR: Is there a part of your career that you enjoy more than others? You've written for films, you've played with many jazz artists, and made your own records, and I'm interested if all of this came about due to your own curiosity or has it happened serendipitously, or because of practical issues like making a living?

DH: Well, I learned early on that the more things I could do, the more I'd be called to work, and making a living is a very big factor for all of us. So I was pleased to learn organ and be on call for all kinds of peculiar, non-jazz organ things, and played piano in very odd situations indeed, and arranging began to come around because I was so active every other way so I began to be the arranger and conductor on dates. But you've asked what I really liked to do. And I think that early on and finally in a sense, what I really like to do is play solo jazz piano. That's really the way I began and it's probably the way I'll end up too. I think I can express myself best doing that. And as much as I love playing with rhythm sections and with great people like Milt [Hinton], the solo piano thing ties in with my earliest piano training. So it's what I continue working on full time.

MR: How about your arranging career? What were some of your first experiences in arranging and was it difficult for you at that time, and did you learn this craft from someone else or was it kind of trial and error?

DH: Well, I studied orchestration for a while, legitimate orchestration, in Juilliard, but really whatever I've learned has come about from being there. I used to play with so many kinds of orchestras that it was bound to rub off. In any case, a pianist is always arranging, because even to play in a non-jazz situation is shorthand, and the figured bass really, and you have to be making up and filling in and amplifying what the rest of the orchestra is doing or not doing. You just have to have some arranging skills simply to play piano in an orchestra. So I began to arrange as the situations came up. It was very hard at first, because it was so much easier to play, but you have to accept the prospect of delayed gratification. And that's still the case with arranging. You'll kill yourself and stay up all night, and then you wonder if it's worth it. But it is when you hear it played back.[2]

Composers and arrangers started as instrumentalists and often paid their dues as sidemen in traveling bands. Pianist Mike Abene's road experience and hassles with pianos helped steer him down the arranger's path:

MA: My big thing on the road was with Maynard [Ferguson]'s band. You know I didn't go through a lot of bands because I was so involved in the writing end of it. But with Maynard at the time it was funny. It was like two station wagons and a panel truck. It was a smaller band, it was four reeds, two trombones, four trumpets including Maynard, and three rhythm. So you'd have usually the band boy and one driver would be driving the panel truck and the rest of us would be split up into two station wagons. Which, if you've ever ridden with five or six guys in a station wagon, six or eight hundred miles—to this day I can sleep bolt upright, in a train or car I can just sit bolt upright. It looks like I'm looking at you and I could be asleep. But the thing is, it was funny with Maynard because I was never really happy with any of the records, first of all. And just the recording quality, it was only one record I felt that the band really sounded good was a thing called the "Blues Roar." And we had enlarged the band for that particular—it's Don Sebesky and I and Willie Maiden did the writing. But in the clubs, when we'd do clubs or concerts, it was wonderful because Maynard would just open up all the charts and we'd play like it was a small band. I mean some tunes were like forty-five minutes, fifty minutes, and the rhythm section just used to be very loose. So if we could only capture that on record, I always felt.

MR: As a piano player, did you ever have to deal with lousy pianos?

MA: God, that's why I prefer writing. You just answered—and you just solved the riddle of my life. People say, don't you miss playing? Yeah I miss playing. But I really love writing because, the first reason being that you know you guys can play your own horns, like the drummer plays his drums, the bass player, but then you're stuck with some of these pianos, they're just hideous. And to this day that's still kind of an occupational hazard for piano players too. The other thing is sometimes you play and you play a great solo, right? So the next night you go back and nobody even has any idea about how well you might have played the night before. It's up in the air someplace. At least you write something—a good band—it's there to remind you if it's really good.[3]

It was a bonus when an arranger could write for the band he played in. Parts were not just written for 1st Trumpet or Trombone 3 for example, but for the man playing the horn. Duke Ellington based much of his success on this practice, and had to recast a composition on the rare occasion of losing a band member.

Saxophonist Frank Foster was one of Count Basie's finest arrangers. On the first page of his score for "You Stepped Out of a Dream" (written to feature Joe Williams) we can see what bandmates he had in mind as he put pencil to paper. I can only imagine what it felt like to write for a team of brass players that included Snooky Young, Thad Jones, Wendell Culley (Prof), Joe Newman, Henry Coker, Al Grey, and Benny Powell.

Frank Foster provided perfect charts to suit Joe Williams, Basie's star vocalist. Some years later, Frank played saxophone in a session that brought together an equally skilled arranger and vocalist. A 1964 recording of "Fly Me to the Moon" featured the best of the best: Quincy Jones, Frank Sinatra, and the Count Basie Orchestra. It's worth taking a look at what makes this arrangement memorable.

"Fly Me to the Moon" was composed in 1954 by Bart Howard,

Arranging the Notes

Score excerpt from "You Stepped Out of a Dream," composed by Herb Brown, arranged by Frank Foster, for Count Basie and Joe Williams, July 19, 1959. (Fillius Jazz Archive, gift of Jillean Williams)

originally written as a waltz and titled "In Other Words." It's a basic song harmonically, but employs an effective songwriting practice, alternating between C major and the relative A minor, a device also employed in songs like "The Autumn Leaves" and "My Funny Valentine." It uses a straightforward 32-bar form divided evenly in half, with a nice outer space/romance metaphor: "Fly me to the moon/Let me play among the stars/Let me see what spring is like/On Jupiter and Mars."

According to the LP liner notes, Quincy Jones flew to Hawaii for a musical sit-down with Sinatra and his accompanist, Bill Miller. He was working under a deadline, and as is often the case, deadlines inspire an arranger's best work. As the needle touches down on this LP, the first thing you hear are Sonny Payne's brushes on a snare drum establishing a perfect tempo. In the fourth bar a subtle skipping lick sets up two E's from Basie, an octave apart. This is Sinatra's cue.

Regarding that tempo, we clock in at 122 beats per minute, a technical number mostly irrelevant to musicians. I have never once played in a band where the leader or the drummer enunciates, "Okay ready? 120 beats per minute" and starts the song. Tempos are felt, and Basie was the master of that. He often noodled on the piano and found that perfect groove before he cued in the band.

Jazz Tales from Jazz Legends

The first sixteen bars of "Fly Me to the Moon" are exquisitely simple, and Sinatra can be partly credited for this. I recently heard an interview with Quincy Jones and a Canadian radio host where the subject of "Fly Me to the Moon" was discussed. Q (as Frank called Quincy) stated that the first sixteen bars of his score were not what they ended up with. Sinatra said, "That's a little dense, Q," and adjustments were made. What we get is basically a jazz combo anchored by Freddie Green's ever steady strumming on the guitar, some tasty flute from Frank Wess, and a relaxed and swinging Sinatra. The saxes eventually sneak in and echo the notes of "in other words." You'll notice throughout that Sinatra, unlike many singers who love the sound of their voice, does not extend his words at the ends of phrases, but cuts them off, leaving space for the band to be heard.

The second half of the song, at :40, introduces a delightful skipping lick from the saxophone section, and a very subtle backbeat riff from the trombones. Harry "Sweets" Edison, a Basie alum and frequent companion in the studios with Sinatra, enters with some muted trumpet at :52. Quincy Jones knew something that the great arrangers know. One of the best ways to get people to listen harder is to write softer. This sparse but swinging musical setting is building a tension that is finally released at 1:12, as Sinatra finishes the first go-round of the song. As Sweets lays into straight quarter notes, Sonny Payne sets up the band with two full bars of one-beat triplets. The ensuing crescendo unleashes the Basie band in all their glory. Quincy writes a paraphrasing of the melody with a wonderful "doit" (an upward fall) from the brass section.

Quincy doesn't beat us over the head for too long. The decibels come back down and Q recasts the song's melody. After a few hearings you literally can sing along with the brass section as the notes and the words match up. Frank Wess adds a bit of flute and the second half of the song is set up with an outrageous brass chord, complete with a downward fall. A more animated Sinatra sings "Fill my heart with song" backed by saxes and trombones, and the song chugs along to its conclusion. The musical term "tag" is a commonly used device as an arrangement nears the end. The last four bars, or the last sentence, of the song is repeated once or twice. Quincy writes a tag for Sinatra, and Frank finally employs his marvelous phrasing that he learned from trombonist Tommy Dorsey early in his career. In the line "Please be true" he holds "true" for two full bars, refusing to breathe, singing straight into "in other words"—a marvelous musical moment. The Basie brass and reeds answer his phrases.

The ending we anticipate in Count Basie arrangements does not disappoint. Most swing musicians know what the "Count Basie ending" is: three rhythmically-spaced chords followed by a low, emphatic "exclamation

Arranging the Notes

point." The word "Splank" for Basie was coined by Sinatra—a good onomatopoeic description of the lick. Splank-Splank-Splank-Boom. In this case, Basie provides the splanky chords and Sinatra provides the closer with "you."

This musical magic occurred in a mere 2:31. I've listened to this cut hundreds of times, thinking as an arranger, listening for something that could have been done slightly different, slightly better. It's not to be found.

Bill Holman, who was capable of writing thick and powerful charts for Stan Kenton, also recognized the need for space when he had his first assignment for a vocalist:

MR: You had quite a list of singers here that you arranged for also. When was your first experience doing a chart for a singer?

BH: It must have been around the middle '50s for Peggy Lee. I believe in starting at the top you know. And I was really scared because I had kind of a crush on her since 1942.

MR: Oh that's nice.

BH: But she's a great singer, so I really took it easy writing the charts. I didn't put a whole lot in there, you know, afraid to get in their way. She told me later after a couple of years, she said, "The thing I really like about your charts is all the stuff you leave out." So I guessed right on that one.

MR: How were you able to hear what you wrote? When was the first time that you had an opportunity?

BH: When I went to that school. Because they had what they called a dance band and a studio orchestra and stuff like that, so you could hear everything that you did, which is really important. Because it doesn't do you any good to just sit home and write charts and never hear them. You don't know what works and what doesn't.

MR: I guess that was the beauty of Ellington's situation.

BH: Yeah. Next day. Well, that's partly why I started my band, in the '70s. Because for years I'd been writing charts and either taking them down to a rehearsal or putting them in the mail and sending them somewhere, and never seeing the music again and not hearing it until I heard this band's particular interpretation of what I'd written. And a lot of times it wasn't exactly what I had in mind. But the simplest thing was to start my band, which Woody Herman told me to do one time. I griped at him about a tempo and he said, "Well, what we tell the arrangers that are unhappy, we tell them to start their own band." So that's what I did.[4]

Jazz Tales from Jazz Legends

Arrangers typically begin their careers adapting music they like for an ensemble of their choice. Once they are hired to write, they lose the freedom to choose their own source material. Sometimes the biggest challenge in a work-for-hire assignment is the quality of the original content. During my arranging/studio experience, the engineer had a phrase we used when we were trying to rescue music that had no redeeming qualities: "putting frosting on crap." Bill spoke honestly about his brief film-scoring career:

BH: I've never gone into actually composing for movies. I did a couple of grade C movies in the '50s.
MR: Did you ever see them?
BH: Yes. One of them made TV and it comes out occasionally as a re-run. It was called *Swamp Women*.[5]
MR: *Swamp Women* with score by Bill Holman. Yeah?
BH: Yeah. Terrible music.
MR: I'm going to watch it.[6]

The previously mentioned phrase "work for hire" is an interesting term. Arrangers may toil for years before they are paid for their writing, but that time is not wasted. The process serves as compensation, especially when the student is fortunate enough to learn from a master.

Derrick Gardner has played in the trumpet section of the Smithsonian Jazz Masterworks Orchestra, the Harry Connick Jr. Big Band, and the Count Basie Orchestra. He caught the arranging bug from Frank Foster, who ably led the Basie band after the Count passed.

MR: I have to say that I'm envious of one of your accomplishments, that you've written charts and had the Count Basie Orchestra play them. People dream about that, you know.
DG: Yeah, yeah. It was early in my arranging career, you might say. When I first joined the band, in 1991, Frank Foster was directing the band. And in between cities on the bus he'd be sitting at the front of the bus in his seat with a pad of manuscript paper, a chart for big band instrumentation, and a black felt-tipped pen, and with no piano or anything you know. And he was doing saxophones, trumpets, trombone. And I was thinking about him doing that and I said wow, that's pretty slick, man. I thought, I wonder if I can do that. I got some ideas about writing, about a tune I wanted to arrange. And so I bought a big pad of score paper, manuscript paper, got my pencil, and I said [scats] and I wrote about eight to ten measures or something. And I figured, I said, man I've got one of the greatest

Arranging the Notes

arrangers in the history of this music at arm's length distance to me. I've got to learn something from him. So after I wrote out my few little measures I went to the front of the bus about a couple of weeks later and I said, "Hey, Fos, would you kindly take a look at this and see if I'm on the right path here?" He said, "Okay." And he took it and looked at it and he says "Um hum, um hum" and he took his cap from his black pen and he went "Um hum," grabbed his red pen took the cap off and he said, "Okay that's all wrong, and this should be a B♮ instead of B♭, and why'd you put a G# there that shouldn't be G#, and make that a G♮. And this thing" he caught a flat five here. "Why'd you put a flat five here when you've got a sharp five, don't do that, that's gonna clash in this chord." And he kind of did this oral thing. He said, "Take that out." And he looked at it and he basically just bled all over my page. I said, "Okay." So we were basically back on the bus and I touched my leg and said "Whew." So we got to the hotel, and fortunately the hotel had a piano. And I played through all the corrections he made, you know. I said, "Okay, I see, oh wow, boy, I sure was off in my thinking here, wow." And so the next thing I did was I bought a little keyboard, you know, and about a month later I wrote about ten or twelve measures or something you know. And we're on the bus and I went to Fos and said, "Hey, Fos, would you take a look at this?" And so he took the cap off to the red pen and he says "Well, that's okay. These ones here, now that's wrong, you should do it like this." Each time, so I'd bring it back to him, so he said, "Okay," and each time I went back to him I had less blood on my page. And so I just went off of his instruction and started learning some of the voicings that he uses and applied them to what I do, and because of that, wow it was like a graduate course in big band arranging, and totally viable, the information that he gave me.[7]

The name Ray Conniff is rarely mentioned when discussions of the largest-selling record producers ensue. Trombonist Conniff followed the sideman-to-arranger path with Bob Crosby and Artie Shaw, then found himself challenged by the innovations of bebop. A calculated move to write for listeners instead of fellow musicians inspired him to create the "Ray Conniff sound." At the time of his death in 2002 his worldwide record sales totaled over seventy million.

RC: We didn't think commercially. I just thought, I wonder how the guys are going to like it. I wrote for the guys. I wrote for Bunny [Berigan], I wrote for Bob Crosby and the guys in the band. I wrote for Artie

Shaw and the guys in the band. I never thought about the people out there that were paying our bills, you know, that were paying our salaries, that went to the dances, that listened to us on the air, that bought our records. You know, I didn't care, I never gave them a second thought. I'd been writing for the Harry James Band, '46. I remember the first thing I did for Harry, I still had my soldier suit on. I wrote a thing called "Easy," an original. I was doing an awful lot of writing for Harry. And I remember he had a song for me to do and the name of the song was "Ruby." And he said, "By the way, why don't you write a little bit, kind of a bop treatment on this?" Bop was kind of a new school of music that was coming along, and I never did dig bop. I liked to listen to it and I think we had some great players like Dizzy Gillespie and Charlie Parker. But it was not my bag. So I says, "Hey, you know, Harry, I just don't feel that kind of music," and, "Maybe it's time you got another boy." And his jaw dropped. He looked at me and he couldn't believe what I was saying. And he said, "Well, okay." So I left the band. For two years I thought all I had to do was pick up the phone and call my old pals, you know, like Sonny Burke at Decca and Paul Weston at Columbia Records. And I called all of them and told them, "Hey, I'm free now, I'm not writing steady all the time for Harry, I'm available." And boy, for two years the phone hardly rang. And finally after sitting waiting for the phone to ring for two years I got so discouraged. I had a wife and a mother I was supporting, and three children, and we were living out in Reseda, and I thought, I've got to go get a job. I can't go on like this. I took a job. They were converting a ten-acre melon field into a subdivision out in Reseda. And I went out and took a job as a laborer, cleaning up the ditches behind the ditch digger. Where he'd make mistakes on the corner, I'd clean the ditches. And I got to thinking, wow, what happened? Which way did they go, you know. In 1940, Artie was paying me $300 a week, which in those days was a lot of money. And here I am out digging ditches for $60 a week. But it gave me a lot of time to think. I started thinking completely different about writing arrangements. I thought, what if I started writing for the people that paid the bills, the people that listened, the people that bought the records. And I started thinking more along the lines of commercially, and I thought about, you know everything in life is rhythm. Our heartbeat is a rhythm, each day is a rhythm, the sun rises and sets to a rhythm, and the ocean tides go in and out to a rhythm, the cycles of the seasons are a rhythm. And I thought rhythm is very important in our life, and I made the rhythm very

Arranging the Notes

predominant. Then I remembered when I first started thinking about the opposite sex. There was a little girl down the street that I had a terrible crush on. I must have been, I don't know, ten, eleven, twelve, something like that. And she was always singing a song, it was [sings] "Ooooh, would you like to take a walk—ooooh, do you think it's going to rain." And to this day, I've heard that song once in a while, people will play an old record. It still moves something. I thought, if I can catch the songs that people fell in love to the first few times, I've got a wonderful idea. And that's what I did. I went back and I thought, when I got my first chance to do an album in 1956, a "S' Wonderful" album, which you heard, or something like it, "S' Wonderful," "S' Marvelous," "S' Awful Nice," there were three of them. I picked songs, and by arithmetic I went back the number of years, the age group I was trying to hit was eighteen to thirty five in the market. So I went back, when were those eighteen to thirty-five year olds hearing, "Ooooh would you like to take a walk" with the little girl down the street, or the boy you know, and so by arithmetic I picked songs from the top ten of those years. So in other words I didn't change my style of writing that much. I still wrote for brass and saxes, big band style, with a predominant rhythm sound, and I added the voices quite accidentally. Voices and instruments and the predominant rhythm sound, and the idea about people falling in love to the songs, and then that album, and the title song of that, "S' Wonderful," that became a turntable hit. It became a gold record. And then we started following it up with a lot of others like it.[8]

Manny Albam has arranged for an impressive list of artists including Gerry Mulligan, Carmen McRae, and Count Basie. As a baritone saxophone player his physical location in the band had an impact on his fledgling arranging career.

MA: As a clarinet player I was almost forced to take up the alto. And I started sitting in a lot of bands as a second alto player. Now the second alto chair in those days, in the four-man sax section, was also baritone chair and so I became a baritone player and I'm glad of it. I finally sold my alto. As a writer from the baritone chair you hear everything up above you. You hear from your position way up to the first trumpet and you hear right through all the chords and the voicings and all of that. It's a great place to live. And conversely, a lot of the arrangers, they were trombone players and they sit right in the middle and they hear it from both sides I guess. That's where their thing is. You know, [Bob] Brookmeyer, Billy Byers, Ray Wright, a whole bunch of them, Don Sebesky, for some reason or other, Nelson Riddle was a trombone player. It seems to be those two chairs are great places to hear what other people do. So if you play other people's arrangements, you can learn a lot from them.[9]

Manny had to deal with a rapidly changing music scene. His career spanned the Swing Era into rock & roll and commercial work. Swing band musicians and studio players were required to be excellent sight readers and Manny became spoiled over the years by working with instrumentalists who could play his arrangements correctly, usually the first time. He had a rude awakening when he started writing for rock groups.

MR: Did it change your work at all when rock & roll became the popular music?

MA: Well, what happened to me a couple of times, there used to be a group in Canada called the Guess Who, and there was another one called the Lloyds of London. They would come down to New York and cut a basic track and then I would go in and add strings and horns and whatever. And that began to become like a joke. They'd go in, first the bass player would come in and play his line. And then the guitar player came in and says, "Wait a minute I can't play with that thing, you've got G♮ and it's wrong—I can't do that." So the bass player would have to make another track. And then the piano player came in and they'd change. So to get one thing down sometimes took three or four days. Finally they got two tracks down and I took them home and I would write "sweetening," is what they'd call it—strings and horns and all that. And we'd call the session and the string players came in and sat down and they played the thing through once and we recorded them the second time and they left and then the horn players came in. And these guys were, "Holy Jesus, you mean you did the whole thing in twenty minutes? I can't believe it." I said, "Well, they're musicians. They read music." You'd have like Marvin Stamm or Bill Watrous or whatever. They'd just come in, sit down and go [scats] and leave, and pick up their $90 or whatever. And the [rock] groups didn't know then who they were dealing with yet. They were dealing with great players.[10]

A select number of rock groups were able to appeal to both pop music and jazz fans, due in large part to their hip arrangements. Blood, Sweat & Tears combined the talents of rock, R&B and jazz players. Trumpeter

Arranging the Notes

Lew Soloff was responsible for a number of memorable BS&T solo spots, and spoke about bandmate Fred Lipsius, who arranged the hit "Spinning Wheel." In April 2000 I was pleased to interview Lew, who spoke about the popularity of the band, his admiration for Fred Lipsius's creativity, and the differences of opinion that arose:

LS: Blood, Sweat & Tears of course was in a class by itself. You know how big that band was at the time? That was a real trip. We were the second biggest band in the world to the Beatles.

LS: The real creative force in that band was a particular arranger named Lipsius. I mean [Dick] Halligan also, but Lipsius was the prime creative arranger in the band. And he is kind of a shy, laid-back sort. And oh man, he would bring in this chart or that chart and instead of saying okay we'll do this, okay we'll record this, it was like nah that's no good, nah that's no good. And finally he just stopped.

MR: Yeah, he had less arrangements on those records than he should have.

LS: Near the end, yeah. Of course. Because he didn't want to bring something in and have it put down. And he was the real, amazing creative energy in that band. Actually so was Al Cooper, before I was there. I loved his songs. But it doesn't matter. I'm always of the mind that if a band is allowed to just continuously try to be creative they're better off than if they have a hit and they try to keep following that formula.[11]

"Spinning Wheel" announces itself majestically. Fred wrote an ear-catching brass fanfare that rips up to what musicians call a sharp 9 chord.

It certainly gets our attention.

After the brass pronouncement, the song builds from almost nothing. In verse one, David Clayton Thomas sings two bars with only unison bass and piano, two measures with cowbell, then two bars with drums, providing a perfect setup for a "whap!" from the brass section. Thomas sings by himself "ride a painted pony, let the spinning wheel ride." In the second verse, our arranger adds horn hits on beats two and four, and a very bluesy riff that climbs up to the flat third blue note.

Jazz Tales from Jazz Legends

The bridge of the song reflects the psychedelia that found its way into pop music in the late '60s. The feel is smoothed out with long and rather dreamy notes, a touch of phase-shifting, and a reverb-drenched echo on the word "real." Horns build up with a catchy triplet figure and lead to a restatement of the opening riff.

In the third verse Lipsius writes two of the most distinctive beats in any BS&T song. It's a wonderful solo spot for the trombonist, climbing from a basement pitch and landing on its target note with the word "drop" sung by Thomas.

When I write arrangements I always arrive at a spot that I describe as "okay what now?" At this point in "Spinning Wheel" we've had a terrific intro, a couple of verses, a bridge, a third verse, and I can picture Fred Lipsius at this "what now" moment. What "now" becomes is classic BS&T. A number of the players in the band were jazz guys, so Fred writes the jazz part. At the 2:00 mark, for thirty-seven seconds, the rhythm section becomes a swinging jazz piano trio, backing up a solo from Lew Soloff that had all my trumpet friends green with envy. At the 2:21 mark, brass chords set up what I can only describe as a demented bugle call that ends on a lip-busting high G.

The final verse has it all, brass hits with "shakes" worthy of the Count Basie Orchestra, the blues riff and the sliding trombone.

Time to end the song. Again, Lipsius is faced with a decision. Rather than a standard fade out or a dynamic last chord, Blood, Sweat & Tears engages in a bit of self-indulgence, which we happily encouraged them to do via our support of their records. As the song reaches its climax, an unexpected switch to a 3/4 occurs. If people were dancing they would have tripped over their own feet. This merry-go-round waltz quickly gives way to a duet of recorders that transport us from a merry-go-round to a steam calliope. There is a brief battle with the brass, trading their measures back and forth. Eventually the brass give up and fade out, leaving the recorders to play a vaguely familiar tune. In fact, it's a melody that's been around for many years, known by two titles: "Have You Ever Seen a Lassie Go This Way and That Way," or "The More We Get Together."

The music grows more chaotic and at 3:56 Fred Lipsius adds a wry opinion on the whole affair with a few sarcastic notes on his alto sax. Drummer Bobby Colomby sums it up with his tongue-in-cheek comment, "That wasn't too good." The jovial response by the rest of the band seems to say, "You're right, let's keep it."

Fred Lipsius can be counted among the arrangers who were indispensable contributors in creating a unique sound for a band. Lipsius won a Grammy for "Best Instrumental Arrangement" for his contribution

Arranging the Notes

to "Spinning Wheel."

The typical jazz combo follows the melody-improvisation-melody format, a standard arrangement that requires no particular assigning of parts. The small groups led by Cannonball Adderley regularly added an extra sense of structure to their performances that helped endear them to jazz fans, including yours truly. One of the most effective passages was preserved on tape at a live date produced by Orrin Keepnews.

MR: My favorite musicians actually are Cannonball and Nat [Adderley]. I think of them together. And I wanted to play something if I could, from amongst the things that you had a hand in, and maybe you can just tell me what you think about him as a person. Let's see if I can find it here.

OK: Well, I'd be more than happy to talk to you about Cannonball and about what I think of him as a person. He was one of the very best people that I've ever known in my life. With that for a teaser we'll listen to the music and then I'll talk to you [audio interlude, "Gemini" from the LP "The Cannonball Adderley Sextet Live at the Village Vanguard"].[12]

OK: Now you realize what just happened there? I mean I was going to point it out but you had the right part of the tune on. This is "Gemini," by another wonderful jazz musician/composer and human being, Jimmy Heath, who fortunately is one of the few old associates of mine who is still with us. And that recording, and you heard a taste of it right there, it's a live recording at the Village Vanguard, and this is the sextet at the time, that Yusef Lateef was added to the body of it, and Joe Zawinul is already in place as a piano player there. But every night that they played this song the same thing happened, it just happened there. In the midst of the solos, after the horn solos and before the piano solo, there's a return to a shout chorus and a secondary melody is played by the band, and invariably what happened there is that ensemble piece gets applause at the end in the same way that a solo does. And it just happened on that fragment of record that you played and that is always—I cannot recall that ever happening before or since, and as I say it became a routine part. Every audience reacted the same way. I mean I can't say that every audience did but I know it happened a hell of a lot and it certainly happens, as we hear now, the night that we were recording.

MR: Well, that's one thing I loved about his bands is, even though it was a quintet or sextet, they had arrangements in there.

OK: Oh they had a very strong sense of arrangements, strong sense of composition in that band.[13]

Dave Rivello and Maria Schneider are two of the most forward-thinking arrangers of today. In order to hear their own work they found it necessary to form their own big bands, just as Bill Holman did. Dave teaches at the Eastman School of Music in Rochester, New York, and leads the twelve-piece Dave Rivello Ensemble. The Frank Foster paper score came to mind when I visited Dave's studio in 2012.

MR: Thanks for taking some time today. And as the camera is kind of catching, you can see sketches all over the room. And I'm really glad to see real paper, to be honest with you, in this day and age.

DR: Yeah, it's part of the process for me and so the computer has its things and in many ways it's made life easier as a composer and arranger, but for me, I have to work on paper. And so I write all my scores longhand, I do all my sketching and my full scores longhand, and then put it into the computer to make parts for the musicians. And I'm still in the quest of the best pencils that I can find and the paper you see, the King brand, this is all King brand manuscript paper. And it was used by Bob Brookmeyer, my hero, and Gil Evans, and Al Cohn, and everybody on the East Coast at least, all use King brand paper. And so I had a connection with the company that was still making King brand paper and because of technology and computers they're no longer producing it. So basically I bought up everything that I could possibly get and I have a stash all over my house.

MR: Is that right?

DR: Don't come rob me. So I hopefully have a lifetime supply of this particular yellow, custom-milled King brand paper.

MR: I had not heard about that. I mean I used to do the paper scores too. But I didn't know King was the—

DR: King was the king sort of.

MR: What does the putting of pencil on paper do for you that the computer doesn't?

DR: A couple of things, and Stravinsky said it much better than I could, but the tactile sense of the hand and touching the paper and so the mind's ear is connected with the arm and the pencil and making the motion. And in the computer there is the mouse, but you're not really making a mark on the paper. And so for me that's a commitment to that note or that voicing or it is saying that I believe in this. And there's a certain strength in that if I'm gambling and I'm combining notes that you wouldn't think should go together but I believe in those and I make that mark on the paper, there's a thing about that. And that doesn't happen the same way on the computer.

MR: Now you obviously would have been writing in the days before you could hear it back. And there's something about that moment when you're in front of the band and you've just written this thing, and you think it's going to work, but hearing it for that first time is like nothing else, right?

DR: It is like nothing else in the world. That's exactly right. And I don't really, even though the technology exists I don't really depend on the computer to play back for me, I still trust my own sense and I still get that feeling. So I might use the computer to play back to check something, but as far as putting in the entire piece and hearing it play back and, "Oh I did good, yay" and then take it to the band, no, it's still that experience for me, that bringing it to the band and hearing it for the first time live with them playing the notes that I put on the paper and it's still that experience, and nothing touches that in the entire world is that experience—the first hearing of something that you created.

MR: How much of what you write can you hear in your head?

DR: I've been writing music since I was in junior high school, not that anybody should ever hear those attempts at that point, but it's been a lot of years. So it's a two-part answer I guess. I can hear a lot of things in my head. And if I were to write something very straightforward then I can hear all of that in my head as I'm creating it. But for me, I'm interested in stretching what I know and what I can do. And so I'm gambling more than I'm not gambling, especially if I'm writing for my own ensemble. So I can still hear that but I don't always know if it's going to work. But I spent fifteen years with the legendary Bob Brookmeyer, and he didn't always know. And I'm good friends with Maria Schneider, and she doesn't always know. And these are people that have been writing music for—Bob especially—for longer than I have been. Bill Holman too, we're friends also. And he sometimes is like, "I'm not sure if it's going to work or not." So part of that never goes away, which is a good thing I think because it means you're trying to expand yourself instead of—if you're just writing straightforward things and banging them out, you should be able to hear those and know that, okay, I can mail it off and forget about it. But I'm not one of those guys.[14]

Jazz Tales from Jazz Legends

Dave spoke of the role of the soloist in big band writing, and methods to ensure that they add to the intent of the arranger.

MR: When I write a chart, I always run into this bit about okay, I've done an intro, done the melody, whether or not it has a bridge, and then you get to that point, what am I going to do now? And Maria Schneider said this to me and I think it came from Bob Brookmeyer. He said, "Wait as long as you can before giving in to a soloist."

DR: Yeah.

MR: Does that sound like something he would say?

DR: That's a Brookmeyer thing for sure. When nothing else can happen, that's when the first solo should happen. So you should do everything you can until then. Yeah, that's from Brookmeyer for sure.

MR: So what are those things that you should be trying to do before you go there?

DR: What I think about is continuing to develop whatever material is going on before I turn it over to a soloist. And so whether that's a melodic idea or if then, oh well, I did this so it was kind of a straightforward thing so maybe I'll do some kind of a counterpoint that's an inversion or a retrograde inversion of what the main material was. I just play around until it feels right to release my thing to a soloist. And what I've begun doing in the last few years, which also comes from Brookmeyer, is when I finally do have a solo, I give them guidelines of where I at least want them to start. So whether that's pitches or rhythmic ideas or I write a melody and then say continue similarly from here, so that they stay in my piece. Because the problem that Bob has addressed in print and lectures and everything is that you turn it over to the soloist and they play what they've been working on in the practice room and it has nothing to do with what happened up to that point. So I try to guide that a little bit and I also try, with my own band at least where I have control over the members of the band, to make sure that they understand that you're part of my piece. You know Brookmeyer said it best when he said, "A solo is a compositional continuance." Those are his words, not mine. But I'll take them, and I use them.[15]

Maria Schneider's writing and big band have earned multiple honors from *Down Beat* magazine and the Grammy foundation. Her big band is one of the few fan-funded ensembles in the country.

MR: How do you impart some of your philosophies to other students? Is it possible to do that?

MS: I try to just show them how I dance around and try to figure my way into music. I try to encourage students to look for something that just feels good, then try to find the logic in it, keep developing the logic, but kind of let their left and right brain work together so that it doesn't become too analytical. And never thinking what do they think I should write, what's going to be hip. What should I adopt to be cool. But try to stay inside. I always feel like the thing that makes each person unique is that you are you, nobody on earth can imitate you, nobody can be more you than you are. So that your job is to become you to the deepest degree that you can, and that's where your beauty and that's where your mastery is, in developing yourself. I think so often it's really easy to look at other people and say, oh he's a master, I have to try to be like that, I have to follow him. No, you have to find the depth of yourself and be disciplined and develop yourself to the same degree that those people were disciplined and developed themselves. And that's the thing that nobody can imitate. And that's where your strength, and that's where your gift is. That's what people want to see, is feel the uniqueness of each other. That's where you really communicate something fresh with somebody. It's hard to do that.[16]

Maria believes a composer cannot operate in a vacuum; that their work must be inspired by living a full and active life.

MS: Music isn't enough for me in life. There's other things too. And I love music but I think what I love about music is it's a valve for other things. I love life, and I want more time to live. And to me one of the problems with musicians is I think they get so caught up in making records and going to the next project that very often the person's first record is the most powerful. Because that record represents years of just working on your own and doing other things in life, and then suddenly you become so busy doing your music you aren't paying attention so much to the other things in your life because they aren't as important as the music. But what feeds the music? Music is fed by a deep and rich life. So I think it's really important to have other things in your life that you can do with equal love.[17]

Authors and poets use words, phrases, rhymes, and imagery in their craft. The arranger's tools include harmony, dynamics, rhythm, sound, and silence. As musical architects, their goal is to combine these elements

Jazz Tales from Jazz Legends

in a fashion that satisfies the assignment and infuses a bit of their own signature sound. Their work is justified and celebrated every time a good band plays it.

Picture Gallery

Jazz Tales from Jazz Legends

Joe Williams and the Count Basie Orchestra, Wellin Hall, Hamilton College, September 7, 1996. (Fillius Jazz Archive)

Joe and Jillean Williams. (Fillius Jazz Archive, gift of Jillean Williams)

Jazz Tales from Jazz Legends

Kenny Davern. The Fillius Events Barn, Hamilton College, October, 1999. Photo by Steve Charzuk. (Fillius Jazz Archive)

The *Tonight Show* Orchestra, New York City, October 24, 1963. *Bottom row left to right:* Benny Goodman, Johnny Carson, Skitch Henderson, Marian McPartland. *Middle row left to right:* Paul Falise, Buddy Morrow, Sy Berger, Don Ashworth. *Top row left to right:* Snooky Young, Clark Terry, Doc Severinsen, Joe Ferranti, Bob Rosengarden. (Fillius Jazz Archive, gift of Bob and Sharon Rosengarden)

Jazz Tales from Jazz Legends

Left to right: Bucky Pizzarelli, Frank Wess, Randy Sandke. The Fillius Events Barn, Hamilton College, October 2007. Photo by John Herr. (Fillius Jazz Archive)

Left to right: Derek Smith, Bob Rosengarden, Joe Wilder, Milt Fillius Jr., Frank Wess, Michael Moore, Kenny Davern. The Fillius Events Barn, Hamilton College, October 1998. Photo by Dave Tewksbury. (Fillius Jazz Archive)

Jazz Tales from Jazz Legends

Left to right: Bucky Pizzarelli, Kenny Davern, Nikki Fillius, Tony DeNicola, Keter Betts. The Fillius Events Barn, Hamilton College, October 2003. (Fillius Jazz Archive)

The Fillius Jazz Archive, Hamilton College. Photo by Marianita Peaslee. (Fillius Jazz Archive)

Chapter 5
Inside the Studio

Historically, every art form has had a tangible goal for the artist. Authors hope to see their writing published, visual artists envision their work in a gallery, and choreographers picture dancers on the stage. Musicians hope to commit their work to records, and landing a record deal has been part and parcel of making it in the music business. Classic jazz recordings have been captured live in concerts and in clubs, but the musicians more often found themselves in the controlled environment of a recording studio. The first jazz recording was released in 1917 by the Original Dixieland Jazz Band. Recording technology was primitive, marginally improved from the process developed by Thomas Edison late in the nineteenth century. Trumpeter Doc Cheatham remembered those days, and his first recording experience backing up blues singer Ma Rainey:

DC: In Chicago [Ma Rainey] used Albert Wynn's Creole Jazz Band and I was in the band. So that's how I recorded with her. She was a very, very nice woman. And we played all of her songs, and that was it. That was about '26.

MR: Our students are used to hearing what is done to make a record these days, in million-dollar studios. What was it like at that time to make a recording?

DC: Well, this place where we played and recorded with Ma Rainey was just a room. They didn't have any speakers. We had a big megaphone we put out in front of the band, but no speakers. And everything was done by wax. You know we didn't have all that stuff.

MR: No fixing mistakes, right?

DC: No, no, no. And my next recording I did in Spain, in Barcelona, with Sam Wooding's band. Sam Wooding was a band in New York and he turned down the Cotton Club, to rather go to Europe with his band than to play in the Cotton Club. That's how Duke got in there. So Sam took the band to Europe in the latter part of '27. And I joined Sam Wooding and went to Europe with that band. The band was so great that no other band in Europe could compare with it. And we just went over there and we played all the big casinos and hotels, because they had a very big name, and we recorded up in Barcelona. It was hot as it is now. And the wax kept melting. And they put ice cubes on the wax to keep it from melting. But they came out wonderful.[1]

For decades, the jazz you heard on records was exactly what was played at the moment. Not only was overdubbing and playing music piecemeal considered counter to the genre, but the technology to even do such a thing had yet to be invented. The recording process was a stripped-down, lean affair. Jazz albums were typically recorded in one day, sometimes in a three-hour session. A second session would be scheduled only if needed. Pianist Richard Wyands describes a typical recording date in 1959:

MR: Do you recall the first recording date in New York that you made?
RW: In New York. I think it was with Jerome Richardson. It was called "Roamin' with Richardson" for Prestige. And that particular date I think the coordinator got me on a lot of other dates for Prestige. That one date I did with Jerome did it, really. I got more calls from Prestige to do more dates. And as a result I did this date with Etta Jones, "Don't Go to Strangers." And that luckily, fortunately, turned out pretty good.
MR: It's curious when a record like that takes off. When you recorded it, did it make a particular impression on you?
RW: No. Well, usually I would go to a date and I would play it and then I didn't think anymore about it because it seems like it would take them forever to release the record anyhow. By the time they released it I'd forgotten all about it really. I knew we did a good job on that, considering in those days you'd just go in the studio, there was no rehearsal, the A&R man as they were known in those days, would bring in some sheets of music and in the case of a vocalist you may have to transpose the sheet and make up the arrangements on top of it, in six hours.
MR: They could do an album in six hours.
RW: Six hours or less. And that's a lot of pressure. We did it though. Everybody did.
MR: So you'd be at the piano and the singer would come over and let's try this—
RW: Well, in the case of Etta Jones, she knew the tunes, she knew the keys, I think she did, and we would get it together and decide on the changes, quickly, very quickly. Figure out an intro, ending, and the solo, and that would be it. Some of those things we did were just one take. I think "Don't Go to Strangers" was just one take. We all made

Jazz Tales from Jazz Legends

our little contributions and before you knew it five hours was up, or six.

MR: Would you go to the union office at some later date?

RW: To pick up the check? Right. The union wouldn't send you a notice that your check, or any checks, were there unless you had so many, like some of the musicians who did recording work every day, but usually you'd have to call them. And usually, "No, we don't have anything for you yet, no," and three or four months had gone by it seemed like.

MR: It might be easy to forget who actually owes you.

RW: That's why I forgot what we played. So one day I was working at Minton's Playhouse up in Harlem and on a jukebox I heard this record "Don't Go to Strangers," and it was Etta Jones. Sounds familiar, I thought to myself. Months later. And it was a hit. I didn't even know it was a hit at the time. I checked it out and sure enough, that was the record I was on. I said wow, a hit. Of course the record company didn't tell me that, no man.

MR: And it didn't make any difference what money you were going to make off it anyway, did it?

RW: No there was no money, no royalties, no. Well, you know how that goes. They made a lot of money on that record. One of the few hits. That was a million-copy hit, I guess.[2]

Richard mentioned the coordinator from Prestige on the Jerome Richardson date. A record label always sent an "artist & repertoire" (A&R) man or a producer to protect the investment and make sure the recording time was used wisely. Producer Orrin Keepnews worked with Bill Evans, Thelonious Monk, and Cannonball Adderley, and confirmed that no one in the jazz business was getting rich through recordings.

MR: What was the typical budget? I don't know if you can say typical?

OK: You can't do that for several reasons. One reason you can't do that is that I'm talking now basically late '50s, early '60s, the value of the dollar is so outrageously different that you can't make comparisons. Even if you allow for this, that, or the other, you lose all sense of—I mean there were no journeymen ball players making over a million dollars a year in those days, just to take an example of the world of entertainment and how things have changed. Also another thing I like to point out was the standard of living was different, everything cost less. It is relevant to point out that union scale for a musician recording, a sideman doing three hours of work in which fifteen minutes of music for an album could be created, scale was $41.25. Now that was not outrageously bad but it just—what is scale today?

MR: It's a lot more than that.

OK: Well, the scale today is several hundred dollars. I must confess I should know better—I mean I still do a certain amount of recording but I've gotten into the habit where you pay sidemen a lump sum that is never going to be as small as what scale is so I don't even deal in terms of thinking about things that way. Nevertheless the whole point is that we did records very economically. Let's put it that way. You could do a trio record and your musicians' costs might total $500. You know you might roughly speaking be paying $125 to each sideman and $250 to the leader and that's probably what got paid on the first Bill Evans album. And nobody was exploiting anybody. It also meant that even though the record only sold eight hundred copies in the first year, so we didn't come out ahead on it, but it was not unthinkable to say let's continue working with this guy. Because he deserves to be recorded. What I do know is this: it was possible to make jazz records without having any significant or even noticeable amount of capitalization. That's the important fact. That a bunch of young guys with a lot of balls and ambition and love of the music and very little capital were able to create record companies. That could not happen today even though people are constantly still trying to do it.[3]

The musicians, producers, and engineers of this era learned to get their music on tape efficiently and with minimal rehearsal. Almost forty years later I was fortunate to have Jerome Richardson sitting next to me when I recorded a CD titled "Jazz Life." Jerome interrupted my explanation of how a particular song was to be run down with the phrase "S'make it." When I looked at him quizzically he said, "Let's make it." In other words, stop wasting time, let's play.

The spontaneity Jerome speaks of is an essential ingredient in a successful jazz recording. In essence, the musicians want to capture what they do on stage. Producer Joel Dorn noticed that jazz recordings often failed to capture this spontaneity, and devised his own way of working with jazz artists:

JD: I was in the clubs for six or seven years in Philly. I saw everybody who was working the circuit. And one of the things that used to confuse me was why do they sound so incredible in the club and then their records, while good, don't have that same feeling. So for instance I saw Les McCann at the Showboat a bunch of times. We kind of became friends when I was on the radio. And his records were okay, but in the club he was unbelievable. So when we signed him to Atlantic I wanted to find out why do you sound one way in a club and another way in the studio. He said, "I hate the studio." He said, "It's always somebody staring at you saying 'take one,' 'we ran out of tape,'" whatever it is. I said no problem. I said I can fix that. And I could. So what I did was I brought a second tape machine in so we never had to stop the tape, we had a half hour's worth of tape. And I said, "Just play, do what you want, forget we're making a record." Now you can't completely forget you're making a record, but if you get out of the way the "okay take three, uh, we're out of tape." Just let the musician do what he does. And if he's got something that he does that works and he's comfortable, you'll eventually get it. So Les went from hating the studio to falling in love with the studio, and then we made lots of great records because we had a way of capturing what it is that he did. That's important.[4]

The heyday for commercial recording studios, especially in New York, began in the early 1950s and coincided with the decline of the Big Band Era. Skilled sidemen were now looking for work and the best of them made the transition from stage to studio. They soon discovered that there was significant money to be made recording jingles, film scores, and the new popular music, rock & roll. Dick Hyman explained:

DH: A lot of us began playing jazz and then got into studio work, and were able to use some of that jazz expertise in one way or another in studio work. The improvisation for a pianist always came in very handy. And then the studio work taught us a lot of other things like in my case I began to play organ as well as to read and learn how to arrange and conduct and so forth. And then the funny thing is, and when I use the plural I mean people like not only myself but people like Milt Hinton and Bob Rosengarden and I'm thinking of present company and certain other guys. The funny thing is that after a while the studio work came to an end and we all became entirely jazz people after that, again. So it was a kind of hiatus that might have lasted decades but it was a kind of wonderful hiatus.[5]

Pianist Derek Smith recalled the post-big band studio days, in his interview from 1995:

DS: Of course all the [Basie] sidemen have been my friends for years, like Frank Foster and Frank Wess, because we were all in the studios together playing all these dog food commercials for years.

MR: Most of those guys that did that, that was after they had had the Basie experience, the big band road thing.

DS: Right.

MR: And they decided they wanted to stay in one place for a little while?

DS: Yes. Exactly. And that's what they did. And at that time you have to realize there was so much work for musicians, especially if you came out of a big band background. Because most of the music was kind of jazz influenced. And there was always big budgets for commercials and they wanted the band to sound right. And so all these guys were coming off the bands and moving straight into this highly paid studio work.[6]

Superior musicianship had to be matched with an equally developed work ethic. When the conductor's baton came down, the studio musician had to be in his seat ready to perform. Trumpeter Joe Wilder recalled some relevant advice from his father:

MR: I wanted to ask you, you've been here for a few days on the campus and you seem to have a very well formed work ethic. And you had told me about a few things that you believe are right in the way you operate your business and deal with other people. I'm wondering, where did you get this work ethic? Was it something from your family?

JW: I guess I got it mainly from my father, who was a musician. My father played with a lot of the bands in Philadelphia and he was a stickler for being on time. He used to pound that into my brothers and me. "You know it's better for you to come one hour early than to come one second late for something," and he would use as an example, there was a drummer that played with one of the bands he played with. And the guy was a good drummer. And he said, "You know the dance starts eight o'clock and we're all there." And he said, "And we're all sitting on the bandstand ready to play and the drummer isn't there. He comes at eight-fifteen." He said, "He knows it takes him at least twenty minutes to set up his drums." He said, "Now what sense does that make? What excuse is that?" And then he would say, "You know just because you're black doesn't mean you have to show up late." And they had an expression that they used to use, they would say you go to work and you come on time,

Jazz Tales from Jazz Legends

and then there's another time that they call "CP time"—colored people's time—CPT was a thing they used to use. The blacks used it in reference to the other people that came late you see? And they would say, well, there is such a thing as the correct time and CPT. So this was a real put down, so you didn't want to get involved with that. But that's basically where I got it from, my father. And the other idea, the deportment of the guys on the job and things like that. He felt that they had an obligation to come on time, perform properly, to dress properly and conduct themselves in a way that people wouldn't have any problems with them.

MR: I've never heard that expression.

JW: Yeah, it's an old expression. A lot of the Latino musicians have an expression that's similar too. The Latino musicians, one fellow was a friend of mine and he was one of the first Latin musicians to play in the Broadway theaters. And we were doing *Lorelei* with Carol Channing. And a couple of times he showed up, the show hits at two o'clock, and at two-thirty he came in and he couldn't walk through the band. Because of the way we were all set up, he had to crawl through the orchestra to get to his seat. And he was so accustomed to showing up late when he'd play a Latin dance some place in some hall, if he got there a half hour late, as long as you got there it was okay. So they had to explain to him that this is not a Latin dance hall, it was a Broadway theater.[7]

Joe's professionalism led him to self-limit his daily schedule in order to maintain his skill level. He observed some musicians who couldn't resist playing every possible session they could, even if it was logistically impossible.

MR: I remember you talking about some fellows who would try to cut corners and play the game of booking two sessions at the same time.

JW: These were guys who were counting every penny they could get. And someone would call you for a jingle date, a television commercial or something. And they would say, can you do a date from ten 'til twelve? And the guy would say yes. And someone else would call and say, I've got a date that goes from twelve until three, can you make it? Now he's got a date from ten 'til twelve, and he's like fifteen blocks away from the other studio. It's no way he's going to get to the other gig on time. And so the guy would say yes to the fellow. Instead of saying I won't be able to make it because I'm already busy, he'd say yes to the guy that has the twelve to three date, and show up on his date at maybe a quarter to one, and say jeez, you know I didn't know that the other date was going to go overtime or something, not calling to warn him of it or anything, just to make the money, rather than saying let somebody else make it. There's enough for all of us, and there was at that time, a lot. Sometimes we did three or four jingle dates on the same day. And it got to the point where, in my case, I wouldn't accept more than three because sometimes you'd go on one and it would be so easy that you felt like you were robbing them, and then by the time you got to the fourth one it would be something so hard that you wish you hadn't started playing the instrument. So I knew that I could handle three in one day, but four was rough.[8]

Musical contractors were the connection between the musicians and the record companies. Their first calls were always to the A-team players, like Joe Wilder, Milt Hinton, Dick Hyman, and a select group of others.

Dick Hyman wore multiple hats in the studio: pianist, organist, orchestrator, percussionist on occasion, and a general get-the-job-done guy. Dick shared his opinion about doing what was necessary to serve the music, regardless of one's personal taste.

MR: What kind of people did you play behind?
DH: Ivory Joe Hunter, Ruth Brown, Lavern Baker, The Coasters, The Drifters. I remember that terrible record "White Christmas" that was so popular.
MR: Did you play on that?
DH: I did. But we did all that stuff. And if you asked me what we thought of it, we always said to each other can you imagine, in twenty years—this was in 1955 or so—people will be saying to each other, "Listen darling, they're playing our song." And you know that's exactly what happened. All of that funny music that we laughed at became classic in rock. And go figure it out.
MR: Well, musicians who've never done studio work may not realize that you don't have to like everything you play on in a studio. It's not possible.
DH: No, no. What you have to like is being able to play it well.
MR: Correctly, yeah.
DH: And you do your best no matter what it is.
MR: So if you listened to the oldies station are you likely to hear yourself?
DH: Very much.
MR: Can you tell me a couple of spots that I might hear?

Jazz Tales from Jazz Legends

DH: Yeah. Johnny Mathis, there's one—there's a famous Mathis record that begins with a piano figure. "Chances Are."

MR: "Chances Are." Yes. That's you?

DH: That's one. Yeah. And then there's another one that I whistled on for Johnny Mathis.

MR: "Wonderful Wonderful."

DH: Right.

MR: That's you whistling, is that right?

DH: That was one of my—well, you know I had made my own, I have to admit—hit record of "Moritat," which then became known as "Theme from the Three Penny Opera" and then finally became known as "Mac the Knife" in 1955 for MGM as the Dick Hyman Trio. And I whistled on it as well as playing an instrument called the harpsichord piano. So it became known around town that I was willing and I was capable of whistling. Willing to undertake it and capable of doing it without running out of breath. So I found myself being called to be a whistler on dates and I promptly joined AFTRA, that is the singers union, because their scale was higher than the musicians union, and on a good day I might collect both scales on a single session. So I'm the whistler on that and I'm the whistler on something with Marion Marlowe, something called "The Man in the Raincoat," one of those spooky third-man theme-type recordings.

MR: Was it a lip whistle or was it a teeth whistle?

DH: No, no, no. The teeth whistling we left to Bob Haggart [as in, "Big Noise from Winnetka" by Bob Crosby's Bobcats].[9]

Studio musicians rarely saw the music in advance that was to be recorded. In the studio, time is money, and even the smallest mistake could require another take. Contractors soon learned which musicians had the chops, the punctuality, the versatility, and the correct attitude. Drummer Bob Rosengarden shuttled between an NBC staff position (including membership in the *Tonight Show* band), recording dates, and the music director position for *The Dick Cavett Show*.

MR: I was going to ask you when you showed up for a day at work at NBC, did you know what was in store for you that day?

BR: I had no idea and couldn't have cared less. I mean I just showed up. In those days, because there weren't that many good musicians, new guys who could play. I always prided myself and it's not false modesty or anything, that I liked only two kinds of music—good music and bad music. So I didn't mind having to play a polka, it didn't really bother me, I can do it well, and I had a classical musical background. So I found myself again slipping and sliding, right back into the NBC Symphony. Because I was one of the new boys. And there was a conductor there at that time by the name of Arturo Toscanini. Dumb luck.

MR: But you were ready.

BR: Oh, yes. I mean you sure as hell better be ready. And the old man couldn't see too far away, you know you had to be right there. So he would look over and he'd make some gesture. And hopefully I'd figure out what it was he wanted me to do or not do. And [Johnny] Carson adopted us. I mean he loved Doc [Severinsen]. And again, slipping and sliding we were doing record sessions all the time, every day. And we all saw each other every day in recording. We used to do three record dates a day, and a television show, every day. Seven days a week. It was a wild and wonderful time.[10]

Much of the music these accomplished musicians were called upon to record was harmonically simple and musically unchallenging. The jazz musicians who stayed out of the studios—either by choice or by lack of qualifications—sometimes looked askance at their colleagues who were thriving in the studio scene. Drummer Panama Francis spoke about his friends' perception of his studio work in rock & roll:

PF: By the jazz musicians, I was called "that rock & roll drummer." It was a put down. Like we'd be in the bar at Jim and Andy's and I'd walk in the door and they'd say, "Ohhh, here comes this rock & roller." They didn't realize how much money I was making, but when they found out how much money I was making, they was knocking the door down to make them records. But anyhow, two years ago they honored me, they gave me $15,000 and a plaque. And I went to make my acceptance speech and all I could say was "Ladies and gentlemen" and I bust out in tears, uncontrollable. Because I was hurt by the jazz musicians who knew me and knew that I worked in bands and heard me in jam sessions, and they went along with the white musicians who labeled me a rock & roll musician. Because they never heard me play no jazz, because I was in Harlem all the time with the big bands. So they didn't get a chance to hear me on 52nd Street. So they thought that this was all I could do, you know, that I was only able to play rock & roll. And my so-called friends and brothers that knew different, never stood up and said, well, no man, he can play something else. I never got called for a big band date, I never got called for a jazz date. That was a label that was laid on me that wasn't fair, because, I mean, I was able to play, you know, at the age of thirteen I was playing in bands. I wasn't playing no rhythm & blues—I was playing in bands, playing arrangements and things. But I knew how to play this music, because I used to play in the church. Just like rhythm & blues became rock & roll. It's like the word "funk." That was a dirty word with black people. You told somebody to "funk," you'd be ready to fight. But the jazz critic heard the term being used by musicians, and they thought it was hip and it caught on. So they said, "He sure plays funky, doesn't he." I remember the time you used that word that you're liable to get your teeth knocked out of you. I mean that wasn't a nice word.[11]

Musicians who grew up on harmonically sophisticated swing music had to make musical and attitude adjustments, and they could go a number of different ways. The inherently curious musician could take pleasure in a new challenge every day. The less curious musician might not enjoy the work, but take pride in doing it well. For the musicians who couldn't handle the monotony, they could keep making the studio dates and become increasingly frustrated or recognize that it was not work they should continue doing.

Piano players in particular were often required to play in an uncreative fashion. Two West Coast keyboardists, Ray Sherman and Paul Smith, both encountered what were called the repetitive "rock & roll triplets."

RS: Funny, that was the days of, I don't know if they even called it rock & roll or rhythm & blues, with the triplets in the right hand. I started getting a lot of calls like that, where that's what they wanted.
MR: Can you recall some of the records you played on?
RS: Well, I think the only hit I was on "Primrose Lane." And I think I faked an introduction on that, and they always say whatever I did was good.
MR: It became a little hook.
RS: Yeah. Because I did a record date after that, it was funny, a friend of mine, Jack Marshall, the guitar player, it was one of his dates. And he came over to me and he said, "Do you think you could play something like the guy played on the 'Primrose Lane' intro?"[12]

And from Paul Smith:

PS: I did one date where the piano was facing the conductor and this whole thing was eighth triplets. And just as a gag I took off my loafer and put it on my hand so I'm playing with a shoe. And he can't see. And I'm going ching-ching-ching with a shoe on my hand. I played the entire date that way and he said great, that's the sound he wants. And I'm playing with a shoe. So I had a faint idea what was coming up. I mean he never knew and I certainly never told him, but I could have sent one of my kids in with a shoe and play duh-duh-duh and that's it. So I could see what music was coming to at that time.

MR: I have to ask the obvious question: what key was that piece in if you were playing with your shoe on?

PS: It doesn't make any difference. It's just the sound, ching-ching-ching. I didn't make any chord changes. The shoe covered part—it was mostly on the black keys, but the lower part was on the white. So you have white and black both. But all he could hear was ching-ching-ching, and that's the sound he wanted. I went up to him after the date and told him not to call me on those kind of dates anymore. I said, "Don't call me on those triplet dates. You've got a musical date I'll be happy to do it." I mean it cost me a lot of money but I'd rather come home happy than irritated.[13]

I doubt that Paul Smith would have been comforted if you told him he was playing on a future hit. Studio musicians, as Richard Wyands reminded us, did not see extra money when a song they performed on became a big seller unless it later was employed for television or film. Two West Coast saxophonists, Ernie Watts and Plas Johnson, spoke of this common occurrence:

MR: When you were doing a particular date did you ever have a sense of this tune is going to last; that it's going to be something that years from now people are still listening to?

EW: No, when you're working you're just working. It's just your work, it's just what you do. I would get up in the morning and I'd go and I'd do a record date. And it could be the Jacksons or it could be Sarah Vaughan or it could be Barbra Streisand. I did pop records, I did jazz records, I'd go and I'd do a record date in the morning and then in the afternoon was the *Tonight Show*. So the record dates usually run three hours so I'd do a date from ten o'clock until one, take a break, go over to do the *Tonight Show*, the *Tonight Show* would be off at six-thirty and I'd do another record date at seven. So I'd usually do two record dates and the *Tonight Show* just about every day, or I'd do three record dates or a big movie date and I'd send a sub to the

Jazz Tales from Jazz Legends

Tonight Show. Because sometimes movie dates are all day long. I did that every day for twenty years. So when you're doing that, all you're thinking about is keeping your health together and going to work. You have absolutely no idea of the greatness of what's going on, or how something is going to last or whatever. What's happening now is all of these R&B records that I played on with the Temptations and Barry White and all of these people, they're being used for commercials, and I'm getting these big checks. I'm getting these checks for Billy Preston things.[14]

And from Plas Johnson, who gave life to "The Pink Panther":

PJ: Henry [Mancini] had the talent of matching the player with the tune you know. He would call just the right saxophone player for what he was writing. Just the right harmonica player. He knew players quite well and he knew music. He had a knack for putting stuff together that matched, and I guess that's how I came to work on his "Pink Panther."

MR: It's a classic. Certainly had a sound to it. Did you have any idea at the time that it was going to become one of those tunes that everybody can whistle?

PJ: No. Of course not. But we did have an idea at the time that it was a great piece of music because it was like eight o'clock on a cold winter morning and I forget how many, it was a full orchestra with strings and everything, and after the tune was recorded, after the performance of the tune, the orchestra applauded.[15]

Guitarist Bucky Pizzarelli has played on thousands of recordings, some of which can kindly be called "novelty records" and others "musical gems." He shared an amusing anecdote that took years to develop:

MR: You never quite know what's going to catch the public's ear.

BP: No. You never know. But in those days a hit record was a glorious thing to have, for an artist to find. Patti Page had a thing called "Doggie in the Window."

MR: "How Much is that Doggie in the Window."

BP: Yeah, we made it in the last five minutes of a three-hour session. So how do you know? I think Doc Severinsen was playing trumpet on it.

MR: I can just picture you going home and saying hey, guess what we did today.

BP: Yeah, and "Itsy Bitsy Bikini."
MR: "Itsy Bitsy Teeny Weeny Yellow Polka Dot Bikini." That was Brian Hyland, wasn't it?
BP: Yeah that's right. And another thing, I made, here's a funny story. I made Ray Charles's "Georgia on My Mind." It was with Ralph Burns, but it was one of those busy weeks where he was farming everything out. And we still don't know who wrote it. Bobby Brookmeyer or Al Cohn wrote the arrangement. So we do the arrangement. Smash hit. Big, big hit. Thirty years later I'm doing the *Dick Cavett Show*. And Ray Charles is going to sing this tune. And the conductor comes up to me and I'm with Bobby Rosengarden's band. And the guy said to me, "Don't play the guitar on this, because it was a certain kind of guitar playing on the record." So he was afraid I didn't know. So I laid out. Do you believe that?
MR: I can't believe that.
BP: I didn't tell him.[16]

In 1969 Roberta Flack recorded the song "The First Time Ever I Saw Your Face," and it was released on her LP "First Take." During a 2015 interview with Bucky and Ruth Pizzarelli, I played the recording from the beginning to get his response. It features his classical acoustic guitar.

MR: Did you get it yet? That's you on acoustic guitar.
BP: Get out of here. What am I playing? Oh yeah.
MR: That was kind of a different date.
BP: Yeah. Well, they asked me to do something without the music, and that's what I did. We had just the chords but they wanted something. That's what I worked up. It was an overdub. She had already made the record. And she wanted something different.
MR: Were you hearing her singing?
BP: Yeah. And I played like I was accompanying her.
MR: Did you come home and say, "I just played on a hit"?
BP: No.
MR: Have you ever known you were playing on a hit?
BP: No.[17]

The recording garnered "Song of the Year" for 1972 from *Billboard*, and the Grammys for Record and Song of the Year for 1972. If Bucky didn't know he was on a hit that day, he certainly wouldn't have sensed that a forgettable jingle date would result in an unexpected bonus:

Jazz Tales from Jazz Legends

BP: We were on the gum commercial. Double your pleasure or something like that.
MR: Double your pleasure, double your fun, with—
RP: Doublemint Gum.
BP: We made a lot of money on that date.
MR: How come?
BP: Well, they played it. Super Bowl Sunday came around and we ended up with $5,000 in the mailbox.[18]

While studio musicians rarely profited from playing on hits at the musicians union rate of $42.50 for a three-hour session, the first-call players were making a significant salary doing three to four sessions a day. In addition, a number of rock bands sought out the best jazz artists to guest on particular songs. The Rolling Stones hired Sonny Rollins, Huey Lewis & the News called upon Stan Getz, and fellow saxophonists Michael Brecker and Phil Woods were frequent soloists on what became best-selling records. These top players commanded a better fee and had the juice to opt for a piece of the royalties. Saxophonist Phil Woods talked about his work with Billy Joel and his monetary decision:

MR: Can you recall when you did the thing on "Just the Way You Are," how many takes did you get on that?
PW: Oh, one or two tops. Oh yeah, it was just me and Phil Ramone in the booth. And he had the changes written on the back of a matchbook cover or something. But it was like a pop tune—a pop tune in the sense of a Broadway, Tin Pan Alley kind of song. It wasn't really a rock & roll song. It's really a pretty nice tune. So it was not a problem. Yeah, I did Phoebe Snow's overdub and Billy Joel in the same day—the same half hour.
MR: Was he producing both of those?
PW: Yeah. And I got $700 for both things, $350 apiece.
MR: I'm glad to hear that. And a Grammy.
PW: You know in those days, I mean from Mike Brecker on, from that period, when they would use soloists, it was kind of SOP, you'd ask for a quarter of a point. If a tune from the album was taken out and made a single, you'd get a quarter of a cent on every single that they made taken from the album if you're the soloist on it. My manager didn't know anything about this stuff and I sure didn't know anything about it. But you know we could have got it, all we had to do was ask. You know how much a billion quarter of a pennies are? That's a lot of money. That record sold over a billion, biggest selling record of

all time. But I mean I would have had the money but I wouldn't have had such a good story.[19]

Just as the big band era passed, the scene that Bob Rosengarden described as "a wild and wonderful time" also ran its course. Derek Smith addressed the change:

DS: Of course nothing stays the same forever, and the studio work disappeared, because: (a) we all got older; (b) technology put us out of work because they can do things with synthesizers where they don't need so many live musicians anymore.[20]

Derek, Bob Rosengarden, Milt Hinton, and most of the interviews thus far in this chapter were mostly New York based. While the scene in Los Angeles remained healthy for a bit longer due to film and television business, technology eventually altered that scene as well. Studio musician Howie Shear experienced the change in his career:

MR: Right now, in 2014, are you doing, in the music business, what you aspired to when you were here [at SUNY Fredonia]?
HS: In 2014? No. No. When I first got out of school [1974], when I moved to Los Angeles, there was a lot of work and what I really aspired to do was play in the studios as a trumpet player. And there was still quite a bit of work back then. And I always wanted to compose and orchestrate and I did a lot of that. There was a lot of work. But as the technology got better and life went on, there was less and less and less real instruments playing in the studios. Instead of four trumpets on our date, there was maybe one, maybe two, but one and sometimes none.
MR: Is that because the parts were being overdubbed with synthesizer trumpets or were they just two guys playing, record them twice or that kind of stuff?
HS: Both that. I still get called to do four parts. But yeah, most of the time it's synthesized trumpets. You get TV themes. Not movies really, but a lot of TV themes that have trumpets on it and they're very synthesized. So there's no trumpets on those. And the movies you do hear that. There's really 10 percent of the epic movies, the big movies like the remix of *Robin Hood* where they need a hundred piece orchestra, where you have trumpets. But that's about 10 percent. The other 90 percent of the films in Los Angeles are done in the home studios. And I myself have done four scores to films. And one

film they gave me a live orchestra. The other three films I had to record in a MIDI studio. So I paid people out of my own pocket to come in and I had a live cellist so it made the other strings sound more real. Or I would put a trumpet over it and maybe synthesized sounds sound more real, and I've got a French horn player or maybe one oboe player. So I hire several musicians to make the synthesized sounds sound a little more real. But that's most of what's going on.[21]

As the commercial work declined, a new opportunity arose for the best of the studio players. Jazz parties began to proliferate, starting with the annual Dick Gibson jazz weekend in Denver, Colorado. In addition, jazz cruises began to hire the best artists to perform in luxurious surroundings, a week at a time. The popularity of these events provided a new venue for some of the same musicians who were doing those multiple studio dates every day. They also returned to playing clubs in small groups, and making jazz records in an efficient and economical fashion.

I'll wrap up this chapter with a brief anecdote of my own. A close friend in Utica, New York, Bob Yauger, operated a respectable studio where I assisted as a producer and studio musician. I often overdubbed a keyboard or sax part for local bands searching for their own moment of stardom. On one session I showed up with my saxophone and the producer said, "All we need is one screeching note in this two-beat break in the song." He did his best imitation of a motivational coach and hyped me for the moment: "You rock, you're the man, you can do it" and other similar blather. Fortunately for me, the note happened to be a high A, transposed to my alto sax, a high F#, slightly out of the range of the horn but a note that I could squeeze out with appropriate intensity. I donned the headphones, and when the moment came I screamed out a high F# for all I was worth. The producer was ecstatic. That was it—fifteen minutes in and out—a first take. The question arose, what do I charge for one note? Do I charge for just the note? What about the money I saved the band for doing my part in less than a quarter of an hour? I honestly can't remember what I ended up making for that session, but I was grateful that the producer did not utter the phrase too often heard in studios nowadays, "That was perfect, let's do it again."

Chapter 6
The Color of Jazz

Jazz did not develop in a vacuum, and musicians were profoundly affected by regional laws and the unwritten codes of society. Their constant travel and visibility as performers exposed them to situations that ranged from degrading to physically dangerous, especially for black musicians in the pre-Civil Rights Era. The same artists we now celebrate as cultural heroes were subjected to treatment that now seems incongruous with the artistic status jazz enjoys today.

Nevertheless I am heartened by the message voiced repeatedly by many artists interviewed for the Archive. Their stories inform us of the racial inequities that accompanied bands in their cross-country tours; the ludicrous situations with venues, restaurants, and hotels; and the social mores of the time that were enforced by peacekeepers and civilians. But the same stories frequently put forth a unified message that once musicians make it to the stage and studio, talent and personality trump all other issues. The worst behavior society offered up regularly inspired a sense of spirit and camaraderie that transcended race, generation, and social status.

Joe Williams and Clark Terry are two musicians who lived through turbulent times. In a conversation in May 1995 Clark and Joe shared similar stories:

CT: You know, Joe, I think that some of the people who will be looking and listening to this wouldn't believe some of the stories that we could tell them about the bigotry and things that we have had to endure in our lifetimes in traveling in the South. And I'm not so sure it was a good idea to bring it up or not. What do you think?

JW: I don't know. As long as it's natural. I think of the positive things that happened. There were negatives of course. I have been attacked. The night Joe Louis beat Max Baer in Chicago I was attacked by four or five white guys with baseball bats. But they didn't run very well. I ran until I could only hear one set of footsteps behind me, and I turned and looked. So I slowed down a little. Nobody ever caught me. But that's one thing. But it never changed the way I am.

CT: It never made you reach the point where you hated people, hated Caucasians, because hate is too important an emotion, right? There was something within you that motivated you to not succumb to the principles or tactics that make you hate people. I'll give you a similar incident. I'm traveling in the South, in Meridian, Mississippi, and I was with a carnival act, Reuben and Jerry Carnivals. So we went in the Deep South for winter quarters. And while playing this show during the week, they always hired somebody in the city as a hired hand to keep law and order on the midway. And the black show was always at the end of the midway. So this cat comes through, now this was closing night, and we are getting ready to go pack up all of the equipment and the crew puts things together, we get on the train and we have our own train and we went on to the next place. So I'm waiting for the drummer, Marvin Wright, who was a good buddy of mine, to pack up his drums, and while waiting for the drummer to pack up his drums, he had met a lady during the week, and she was of fair complexion, and you know what the situation down there with the—

JW: Almost white, you mean.

CT: That's right. So I'm standing there with Marvin's lady friend, waiting on Marvin to unpack his stuff because the Mills Blue Rhythm Band was playing in town that night, so we're going to that. Well, here comes this little cat, and I'm standing there. He said, "What are you doin' standing out here after the lights is out, Nigerian?"[1] So I said, "Well, I'm waiting on the drummer, actually." "You with this here show, boy?" I said, "Yes, I am." He said, "What'd you say?" I said, "Yes, I am." He said, "Do you realize what you said?" I said, "Well, you're asking me a question, and I answered it." He said, "Did you realize that you said 'yes' to a white man?" And that's all I remember. I have a blackjack at home right now, to remind me of this—one of those lead things, covered.

JW: He hit you?

CT: Did he hit me. Right here man. Bamm. And my head got so big, I don't know what happened after that except what I was told by the train crew. Now this is an example, I could have, that could have motivated me to hate Caucasians the rest of my life, but it didn't.

JW: He could have killed you.

CT: But what happened, he left me laying in a puddle of mud and the work crew was all Caucasian. They picked me up, took me back to the show trains, and by the time they got back this dude comes back with about twenty people with axes and sledge hammers and chains and saws and picks and shovels and everything. Said, "Where is that Nigerian we left laying down there in that mud?" And the Caucasian

The Color of Jazz

said to him, "Oh he was some smart aleck, we just kicked him in the pants and sent him up that way." So they ran up that way looking for me where in reality I was back here in the show train. So that's one hand washing the other. And this is long before I realized the importance of love and was motivated by love after that, but this was something within me that helped me to balance out decency and right from wrong. Makes you keep on keepin' on.[2]

In 1994 Jean Bach presented jazz lovers with a unique gift: the film, *A Great Day in Harlem*,[3] which told the backstory behind the 1959 *Esquire* magazine picture of fifty-seven jazz artists photographed by Art Kane.[4] Jean was a self-described "jazz groupie," especially for anything Ellington. Her interactions with the musicians in the '40s help us to understand the social guidelines imposed on her musical heroes.

MR: You just started to touch on a subject that I find interesting and that is the racial thing that was happening at that time, with this music and the fans, and how did that kind of balance—

JB: Very, very heartbreaking in a way, but somehow—as you look back it was terrible—it was a given. And I was interviewed by somebody from the Black Entertainment Network, she came to my house. And she said, "You don't look like a jazz groupie, to be following the band." Well, boy, I was. I was the first jazz groupie. I mean I'd hear Ellington was playing in Rock Island, Illinois, and if I wasn't doing anything that day, I'd get on the train and just go and hear the band. So I heard him quite a lot. They played at the Sherman Hotel for— was it a four-week period or maybe a little longer. And Harry Lim, the jazz critic from Holland was living in Chicago at the time. And he and I went every night to hear Ellington. Then we would go out afterward, and you didn't go out in midtown Chicago, you went to the South Side. There was a drug store out there called The Ritz Drugstore. And they had something like twenty-seven flavors of ice cream. So we'd all sit around, the whole band and Ellington, and we'd be dipping in each other's ice cream, very unsanitary. Ellington coined a word: "seagulling." And he said that's what you do when you steal something off someone else's plate. And he said, they had their own private car. They had to travel that way because they couldn't stay in hotels. And I think they had their own diner too. And he said at mealtime, the master seagull doesn't order anything for dinner, he just orders a service plate, and he just walks down the aisle and says, "What do you have that goes good with my dinner," and helps himself. But Bobby [Short] tells me a lot that's like childbirth. You forget all the terrible stuff. I don't remember it. But Bobby said, "Don't you remember, we had to meet in the stairwell and all that stuff?" He said it was really kind of bad. But I remember a few moments of anxiety. [Vocalist] Lee Wiley was living in the Rockefeller Apartments, not far from where we are now. And it's kind of a tony building. I don't know if they called it the Rockefeller Apartments, but it's across from the Museum of Modern Art. And she had invited the gang from Nick's to come over. And she suddenly said, "[gasps] Zutty Singleton—they won't let him through the lobby." And I said, "Let me handle this." And my mother was sort of a Grand Dame and she'd "brook no nonsense" as we say. And I suddenly became my mother. And I said, "Give me the doorman, please." And I said, "What's his name, James?" I said, "James," I said, "This is Miss Wiley's apartment. She's expecting some guests. Will you see that they're ushered up right away, and make sure that Mr. Singleton comes. You'll recognize him. He's colored. Thank you very much. Good-bye." Because to have to go up the service elevator kind of breaks your spirit and that happened all the time.[5]

Black musicians most assuredly embarked on southern tours with trepidation. Even an artist like Art Tatum—whose reputation is beyond category by any standards, jazz or classical—experienced the humiliation of having to depend on white musicians for basic daily necessities. Veteran big band drummer Sonny Igoe described a 1954 tour with a mixed group of musicians:

MR: When you were touring with Benny [Goodman], or later Woody Herman, were you playing for integrated audiences?

SI: Oh yeah. But the problem was that when you got down South they couldn't mingle. Of course then everybody was colored. The term was colored. So the coloreds would be in the balcony. They could listen but they couldn't come down and dance. I don't know if they danced in the hallways or anything like that because they couldn't see. But they were definitely segregated. And we didn't have any black guys in the band with Benny in the year—I was on tour with Stan Kenton in 1954 when I was with Charlie Ventura. And there was two buses, there were so many people on this tour. It was a great—he called it the Festival of Modern American Jazz. And it was Stan Kenton's band and Shorty Rogers and Shelly Manne, Art Tatum Trio, June Christy. And Lennie Niehaus was in the band. But

The Color of Jazz

anyway a whole bunch of people. It was almost a three-hour show. And Charlie Ventura's group with Mary Ann McCall singing. And so we played down South. We went on a sixty-eight-night tour with no breaks. No nights off. And two buses. And I was in the bus with Art Tatum and his trio guys and a couple of other fellas, a band boy and a couple of others. There weren't as many people on our bus. So we would get down South but Art and his guys couldn't—we stopped for a rest stop thinking we'd get off the bus and we'd stop to eat and they couldn't get off the bus. I used to bring them coffee, sodas and stuff, we all did. Everybody catered to those guys. Because they didn't want to get involved in anything because it was still like that that down there. I remember when I was in the Marines it was terrible, during the war, in the southern cities.

MR: They didn't even respect that they were servicemen.

SI: Nah, nah, nah. Terrible. As a matter of fact we used to get sometimes in trouble. There would be two drinking fountains. Whites only. Colored only. We'd always drink out of the colored. People would say, "Get out of there you white trash" and that kind of stuff. That was the '40s. You can't imagine that today, actually. Terrible. But they couldn't stay in the same hotels, they had to have them in the section of town where they could stay. Some of them stayed like in boarding houses. But that was the way it was back then. And even though Gene [Krupa] had Roy Eldridge in his band for years, that was before that time in the late '30s. It must have been terrible for those guys back then.[6]

Milt "The Judge" Hinton played bass on thousands of recordings, circled the globe with Louis Armstrong and Cab Calloway, and blessed us with photographs of his fellow musicians that only an insider could have taken. Milt and his wife Mona opened their door and hearts to countless musicians and could invariably be found at the center of a circle of friends and admirers. Mona Hinton accompanied Milt on tours with the Cab Calloway band in the 1930s and spoke of those travels in this interview conducted in March 1995:

MH: Well, unfortunately, due to the climate of our society, the blacks and the whites were segregated. And it made it very difficult, especially when we were traveling in the South. Because frequently we would run into Glenn Miller's band or Tommy Dorsey's band, or some of the well known white bands. They were staying in nice hotels. And unfortunately the black musician would have to stay on the other side

Jazz Tales from Jazz Legends

of the tracks, usually in someone's home, or in a hotel that was not very good. And as I say, unfortunately, frequently the owners of the hotels, they would take advantage, I mean of the black musicians. They knew that we could not stay in places, and we'd run into places with rats and with the roaches and with the bed bugs and whatnot. So under those circumstances it was not good. Frequently we would go in towns and I would have to go out in the black community and try to help find rooms for the musicians in Calloway's band, and sometimes the places where we had to eat were just intolerable. And as I say, we made it.[7]

Both Cab Calloway and Duke Ellington often dealt with this problem by hiring their own Pullman cars enabling the bands to travel, sleep, and eat on their own terms.

At times, managing to arrive at a gig could present an obstacle. Trumpeter Joe Wilder was a member of the Lucky Millinder Orchestra in 1947. Like Milt Hinton, Joe Wilder lived his life with dignity and class, and with a wry sense of humor that served him well throughout his career. I asked Joe about touring the South with Lucky's group in this interview from October 1998:

JW: We were in South Carolina [with] Lucky Millinder. Lucky was a very nice fellow. He was not a musician, but he had a lot of natural talent for selecting the right kinds of tunes and tempos and things of that nature. But I think six of the members of the band were white. And we arrived early in South Carolina at this hall where we were going to play, and suddenly up drove the sheriff with his deputy in the police car, and he says, "Who's in charge here?" And Lucky said, "I am." He said, "Well, I'm just here to tell you there's not going to be any mixed bands playing down here in Charleston." And Lucky looked at this guy, and Lucky—you know the reason I think they called him Lucky, he would take a chance on anything—he looked this guy dead in the eye and said, "This is not a mixed band." And some of the guys were blonde with blue eyes, there was no way in the world anybody would have mistaken any of these guys for being black. And so he went to each guy. I think if he had said, "Are you black?" he might have gotten a different answer. But he went to each of these guys and asked, "Are you colored?" And each of the guys, going along with what Lucky had said, would say yes. And so he would shake his head. And finally the last of the guys he asked was Porky Cohen, who was our first trombone player. And he had a

The Color of Jazz

slight lisp. And when he asked him, now Porky is responding more emphatically than the other guys, and he said, "Why thertainly" with this lisp. And at this point we had all been starting to chew on our tongues and everything, trying not to break up because it was so ludicrous. And you could see the ground tremble, we were trying not to let the sheriff see it. But anyway he turned to the deputy and he said, "Well, I guess if they all say they're colored, there ain't nothing we can do about it, is there, Jeff?" And so he said, "No, sheriff." And they got in the car and drove off. And we played that dance that night. It was very funny. And it might have been the first time that an integrated band played there. It's very possible that that was the first time.[8]

Despite the best efforts of law enforcement and promoters, the music had a way of overriding the rules, both explicit and implicit. Vocalist Ruth Brown made her mark in jazz, blues, and R&B. As a band leader, she experienced her share of trouble on the road. Arriving at the gig did not mean those situations ended for the night. In March 1995, Ruth related what a typical gig was like:

RB: Well, most times we worked warehouses and barns, and nine times out of ten that didn't have what you call the "second balcony." If we were lucky to play a county hall or an auditorium sometimes they had a balcony, and in that balcony was called the spectators. These were the whites who bought tickets to come in to hear the music but were not allowed to come on the dance floor. Sometimes it was vice versa. The whites would be down and the blacks would be up in the balcony and not allowed to come down. But in places such as barns, warehouses, where there was just one level, they would separate the races with a rope, and I say, a clothesline was what it was, an oversized clothesline. And most times someone had taken a huge cardboard and written "colored" which was the definition of our ethnic group at that particular time, and on the other side the card would say "white." And the white spectators were allowed to dance on that side of the rope, and the black on this side. But what they did not anticipate was that the music generated such a joy, people got to dancing, the ropes would fall down, I seen it happen many times. And people would continue to dance, and just wander in to each other's space. Nobody would say a thing for a moment, and then it would occur to some official that, uh oh, the rope is down and they're dancing in the same space, and we can't have that. And then somebody would run up on the stage and say, "Stop the music," and they'd just stop the music and go back and put the rope in place, and you had to go back on your given side.[9]

Ruth and her band were once pulled over for going five miles over the speed limit. Suspicious because of the luxury car they were in, the troopers made the band prove they were musicians by getting their instruments out and playing on the side of the road. The pianist, Lee Anderson, "played" on the hood of the car.

The race card could be dealt both ways as drummer Louie Bellson learned. He was the only white player in Duke Ellington's Orchestra in the early 1950s and was once asked to become "non-white" so the band could keep him on stage.

LB: In 1951 they had the Big Show of 1951, which consisted of Nat King Cole, Sarah Vaughan, and Duke Ellington's band. They were the three big stars. Now besides that they had Peg Leg Bates, Timmy Rodgers, Stump and Stumpy, Patterson and Jackson, all these wonderful acts—tap dancing acts. It took us a week to rehearse that show, playing with Nat King Cole and Sarah, Duke, and all these acts. So after we finished rehearsing for a week, Duke finally discovered that hey, we're getting ready to go down to the Deep South, you know? And in those days, you had segregated audiences. The whites couldn't play with the blacks at that time you see. In those days it was "colored," you didn't use the word "blacks." So now the big problem is, Duke called me in the dressing room and says, "What are we going to do? I can't find a drummer to take your place, because it would be a week's rehearsal and the guys that can do it, they're all busy." So Duke says, "You mind being a Haitian?" I said, "No, okay, that's all right." So we got through it okay. It was a little tense, because the situation was still down there, and the audience, because they told [percussionist] Jack Costanzo with Nat King Cole he couldn't appear because of the racial thing. But some spots it was a little rough. But we got through it. I think through Ellington's peaceful ways and the wonderful attitude that the band had kind of rubbed off on everybody. But still it existed.

MR: Well, it's nice that the music had a part in helping that situation to move along a little faster.

LB: Well, we played a gig in Mississippi and there the townspeople were wonderful, they came to the rescue, where we couldn't stay in certain hotels and so forth. I mean these people came from wealthy

The Color of Jazz

families too. They had Strayhorn and Duke and Clark Terry stay in one house, and [Harry] Carney and Russell Procope and myself in another house, and all on down the line. Beautiful homes and they fed us. So along with the bad there's some good too. And these were situations that we got over, we dealt with it. Sometimes it's almost like a slap in the face but you realize what the situation is and you go straight ahead because you've got something to do that's valued and I think when you do that you realize that none of those things should bother the musicality of something. It's the fact that whoever's playing that music doesn't make a difference, let's play it and show where the peace and love is.[10]

Trumpeter Red Rodney pulled off the opposite ruse when he became "Albino Red" for his southern tour with the Charlie Parker Quintet.

In the 1930s, when big band jazz was the popular music of the day, an important breakthrough occurred. Pianist Teddy Wilson often played intermission piano between sets of the Benny Goodman Orchestra. Because he was black, he left the stage when Goodman's musicians entered. At the urging of jazz promoter Helen Dance[11] and despite warnings from his management, Benny Goodman thwarted convention and hired Teddy Wilson and Lionel Hampton to perform with his band. With drummer Gene Krupa, this quartet become one of the most recorded small groups of the decade. Jackie Robinson's entry into major league baseball nine years later drew more press, but Lionel Hampton and Jon Hendricks both touted Goodman's integrated quartet in their interviews, conducted back-to-back on October 18, 1995:

LH: I was the first black musician to play in a white band. See, and Teddy Wilson was playing with Benny, but he used to play when Benny used to take intermission, and no white musicians was on stage, then Teddy would play by himself. So I was the first one, legally, to break that tradition down. But the funny thing about it, there wasn't no black and white playing together no place. Not in pictures, moving pictures, not in baseball, or football, no kind of sports. The Benny Goodman Quartet was the first mixed group and we were the first integrated group, the first black and white group.

MR: Was that ever a problem playing in certain parts of the country?

LH: No, no. Because we all played good music. And Benny presented us in a professional way. We were four in his organization, and it would be noticeable that we were soft. And the people liked that. Some of the ovations that he used to get, it was the sound.[12]

Jazz Tales from Jazz Legends

And from Jon Hendricks:

JH: Benny Goodman is an American social hero. He is a hero in the development of American society. Outside of music, Benny Goodman is a social hero. Because his love for the music was so pure that he just did not understand why he couldn't have Lionel Hampton in his band, and then Charlie Christian and then Teddy Wilson you know. He just didn't understand that. And the bean counters and the accountants and the lawyers, they tried to explain to him, "Benny, you'll lose your show, they will not renew you on the 'Camel Caravan' if you do this." So they gave him all those very hard-and-fast business reasons. But he refused to understand it. He said, "I like those guys." So he did what people have to march now to achieve. And it's because of the power of the music, a love of the music.[13]

Eventually the integration achieved on stage found its way into the New York City recording studios by way of Milt Hinton. At a record date, every studio musician had to prove they could get it right the first time, could handle any kind of music placed on the stand and be punctual. In the studio, ability is color blind. In his book *Bass Line*, Milt related how a chance meeting with Jackie Gleason helped make this happen for him:

MH: It was during my slow period that I ran into Jackie and his manager, Bullets Durgon, on a street corner downtown. He asked me the usual kind of questions, "Whatta ya doing? What's going on?" Instead of giving him the standard show business answer I said, "Nothing." Jackie turns to Bullets and said, "We're doing a record date tomorrow, put Milt on it." Bullets tried to explain about contractors but Jackie didn't want to know. "I don't give a damn about contractors. Call whoever is in charge and tell him I want Milt there tomorrow." The next morning I showed up at Capitol. There must have been fifty musicians in the studio. I'd recorded before but never anything this size. Besides, I knew from the minute I walked in, I was the only black. After the first few takes, we took a break and a couple of the musicians came over and introduced themselves. By the time the date ended I felt much more comfortable. The contractor came over, complimented me, and asked if I'd do the next session to finish the album. I didn't even wait to get the date and time—I just nodded yes.[14]

The Color of Jazz

The comments and anecdotes I heard in these interviews on this subject seemed genuine and heartfelt. The experiences and influences that set these musicians on the jazz path ran the gamut from the church they attended as a child to what station the radio was tuned into at night. To these artists, qualifying a jazz musician's success by adding or subtracting points because of their race is an insult. By championing the ultimate importance of the individual, these musicians bolster their own accomplishments and give us a reason to take faith in the power of the art form.

Saxophonist Frank Foster visited Hamilton College as an artist-in-residence after stepping down as leader of the Count Basie Orchestra. He shared his opinion on the subject of race and talent:

FF: I don't think every person born into this world is a jazz musician, and I don't agree with—somebody's got something out that says anybody, everybody can improvise. I don't go with that.

MR: Oh that's right, there's a series, *Anyone Can Improvise*.[15]

FF: Yeah. I don't subscribe to that. But it's an individual thing, it's not a racial thing. We have such a melting pot here, we're all into each other's culture. Okay, I contend that jazz was born in America as a result of the black experience. Now nobody in the world could ever convince me that that isn't true, okay? But now as I said before, we've got this melting pot where we're all into each other's culture. We can emulate one another, and we can relate to one another, and talent wasn't just given to whites or blacks or Latinos or Asiatics or whatever. Every racial ethnic group has talent. And all God's children got rhythm, some more than others. Look man, I know some black folks who can't clap on two and four. ONE two THREE four. I know some cats who can't do this [claps one TWO three FOUR]. On the other hand I know some white folks, every time will say [claps one TWO three FOUR] and vice versa you know. So we've all got talented people and we've all got some no-talented people. Every ethnic and racial group has somebody blowing a horn that should put it down and forget it and be a plumber or a postman or something. But when I hear somebody who's not black perform on an instrument and that person is good, they are good, regardless of what somebody else black might say—oh he can't play, she can't play, that's it. Man, it hurt me years ago, one of my trumpet players, are you familiar with Lew Soloff? Well, this guy just put Lew Soloff in the garbage can, "He can't play, he never could." And Lew Soloff is a monster. Lew Soloff can play anything, can play jazz, can play lead trumpet, he can play in a section, you know, he can just do anything that's necessary for a jazz trumpeter to do. Big band, small group, whatever. So when one of us can do it, give us the credit. When one of them can do it, give them the credit. I don't feel threatened by anybody. If you can play and you're white, great, let's play together. If you can't play and you're white —

MR: Go play with someone else.
FF: Yeah. If you can't play and you're black, get out of here.
MR: Go play with that white guy that can't play.[16]

Frank's comments remind me of my own feelings about playing music when I had the good fortune to play a series of gigs in 1998 with Claude "Fiddler" Williams. If you had attended one of our performances you would have seen then twenty-year-old blonde bassist Genevieve Rose swinging next to "The Fiddler," who toured with the Terrence Holder Band in Oklahoma in 1928. Claude and Genevieve were bookended by two middle-aged white guys, Syracuse guitarist Mark Copani, and yours truly. The dynamic quartet was the perfect blending of musical and cultural elements, and musically one of the most satisfying of my career.

At jazz education conventions we can witness the melting pot to which Frank Foster refers. Throngs of musicians, educators, students, promoters, producers, and publicists of every race, age, and gender converge in the name of jazz. Many of them hope to grab a piece of the small pie that jazz occupies in the music marketplace. It is an uphill battle, but as in any artistic endeavor, originality and skill will earn the spotlight.

The music, wit, and wisdom of Jon Hendricks is worth studying, either in the recordings of Lambert, Hendricks & Ross or with his own recent releases. In our second interview in January 2000, he talked about his father (a member of the clergy), his hometown, and the big picture:

JH: My father had an aura and an authority about him that people immediately respected. When he died, by that time I had married an Irish girl. When he died I took my wife to the funeral. And when I drove into town the town was buzzing, because it was in Kentucky. And they stopped me a couple of times and says, "Whatchall doin' here boy?" And they're looking at my wife. And I says, "I'm Jon Hendricks, I'm here for my father's funeral, Reverend Hendricks." And they said, "Oh Reverend Hendricks, okay." And I went to the funeral. It was incredible. And at the funeral, half the town was there, and fully half of the people in the church were white people. That's how respected my father was. And I remember sitting with him one night and there was a local white preacher who used to

The Color of Jazz

come over in the evenings and sit and talk to my father. They would be sitting in these rocking chairs on the porch. And one night the preacher says, "Reverend, I just wanted to discuss something with you." And my father says, "What was that?" He said, "Well, I just can't help it," he said, "I just feel that my people are better than your people." And the rocking kept on, and I'm waiting. And my father said, "Well, Reverend," he said, "do you believe in God?" And so the white preacher said, "Well, you know I do." And my father said, "Well then, what's your problem?" And the rocking kept on. And not another word was spoken. And I said whooooh. He got right to the heart of the matter. Because that's the key. We still talk about a problem. There is no problem. There is no racial problem if you acknowledge God. Because if you acknowledge God then you are looking at another child of God. So what are you talking about? If you're going to separate from that other child of God because of this mythical term you have here, you are acting in an ungodly way. So when people ask me about race, I say, "What time does it start?"[17]

Chapter 7
Thoughts on Improvisation

I try to avoid absolutes when talking about music, but it's safe to say there would be no jazz without improvisation. Improvisational technique is not exclusive to jazz; musicians who play rock, bluegrass, and jam band music all employ it, and according to historical anecdotes, both Bach and Mozart improvised in their own way. But jazz, more than any other musical genre, depends on the extemporaneous creation by individuals. Listeners can be puzzled by these musical explorations, and it is no accident that big band swing, arguably the most popular style of jazz, relied the least on improvisation for its success. When non-musicians listen to jazz, a common complaint is: "After they play the melody, I don't get it. They're just playing what they want I guess." Part of that statement is correct. They are playing what they want. But their choices are based on surprisingly cogent structure of time, harmony, and form.

Consider the song "Take the A Train." It consists of four 8-bar sections, which equals thirty-two measures in A-A-B-A form. It's really sixteen measures of music cleverly organized to create a song twice as long. When performed by a small jazz unit, the typical format will be: melody, multiple improvisations based on the form, and ending with a return to the melody. Creating new melodies and variations on the fly is what jazz musicians learn to do. As jazz progressed, forms and harmonies shifted, becoming either more complex or simpler.

The First Steps
The basic goal of starting young musicians is to put them at ease by creating a scenario that guarantees some level of success. The typical young student at the first improvisation lesson is probably feeling shy, intimidated, and unsure. At this early stage, asking them to play what they feel is counterproductive. Junior high students are reluctant to express their emotions, especially to a stranger. I leave that concept to much further down the line. At all points during the process I offer praise and constructive ideas about the way they are playing. In her interview in 1997, Marian McPartland discussed the process of students learning to improvise:

MR: Do you think that jazz can be successfully taught to play [to children]?

Thoughts on Improvisation

MM: Sometimes I think it can. I actually did a three-month period in the Washington, D.C. schools and we got a huge grant for this, to go around to the public schools with just this thing in mind, to teach kids to play jazz. And I used all the local musicians, and one of the best tunes I thought to get the kids started to play would be a blues, and then we picked "C Jam Blues" because it's so repetitive, and the kids had these little instruments like a vibraharp, with two octaves they all had to play on. And we did in fact get kids to not only play this tune but to improvise on it. And we culminated with a concert with Duke [Ellington], he came down and played with a small group for the kids in the school And it was one of the great experiences of my life. So at that time I thought that they really had done some good things and it was a shame that they couldn't follow through, like after we left the program just fell apart. I mean it broke my heart because we really had kids improvising with the Navy band, what an experience that was, I'll never forget. Anyway, I basically think that you can, if somebody is interested, you can point them in the right direction. Kids have to be motivated. And I think if they really want to do it that's half the battle. Then they will investigate and listen and that's a part of it. But I have seen and done workshops and stage band clinics and things where you think these kids will never play. Next year the kid comes back, having listened to Bill Evans or somebody, and is playing away, and I'll never say never to anybody, because I think it takes wanting to do it, and motivation, and that's about it, really.[1]

The subject of improvisation was discussed during many of our interviews for the Fillius Jazz Archive. It's worth noting that the majority of these accomplished improvisers do not dwell on technical musical terms to explain the process of improvisation.

In the Beginning
Clark Terry responded to a question posed by Professor Michael Woods about the role of music theory in creating an improvised solo. He takes us back to a time before musical terms were labeled and intellectualized.

CT: You have to remember that years before people who came into this field, years before they knew anything about theory or harmony, composition, counterpoint, etcetera, they gave in to their feelings. And they were indulging in, for lack of a better term, they called it "get off." This is long before the term "improvisation" was coined, pertaining to playing music. They used to call it "get off," which simply meant that the first chorus you played a melody, and thereafter you'd use the melody as a guidewire to simply superimpose extemporaneously a melody around this given melody. So you "get off" the melody. Even then the guys were giving vent to their feelings and expressing themselves and they would use certain things that would help them get from point A to point B. First of all the one thing that we teach our students today regardless of how much theory or harmony or composition will get in their brain, they've got to know when to use it. They've got to listen for when to use it, or how to use it. Heads loaded with something they don't know how to use it, don't know where to use it or when to use it. So this is a lesson that we try real hard to get our students to understand. Back in those days, they didn't know anything, as you mention, about technical terms. They had nobody around to teach it. But they were determined to give in to their feelings and express themselves, and "get off." So what'd they do? They played the blues as the main vehicle, and they played the standard tunes, and then superimposed melody around it. But on the blues they figured out a good way to give vent to their feelings is that somebody had to change the melody, even without knowledge, to figure out, there's the tonic, that's the one; then you go up the scale, one two three, that's the third, they'd lower that a half-step, that's the minor third; you go up one, two, three, four, five, lower that, so you've got a tonic, a minor third, a flatted fifth, and they didn't know then that it constituted a half diminished. All they knew is they called them the "blue notes." "Man you've got your blue notes?" "Yeah, baby I've got 'em down, I'm working on F# now, I'm going to have that tomorrow." Now you can't pick out more beautiful and important notes in playing the blues than those three. Then you go into your seventh. That's all. Just that one note, those two notes, or those three. Because after a while they begin to hear all of the relative notes that constitute the scale, and then they're going to hear the four, they're going to hear the flat five, some people call it the augmented seventh, the flat sixth, the major seventh, they'll hear the whole scale then. But after a while they're going to be involved with playing those blue notes. The tonic, minor third, and the flatted fifth, and they got it.[2]

Pianist Bill Charlap grew up in a musical environment well after the era that Clark Terry describes. Music is often called the universal language and he finds the use of language an appropriate metaphor in describing

Thoughts on Improvisation

his thought process (or lack thereof) when improvising. He also emphasizes the importance of listening to the sounds and the space that surround you in any given situation.

BC: One should not be sitting there doing analytical thought when you're improvising. It's like language. You don't think about the next word you're going to say, you don't think about how to spell it or what that word is, you just say it. It's the same for me at the piano. Same for any musician worth their salt as a jazz musician. You think a phrase and you play that phrase. I don't think, gee that's the third, that's the seventh, that's a dotted eighth, sixteenth, there's a whole rest here—all the technical things. I hearken it to language because in language you have to know how to conjugate, you have to know how to speak properly, how to get your ideas across in many different ways. You might say I walked up the mountain, and you might say I slowly walked up the mountain and then I ran and then I stopped and I took a rest, I had a ham sandwich, and then I got to the top of the mountain. There's a lot of different ways to get there. And I know many different ways, just as you would in a conversation, but you don't think about it, you just think of what you want to express. That's the best analogy I can give for what happens when I'm improvising. Behind it is a great deal of knowledge and experience and the ability to listen. The most important thing is to listen to the players around you, or if you're playing solo, to listen to the air. Listen to the space, and listen to what the space needs. And if it doesn't need anything, don't play anything.[3]

Although they are a generation apart, like Bill Charlap, saxophonist Charles McPherson also used a language analogy to describe the improvisation thought process during his interview in 1998:

MR: If you're playing on "All the Things You Are," have you internalized that tune enough over the years that you don't have to think about this Two-Five-One and that?
CM: Oh yeah. In pretty much all music. You have to do that when you're learning a tune. But once the tune is committed to memory, the form, the structure and the elements that make the tune what it is, I don't think any real pro that's been playing for a number of years really thinks about that. It's like when you're getting ready to talk you don't really say I'm saying an infinitive, I'm saying this is a verb, this is an adjective phrase, you don't really say that. You just need to

say whatever it is you want to say and then you try to do it. And you do do it. So it's pretty much the same way.

MR: I'm wondering if that's something that would be really important to pass on to a student, not to neglect learning songs really well because all the theory will not come into play until you know the song.

CM: Right. Yes. You have to know the literature that you're dealing with. So it's just like anything else, you might go to school for journalism or for whatever. It doesn't make any difference what it is. You have two dimensions to conquer. You have the physical dimension or the physical media that you're dealing with, whether it's music, if it's writing, it doesn't make any difference. There's a certain thing that has to be overcome and you have to get the professionalism and the command over whatever medium it is. And then after that's done then that's not really the real main event. The main event is what do you do with that now? What kind of pictures do you take, or what kind of story. You can go to school and learn how to write, but okay now after you know the elements of how to write a short story or a long story, essay, this and that, all right, you know mechanically what to do, you know this is supposed to unfold in this manner and climax here and this here. But now that doesn't mean you're going to be a great writer. It just means you know the elements of writing. It's the same with music. You can learn Two-Five-Ones, chorus, and yes, you should learn that and you will learn it and you do learn it. But that doesn't mean you're going to be a great soloist. It doesn't mean you're going to be a great artist. It doesn't mean any of that, because there's another aspect of all of that that has nothing to do with the physicality or the medium through which you're dealing, it's got something to do with all that other stuff, all that abstract stuff that you can't hold or touch, that there's no way in school they can show you. You can learn facts, figures, and knowledge. But discrimination and wisdom cannot be taught. That is something that you come wired with, or if indeed there is such a thing as people learning how to do it—I'm still out on that, I don't know if you come wired with it, or if indeed there's some way of learning, or your environment. I don't know that you can teach these things. How to write a great story. How to play a great solo. How to write great music. That's something else, and that's something that you deal, as an artist, this is what you're dealing with after you get past academia and all of that stuff. Then it's like how to get the best out of yourself when you want to, all the time.[4]

Thoughts on Improvisation

Intuition plays an important role in creating your own sound, according to saxophonist and clarinetist Ken Peplowski. Ken also belongs to a younger generation of jazz artists who had access to the growing body of codified information about how to play jazz. His advice on the subject of jazz theory is basically, "Learn it then forget it," a phrase that most teachers would find difficult to pass on to their students. Ken speaks about dealing with "mistakes" and the opportunities they may present. He compares the best improvising to a mystical experience.

KP: A big part of improvising is forgetting what you know and just using your ear and going on intuition. Because sometimes they get very hung up in the schools on, if you have this chord you have to play this pattern over it, this is what John Coltrane did when he played. But the reason why those musicians were famous and why they were so loved is because they were individuals, with their own style and their own sound. And you have to encourage students to explore on their own also. It's great to learn all this stuff because any knowledge is good knowledge. The trick is later to forget that. It's like things you feed into a computer and then out comes something else. Whatever you read or whatever you live, it all comes into your music. So you can't sit there while you're playing and think about every single chord and what can I play over this? Because the best moments when you're improvising, you're actually—I hate to say this—but it's almost an out-of-body experience. You can actually listen to yourself playing. You're just sailing through the changes and saying oh, hey, how did I play that?

MR: And how do I get out of something that I didn't mean to play? Did that ever happen to you?

KP: Oh, of course. In fact sometimes you can do that. You play little tricks on yourself. You paint yourself into a corner and then you try to get out of it. But as Dizzy Gillespie said one time, you're only a half step away from salvation at any given moment. Because when you look at a chord and you look at extensions of the chord, you keep adding thirds onto the chord, you have every note in the chromatic scale anyway. So it's all how it comes out at the end, how you resolve a phrase. So to me the object is not to think about every chord as an individual thing, but the whole thing is a big picture. And your object is to get from point A to point B and tell a story and have a flow to it—a beginning, a middle and an end. And getting back to the schools, that's what I try to bring to the students, to show them how they can maybe assimilate these bits of knowledge they have, and try to find their own way of negotiating these chord changes, not forgetting the knowledge that they have. It's important to learn that stuff but sometimes individuality is not stressed enough.[5]

Trumpeter Joe Wilder echoed Bill Charlap's comments about the importance of listening and reacting to your musical surroundings and reminds us that a bit of mental preplanning can go a long way in creating effective improvisations. When asked about his thought process he offered his own connection to language and added an athletic metaphor:

JW: These things come to you automatically. I mean usually if I'm going to play something while someone else is playing, I'll try to think of something that I would like to start, to introduce my solo with, and it's something that's relative to the nature of the piece itself, and something that fits kind of harmonically with what's going on. And I usually try to think about that. And I also think it's just—improvisation it's like giving a speech or something like that. You have a subject, and your interpretation of it may differ from mine, but it's still basically the same subject so that's a theme that you're improvising around. And you try to play something that enhances it, and also adds a little different flavor to it. So you don't come in and play exactly what the person played before you. You may even extract some of what he played as a lead in to what you're going to do, so you get that dove-tailing, and it's like passing the baton in a relay race. You do it smoothly. You're running and you pick up the same speed as that person whom you're going to accept the baton from or pass it to, and you get that smooth transition. If you listen to a lot of improvisation in different groups, they have that smooth transfer from one to the other. That's the way it comes off.[6]

Drummers too internalize a similar thought process to what a horn or piano player might. In this interview from 2014, Winard Harper related the thinking process in his solos, remarkably similar to Joe Wilder's:

MR: I read a quote in the *Washington Post*. You were playing with someone and it said you played "wonderfully orchestrated solos." When you're doing those 4-bar breaks, 8-bar breaks or whatever, do you plan ahead for the next break?

WH: When it comes to solos I'm still trying to compose, you know, like Max [Roach]. I'm trying to say something. So in my solos, I may have some ideas and then I'll go forthwith, and then from that

Thoughts on Improvisation

something else comes. But on the trading, for me it's always based on what the horn player plays or the piano player plays, whoever is taking the fours before me. Because if they've said something I'm either trying to continue the statement or answer the statement. So sometimes rhythmically I may hear something in what they played and I may borrow from or take that and start it and go from there. Sometimes it can be a conversation. And then everybody looks and says wow, he hears me. You know what I mean? And then all the doors start opening up with everybody, everybody's giving and taking. It's a wonderful thing playing music. If you think about it, all those things are fundamentals for life. Because you know what it does to somebody when they realize and they find out somebody hears me. I've talked and he's listening. For families, for everything else. Some of it doesn't happen as much as it needs to, even in society. You know that's a lot of what's going on. People are talking and they feel like nobody's listening. Okay, like who hears me? And that's what happens on the bandstand a lot of times. I always tell a lot of my students, once you start playing with people, people you've never played with before, you're going to find that once they know that you're listening and you hear them it's going to open up a door. I mean it always happens. You might be playing with somebody and they're just thinking about playing the music. And all of a sudden they play something and you catch it and all of a sudden they look up, oh, we're "conversating."[7]

Serious students of jazz hope to make the majority of their income by playing it. Those of us who are working musicians know that what you like to play and what you need to play are not always the same thing. Trombonist and arranger Dan Barrett is a frequent guest at jazz events across the country and a recording artist for Arbors Records. When asked about what students should practice in their study of jazz he offered some practical advice:

DB: I would advise [students] that in their practicing as they're playing scales and as they're playing exercises and trying to improve their technique, I would take about 25 or 30 percent of that time and use it to study songs. And go out and buy sheet music, not just lead sheets with the chord symbols, but shell out the bucks that it takes and buy Cole Porter and Gershwin songs. Look at them and look at the piano parts, even if you don't play piano. And it takes forever if you're not a piano player, but it's worth the effort to sit at a keyboard and hear how those inner voices move. And if the student spent a little bit of his practice time, doing that, analyzing these songs by these great songwriters he'd learn how to construct a line. Because after all these are great composers. And what we're trying to do in jazz ostensibly is to compose, even though we're composing spontaneously. And I think what better way to learn to compose then examining music by a great composer. So not only would you profit from that knowledge that you can gain by analyzing that music, but also you'll learn these great songs. One student said, "Well, this is all well and good, but when are we going to get into the Lydian modes and all of that?" And I say, "Somebody else can teach you that better than I can," and I said, "I think any knowledge is good." And I said, "It'd probably benefit you greatly to know about that. But I'll tell you something. Playing in clubs, I've received $5 here and there to play 'Body and Soul' and I've received $10 tips to play 'Stardust,' but I don't think I've ever made a dime to play a Dorian mode or a Lydian mode. So it's great to know about that stuff, but I think you'd be better off and stand a much greater chance to make a living in a fairly competitive business if you learn these songs and learn them correctly, so you make people happy.[8]

A number of years ago I had the great fortune to be able assemble an all-star group to record "Jazz Life" which contains some of my own compositions, and trombonist Bill Watrous and trumpeter Wendell Brunious are on the recording. In one instance, on a tune they had never before seen, they were able to pull off a seamless transition between solos that reminded me of Joe Wilder's description of that moment soloists face. The tune is entitled "Beyond Category" and was written for Clark Terry. There are eight bars from Wendell followed by another eight from Bill. In addressing my question about improvisation, Bill referred to that 16-bar moment in an interview which was conducted in March 1999, on the day after that session.

MR: Is it possible for you to describe what you think about when you improvise? Is it the chords that are behind you? Are you thinking about what you played six measures ago and where you're going with it? Is it possible to put that into words?

BW: I'm thinking ahead frankly. And what I'm basically doing is I'm thinking counterpoint as I'm going. And I'm listening to the textures that the rhythm section is putting out. I'm listening very carefully to the bass and drums and the piano and trying to get a mattress to

Thoughts on Improvisation

bounce on so to speak. And if everything is planned, understandable, that's coming down, then it's not difficult, no problem at all to just close my eyes and go and play. It's the same with Wendell. Both of us played on one of those tunes that you had the other day, when it was not clear who was going to play, and the changes weren't necessarily—

MR: I was blown away by that.

BW: Both of us just closed our eyes and just went with it. See, if you blunder ahead all the time, you'll never get anything. But if you play a little bit and then stop for a second and listen to where it's going, and go there, there's no problem. That's the secret. But people that are trying to have this constant ongoing flow, you can't have an ongoing flow if you don't know where the heck you're going.

MR: To go there, as you say, you need to have spent some years developing your ear.

BW: Oh yeah.

MR: What do you suggest to players to do that?

BW: I would suggest this: I would suggest that they take those Aebersold CDs and play along and put them on, even if they don't know the tune, and just try and feel their way through there, not getting into a panic but just going where they suggest that you go. And if you listen, if you really honestly listen, and have the ability to listen, of course that has to be developed too, ear training is one major part of this thing, if you can teach them to hear a tone and produce it on their instrument, and then hear a series of tones and do that. And if you equate what you hear with what's coming out of your instrument, it makes it a lot easier. It makes it a much simpler job than if you're just shooting in the dark. You have to close your eyes. I tell a lot of young players, don't have your nose dripping on the paper man, listen to what this thing is doing, close your eyes and get into the capsule and go there. Just let your ear and your feelings sort of take you someplace. It's worth trying. And I always get people to try to do that.[9]

Bill also addressed the issue of "playing outside" or "playing free," phrases that I feel are too frequently used to justify unfortunate note choices. I'm reminded of Dizzy Gillespie's description of an unwanted tenor player nicknamed "The Demon," who dominated jam sessions at Minton's. Dizzy described him as "the first freedom player—free of harmony, free of rhythm, free of everything."[10] Bill was addressing a question about the times when he himself might go outside "it"—"it" meaning the song and

Jazz Tales from Jazz Legends

its chord progression.

MR: Do you feel compelled to bring it back in?

BW: I keep it in sight. While I'm doing it I keep it in sight all the time. Because I feel that if you don't do that then you're just B.S.-ing everybody. I really believe that. I think that if you're going to play outside, you better damn well know where the inside is while you're doing it and keep it in mind and have at least a smattering of an idea as to where you're coming from. If you're going somewhere, you better have roots. You've got to have them. I think you really do. Yet there's a lot of players that absolutely don't care. They have no roots, I mean there's no anchor anywhere, and they don't want one. You've heard them, you've heard these type of players that just ramble on and they hope for a series of happy accidents. And sometimes you get them.[11]

I know many listeners and non-improvising musicians have the impression that after they state the melody, jazz performers just proceed to play in a random fashion. But only in what is called "free jazz" is that even close to the truth. Improvising—making it up as you go along—in the context of most jazz performances is accomplished within a structured framework. The improviser first needs to be aware of the time, the beat, and the rhythm, or even the most astute note choices will sound off. Even if an improviser chooses to create phrases that seem to conflict with the steady beat—to play "against the time"—they are acknowledging where the time is. Second, the soloist is trying to choose from a pallet of notes that match the chords on some level. Depending on the number of chords per measure and the tempo of the song, this can be a daunting task (think bebop!). Again, the improviser may choose to play "outside the chord" but in doing so acknowledges what is inside. As Bill Watrous said in the last excerpt, "If you want to go outside, you better know what's inside."

The soloist is trying to "get off" the melody but has to be aware that the melody was written within a defined and repeated structure—typically a 32-bar A-A-B-A form or a 12- or 16-bar blues. Losing sight of this may find you committing a classic faux pas, ending your solo in the middle of the form thus garnering mystified looks from the bandmates, who know where they are in the structure.

Here is trumpeter Randy Sandke's thought process during improvisation:

MR: Can you articulate what you're thinking if you're playing "Ain't

Thoughts on Improvisation

Misbehavin'" for instance, and you're improvising over the changes, is there a thought process you can talk about?

RS: I've never been interviewed myself on this subject, so I'm just speaking off the top of my head. But from my own experience the less thinking the better. The more you feel like you're part of the whole group, and that the music is just kind of there, you're just sort of pulling it out of the air, the better you are. And I have that feeling when I write too, by the way, which is not that I am really creating it, but it's like the thing is there. It's like you talk about Michelangelo's "David"—it's like the stone is there but he sees the thing. It's already in there, he just chips away to get at it. And that's the way it always feels when I'm writing. It's kind of like prospecting. It's like the gold is there. It's like all these great compositions that have never been written, they're all there, you just have to find them. And it doesn't feel like I'm the one that's doing it, something unconscious is deciding what's gold and what's not in there. But you have to kind of have some sort of discrimination, some kind of feeling for this does something to me and this doesn't. Because what one person considers gold, another person might not. And that's kind of the beauty of it because that's why everybody plays differently. I guess the important thing is to have that feeling that for some reason this really turns me on, you know these notes, but these notes leave me cold, or this rhythm or something like that. It's that kind of feeling like you're not really doing it yourself. It's not a conscious thing, it's just sort of there, which is a pretty vague answer I guess.

MR: Some people have used the word "Zen"—it's a Zen experience. I think the challenge with that is to try to relate that to younger players. Because some of the veterans complain that the younger musicians are just playing scales and they've got all this knowledge of chords and modes but they're not creating melodies. And how do you tell them how to do that? Maybe it's not possible. Maybe that's what makes the jazz cream rise to the top.

RS: I don't know that that's so much a generational thing because I think it's always been like that. There've been a few players that can just make it sing and take wings and whatever, and a lot of people for whatever reason, it's just less than that. And there are some players these days that I think are quite lyrical, and even younger players, and then guys who are not. Going back to another thing about playing, one thing that sort of interests me is that Louis Armstrong for instance, he could play with the worst band in the world at times—guys that were just on a totally different—I mean nobody was on his level, but way under. And he would say that he didn't even hear the band. Like he would just play, he just had such a strong feeling inside him that he would just charge ahead and it would just fall into place. And of course, that's him. I cannot do that. I mean I can do that to a certain extent, but I always feel very much like I'm playing *with* the guys and that my playing is affected, for better or worse, by what's going on around me. Sometimes I feel like it's very difficult for me to really get it happening if it doesn't seem like it is around me. If you're just doing it a lot you just have to do it regardless of what it feels like. And know that it changes. You can start off feeling like you're kind of beating a dead horse or walking a mountain uphill. But then it can catch on and then you forget it.[12]

Denny Zeitlin, psychotherapist by profession and pianist by avocation, shed a psychological angle to the subject of improvisation:

MR: Is there something that makes one person more able to learn improvising than another? Or be less afraid of it?

DZ: It's a good question. I do believe that there is a certain inborn talent for improvisation that helps a person if they're interested, if they can draw on that genetic advantage that's helpful. But an awful lot of it is interest in it, access to opportunities to learn it, permission to have that experience, and not having any kind of psychological obstruction that gets in the way of allowing yourself to enter that terrain where improvisation is possible. And the kinds of psychological issues that frequently do get in the way of people doing that are people that have big issues about losing control, that have tremendous need for structure and reassurance that what they're doing every moment is right. It's one of the things that makes it very hard for classical musicians to make a transition into also being able to improvise, that they might play a wrong note, how do you know? You have all these possibilities. What makes that note better than another? And they can be paralyzed by that. I've probably worked with a somewhat higher percentage of performing artists in my private practice than other psychotherapists, and I've seen certain themes repeat, that seem to get in the way of people being able to improvise well. One is this control issue that I mentioned. Another theme is the fear of failure. People who have tremendous concerns about public humiliation, that they're going to do it wrong and they'll be blamed, or that they'll never be able to feel good about themselves. It's hard to take a risk. Improvising music entails a certain amount of risk taking if you really want to get into something new. You have to be willing to break new ground, you have to be willing to fall on your face, to make an error, and for that not to be disastrous. For some people psychologically that's scary territory. Then there's another whole group of people with a different theme that gets in their way, people who feel very guilty about being successful, which is actually a very common theme in human life. People who feel on some level they don't deserve to be powerful. They don't deserve to be successful. Often it entails a belief acquired in childhood that for them to be powerful and successful means taking it away from someone else: from a sibling or from a parent that was hurting or a father that was depressed. So they end up feeling they have to hold themselves back. These people operate as though there's a governor on their motor all the time. They're able to brilliantly snatch defeat from the jaws of victory. So those people have trouble getting up on the stage and letting themselves play as good as they can. They end up making mistakes, self-sabotage. In the course of psychotherapy they may be able to understand this theme and rework it and get freed up and I've certainly had patients who were performers who have done just that.[13]

So Are There Wrong Notes?

This question produced interesting answers from our interviewees, but first we need to look at what constitutes a wrong note in music. A wrong note in classical music is much more apparent than in jazz, especially in jazz improvisation. In classical music, if a performer plays a note not written by the composer, it's a wrong note. Even people who take a certain perverse pride in saying they're tone deaf, can sense an incorrect pitch in a familiar classical piece. Victor Borge, the highly accomplished pianist/comedian, made a career out of well placed mistakes; incorrect notes that people could identify in the midst of classical performances.

I recall listening to both Miles Davis and Dizzy Gillespie, two trumpeters with vastly different sounds and approaches. Both of them often played notes that struck me as being incorrect, unintended, and from my definition at that time, a "mistake." However, if Miles Davis played a note, with that fragile tone of his, it took on a certain extra poignancy, whether or not he intended it. When Dizzy Gillespie played a questionable note, like a flatted fifth (famously called "Chinese music" by Cab Calloway[14]) he was entitled. After all he was Dizzy Gillespie and he was making jazz history.

Baritone saxophonist Gary Smulyan spoke of his deliberate choices

Jazz Tales from Jazz Legends

in improvising, though they may sound dissonant; he then differentiated deliberate dissonant note choices from mistakes.

MR: When I heard you play, you did these really cool sequences and both of them ended on this weak note. I think it was the flat nine or something. I could tell that this was not an accident, that this was the way you play.

GS: It's deliberate. It's not planned, but I'm really fascinated with harmony and I spend a lot of time at the piano and I think all of the solo transcribing I did when I was younger has really been instrumental in helping me develop that kind of harmonic sense. I think it's important for musicians to have that. It's almost like they have to know what they're doing. You know jazz is a lot more than just playing by ear or by feeling. There's this misconception [beatnik rap, sings] oh I'm a jazz man, I play what I feel man. And that's not what it is. I mean jazz is really, four things have to hook up, right? What you can think, what you can hear, what you can feel, and what you can execute on your horn. But the thinking part is really important. Because unless you're really thinking about the music you can't really manipulate the changes, right, if you want to put substitutions in or if you want to kind of play a different key or you want to just kind of use some harmonic devices to kind of accentuate your playing. That requires some thought.

MR: One of the really uptempo tunes you were playing, your solo had a nice arc to it, and about three quarters to the end you were playing really quick. And I'm wondering how many of those notes are deliberate?

GS: They were all deliberate. I knew exactly what I wanted to play. I didn't plan anything out in advance, but at the moment I knew exactly what I wanted to do.

MR: Okay. What do you do if you make a mistake?

GS: I make a lot of mistakes. Right? Jazz is made by human beings. We're flawed fundamentally. So like I said before, there's no perfect solo. So you make a mistake you go again.

MR: Well, what constitutes a mistake for you?

GS: Well, that's a good question. Playing something that I didn't really want to play. Making a wrong choice. Not ending the way I want it to end. I think for me the most important part of your solo is how you end, because that's what people are going to remember. You could play a great solo, but if your ending is weak and you're not committed in terms of how you want to end, you kind of just peter out or your cadence is not strong, that kind of weakens what came before. To me.

MR: I wonder if part of that is thinking ahead. Like should I do one more chorus or should I end here?

GS: Well, yeah, that's hard, that's a hard choice to make, and there's been many instances where I should have stopped where I kept going. And there's been other instances where I should have kept going and I stopped.[15]

Tenor saxophonist Ralph LaLama provided his perspective on wrong notes, in 2010:

MR: In jazz improvisation, to you, what constitutes a wrong note?

RL: That's a good question. It's like beauty is in the eyes of the beholder. I think there are wrong notes. A lot of people don't. I do. I really do. Because you have a background, you have a chord, and then you could use all twelve notes but it's how you organize them. Sometimes you might put a wrong note in a wrong part of the beat or something, and it sounds wrong. And I just get this tension up my spine. But, then technically you can play a wrong note, technically meaning theoretically it could be a wrong note but it sounds right. You know, because of the placement. You know Thad Jones was the master of it. Coltrane too. Sonny Rollins, all those masters, Joe Henderson. As far as theoretically, in other words we have a chord, we have a scale and we have the chord tone[s]. So if you play outside of that, it could be considered wrong. But if you know how to phrase it exactly right and resolve it right that's another thing. It's in the resolution. You can resolve a wrong note and make it right see. And then sometimes I know when I hit a wrong note, you know like I say I feel it up my spine, and I usually hear it from my wife. My wife is a great singer, Nicole Pasternak, and she has great ears too. She doesn't actually holler at me, but I know she can tell when I hit it. But when you're trying to improvise, sometimes you get hung up. So if you just play all your licks that are comfortable, all your stuff, then you're not going to mess up. Then I don't think you're really improvising. Let's put it this way: there's tension notes, and there's wrong notes.

MR: But I noticed yesterday in listening to you—

RL: A lot of wrong notes.

MR: Well, every once in a while you would end a phrase with a note that made me go, like literally, I wish I would have thought of that.

Jazz Tales from Jazz Legends

RL: Well, that's what I mean. That was tension. That wasn't wrong, hopefully. I mean that's the way I would interpret it. I don't know, I've been doing that a lot more lately. I've been trying to get a little bit more modern. I'm just experimenting. And hopefully if all these improvisers do, you know, you don't want to be complacent. I don't. That's boring to me. So I started very consonant, I was more consonant when I first started playing. Well, this was actually a lot of my upstate [NY] influence. And as I got older and you start hearing more, and you hear other guys too, I get influenced by other people too. I'll be honest about that. I'm definitely influenced by what things are around me at the moment and at different places and in different cultures. Because I'm lucky. I get to go around the world.[16]

Virtuoso pianist Jon Weber offered specific examples of how seemingly wrong notes can be manipulated into a solo, then turned the question back to me:

MR: Is there such a thing as a wrong note?

JW: No. No. No. Well, if you're playing—okay—if you're playing Beethoven's Ninth Symphony yes. There's a wrong note there. If you're jazz—there was a great TED feature that Stefon Harris did called "There Are No Wrong Notes on the Bandstand"[17] meaning in a jazz combo setting they were playing kind of an F suspension thing together with a little quartet. Stefon was playing vibes and there was a pianist and a drummer and a bass player, and he asked the pianist, he said, "F#" which is about as harsh as it gets okay, to most Western ears, out of the twelve possible notes of the scale, that's the hardest. He played that and everybody kept on playing in F and he said, "Now, to most people that sounds wrong. However, let's do this—they did the same thing, they vamped this thing in F and he played the F#. But he followed along in the F# thing this time. He said, "Now, the only reason this sounded wrong in the first place is because we didn't follow it." But when you follow it, and Frank Zappa says exactly the same thing. Whenever they made a goof on stage, and they always had these very intricate arrangements. If somebody had a goof, the goof became the new thing. They said, "Oh we love it, we love it." They followed the mistake. The mistake became the thing, until another mistake came along. They lived for mistakes. There'd be no laughter in a perfect world. So are there any wrong notes on the bandstand? You know something? If you're playing a tender ballad, that's being obnoxious about it. But in a

>   hard bop kind of a situation I don't think so. And in most situations I would say no. I would say a wrong note is a rarity. I'll compromise that much.
>
> MR: All right. I like the description. You know there's a lot of different thoughts on it. You can go on the Internet and get all kinds of people talking about it. And some people have said you have to keep working on that note.
>
> JW: What do you think? Are there any wrong notes?
>
> MR: Well, I'm changing my mind some. I used to think yes, there's definitely wrong notes that you can play. And I've heard people play them. But if Stefon Harris plays an F# in that thing, it's different than when a junior high kid plays an F#. Because Stefon will do it with attack, with purpose. A junior high kid maybe just is hitting a note and he doesn't know what exactly to do with it and so then it sits there feeling wrong.
>
> JW: I guess I was thinking about being in a gig situation somewhere. But when you're learning, oh my gosh yes. And then transcriptions. I mean when I was coming up I would transcribe solos note for note and learn them. Yeah. At that stage yeah, I would say stick to the ink at that stage, early enough. And then learn what it's supposed to sound like. I guess again, what it's supposed to sound like. I don't know, maybe the wrong note thing is going to be the next big thing. I don't know. That's a possibility.[18]

For me, improvising is an intense exercise in problem solving, not a particularly romantic description I admit. But if the "problem" of creating something new within the aforementioned parameters is solved melodically and memorably, the romance will come along with it.

My favorite improvisers have had a rare ability to spontaneously create mini-melodies, licks, or phrases that somehow sound just right for the moment. There really is no explaining it, and that is what makes it magical. A well known jazz method declares, "Anyone Can Improvise."[19] Maybe. And perhaps anyone can sculpt a marble statue, compose a sonnet, or choreograph a ballet. But what elevates the very few into that rare place that makes us pay repeated attention? What inspires us to imitate their innovation? If someone figures out what exactly that is and codifies it, I would rather not know. I would rather preserve the magic.

Chapter 8
Motivation and Inspiration

Successful musicians rise to the top through a combination of talent, perseverance, and a healthy dose of luck. When discussions ensue about where this all starts, the nature versus nurture question inevitably is raised. I feel that it has to be both. A musical seed has to be present in a child, and that seed then needs to be nurtured. My own interest in music surfaced at an early age and was eventually influenced by an odd assemblage of recordings that included Glenn Miller, the Tijuana Brass, Cannonball Adderley, and Dave Brubeck. Supportive parents and a fortunate association with two fine Rochester musicians, Roger Eckers and Chuck Mangione, helped set me on my path.

The experiences, encouragement, and serendipity that occurs during childhood can have far-reaching consequences. We may forget that children can be profoundly affected by simple things that adults take in stride. Many of our interviewees cited moments from their youth as motivation for a life in music. Bassist Keter Betts actually started out as a drummer after an encounter with a marching band:

KB: I started out on drums. I was in the fifth grade. And we had an account at a little Italian store around the corner and my mother sent me to the store to get a loaf of bread and a bottle of milk. And an Italian parade came by. And I came back about four hours later with the milk and the bread, and my mother liked to kill me, because she was worried, you know, one block away and I was gone all over town following this. I realize now that it only takes a second for you to see something to impress you and then you want to investigate what is this, and I was following this parade all around town, fascinated by that. And so I did get a whipping, because at least I could have come back and said, Ma I wanted to follow the parade, instead of just going. After the whipping I said, "I want to play drums." So I guess she figured, well, if he takes a lickin' and keeps on tickin' he must really want to do it.

MR: Well, this had to be great preparation for your eventual career as a bassist I would think.

KB: Well, I switched to bass through Milt Hinton.

Motivation and Inspiration

MR: Because of Milt Hinton?

KB: Yeah. I'll tell you what happened. I was always watching every drummer. That's what I went to see. And I saw Cab Calloway was going to be at a theater and I'd never seen Cozy Cole, because I tried to study with him but he was very busy. But I'd never seen him play. And I knew he was working with Cab so I said I'm going to go see Cozy Cole after I take my lesson. And I went to the theater, and a new drummer had just joined the band, and I didn't catch his name. He took a drum solo and it was fascinating. And I said I've got to meet this guy, I've never even heard of him. So I asked the usher, how do you get backstage? And by the time I got back there he had left on their break, and I ran into Milt Hinton and we started talking. And I told him I'd just graduated from high school last month and he said, "Come on, I'll take you to lunch." And we started talking and I told him I tried to fool around with the bass in school and we didn't have many bass players, in fact we didn't have any bass players in school. And I could hear all of this because of being in the chorus. And he said, "Well, if you ever decide to take bass, I'll give you the name of a good teacher here in New York." And I thought about it and about a month or so later I went to this guy and it was Al Hall. And he was in the [orchestra] pits. He was like the first black bass player to get in the pits, and that was in 1946. So he told me he was very busy but he recommended a guy in Brooklyn. And so I called the guy in Brooklyn, and he said, "Well, come over," and I did. And then I decided, I think I will play bass. And I borrowed some money from mother and I also bought a bass, and two other guys started at the same time, Red Mitchell and Kenny O'Brien. We started with this guy in 1946.[1]

John Pizzarelli Jr. could not have grown up in a more stable and musical environment. His father (Bucky) is one of the most respected guitarists in any musical genre, and was wise enough to let John find his own way, but offered timely suggestions:

MR: You grew up in a time when you had a heck of a lot of musical influences to choose from, in addition to your father. What made you gravitate from one thing to the next? Did you latch on to something before jazz?

JP: Oh yeah. I think the sound of the Beatles was in our house from when I was born. I was born April 6, 1960, so when I was about four my sisters had all those Beatle records. That stuff, that sound. And I clearly remember singing along with those records at a very young age. And I remember a little later on, I was six or seven, my father bringing the tenor banjo downstairs because it was his father's; and my father's uncles, Pete and Bobby Domenick, were banjo players and guitar players. And he said, "You're going to go to Victor's House of Music in Ridgewood and you're going to play, they'll give you some banjo lessons." Cool. So I went down, we went through the book, and at the end of the lesson he'd go, "Okay, today we're going to learn 'Bye Bye Blues.'" And he'd go, "Put your fingers here," and we'd go through the songs. So that was about a year or two of that. Maybe just a year, I don't remember how long it was. And that's the summer of '66, '67. And I played for a year or two, and then I put it down for a while and then I studied with Pete, the older brother, who was the most accomplished musician I've ever known, who was just phenomenal. And he was the oldest brother of all my father's uncles and aunts. And he stayed home, worked and did club dates on the weekends but he was fabulous, I mean remarkable. I was now ten, and then shortly after that, there were always guitars on the couch at our house, so I'd pick up the guitar and start playing along to records, Elton John records, because I discovered the books with the dots.

MR: Tablature?

JP: Yeah. And so there were the chords, now see? And it works with the records. So I'd play along with records. And gravitated toward learning Peter Frampton solos and all that went along with that. I mean my father had amps and guitars, so I was the guy. "Come on over, we've got the equipment." Plugging everything into one amplifier, the whole band came out. And so along the way my father said, "Well, okay." Actually he tells it, which is strange, is that there was a trombone player a couple of towns over who wanted to play "Spain" at a talent show at his high school. So we had this record and I had to go [scats the line from "Spain"], that was the fastest thing I'd ever played in my life. So it was a big deal. So I learned this thing and my father was amazed. And so he went, "Okay, here's a Django Reinhardt record. Listen to 'Rose Room'." And here's this guy going [scats]. Jeez. Okay. Well, I'll try some of that. And then we started in with the George Barnes/Bucky Pizzarelli records. And he'd say, "Why don't you listen to George?" And I'd start to learn George's parts, and we'd play them around the house. And so the jazz vocabulary was making its way into my head. Whenever he'd play a concert somewhere I'd go and play "Honeysuckle Rose" at the end of the concert with him, because I knew George's part and I could play his solo pretty poorly, so, hence, that was my thing. And then he taught me "Chicken a la Swing," that Carl Kress/McDonough duet, and I played the second part. That was sort of a rite of passage for the Pizzarellis. Because Mary had learned it previously when she was fifteen. A very hip family. And long story short, when I came back from college I started playing duets with my dad—concerts—so I knew six more songs so I came up earlier in the show. Sometimes we'd do the whole night together. And then one day we were doing a concert out in Morristown at a library, and he said, "Play the seven [string guitar] today, we'll both play sevens. This way when I solo you accompany me, and when you solo I'll accompany you, we'll have the two sevens going." Sure. So the hardest thing was playing "Chicken a la Swing" and forgetting about the other string. And it was fun. And from there on in it was two times seven.

MR: Doing more bass lines with that?

JP: Yeah. You play the chord and so if you had a D minor chord, now the bass note was an octave lower than where it would be on the regular A string because of the low A. And it was great. It was so simple and it's still—a lot of guys get too wrapped up in harmonizing the seventh string. Don't worry about it. Don't use it for anything but that kind of stuff. Playing great chord melodies and things. That's what it was for, you know.

MR: Did you get to a point on a particular day or time when you said I'm going to make my living doing this?

JP: I never did. The only thing that I wanted to do was to somewhere along the line write a lot of pop songs and I thought maybe there was going to be some pop music in my future, performing my own songs and being Billy Joel or James Taylor. And it's interesting you should ask that question because I never ever realized that I was making a living doing what I was. I was playing with my dad, and I'd be getting these $600 checks and $1,000 checks or whatever, $250, whereas when I was playing dances with my band, I'd be getting $25. And that was like wow. If we had $50 for the gig we were going crazy. And I still had the rock band, because we had fun doing it, and we'd have stretches of down time and I was playing solo gigs and then on the weekend I'd take a rock gig with my band, just playing four-chord songs, three-chord songs. And my father said, "You're the only guy playing jazz to support his rock & roll habit." And he was right. I mean I'd be playing gigs and I'd be giving the money away. Ah, we're having fun here, Doug had the van, give Doug the gas money, I'll take five bucks and I'll have another beer. And the drummer, he had to come alone, give him the toll money.[2]

Not all jazz artists enjoyed the parental support and musical environment that John described. Clarinetist Kenny Davern lived in nine foster homes before the age of six.[3] Fortunately, a distinctive sound emanating from a kitchen radio grabbed his attention:

MR: Was there a point where you said music is going to be my career?

KD: Right. I can remember it like it was yesterday. There used to be Ted Husing's bandstand. Ted Husing I think originally was a sports car enthusiast or whatever. And he played popular music like from three to six everyday, I forget what the station was, WJZ or WOR or something like that. And the last fifteen minutes he played Dixieland band music. And I liked that. I liked the way those bands sounded. I liked it especially because the clarinet was free. And then on Saturday mornings from eleven o'clock to twelve he'd play a whole hour of all these different people—Dixieland jazz bands—whether it be Tony Parenti or Wild Bill Davison or whoever was around at that time. And one day he played a Muggsy Spanier recording of Muggsy Spanier's Ragtime [Band] and they were playing "Memphis Blues." And I was just standing in the kitchen listening and I heard this, because the radio was on top of the ice box. And I heard this instrument growling and grunting and this beautiful background like the band playing whole notes. And it was Pee Wee Russell playing clarinet. Well, you know you can go look at paintings, you can read books, you can see movies, you can listen to music, and if you haven't had a meaningful experience from any one of those things you're never really going to be hooked. I mean if a book can make you laugh and cry, and the same with a painting or whatever, if you can experience something—prior to that you just listen, you know, like a fan. Yeah that's good, yeah. But if it doesn't really grab you emotionally—and I stood there transfixed looking at that radio. And I said that's it, I want to do that for the rest of my life. I was about fourteen.[4]

Pee Wee Russell remained Kenny's favorite on the clarinet. Although he would not have described his own playing as an imitation, he did achieve the same level of individuality.

Radio played an important role in the formative years for musicians born in the late 1920s and 1930s. With fewer stations to compete, the powerful AM stations broadcasting at night could be heard hundreds of

Motivation and Inspiration

miles away. When I interviewed pianist Junior Mance, I was eager to relate my radio experience and was delighted in his response:

MR: An interviewer isn't supposed to tell his own stories, but when I was a kid in high school, I used to hide under my sheets and listen to this all-night jazz station. Well, one night this tune came on, it was a piano, it was going [hums], and there was just something about this tune, I thought wow, it was beautiful. And they said, "This is 'Harlem Lullaby' by Junior Mance." So I got that record. You really captured something there. Can you tell me when you wrote that? This must have been in the '60s when I heard it.

JM: It was in the '60s when I wrote it. I just recorded it again on an album that's coming out with a quartet.

MR: Can't wait.

JM: But what you say about under the sheets, well, I guess I was about ten years old and my dad asked me one Christmas, "What do you want for Christmas?" I said, "I want a table radio." You know this was before they had the little battery portables and all of that. And he was shocked. He thought, what does he want a radio for? Well, they would listen to all the broadcasts at night, you know like Earl Hines would broadcast from the Grand Terrace. And there was another place in Chicago I think called the Garrick Show Lounge, where I remember Don Byas and J.C. Higginbotham were in a small group there. That was the days when there were more radio broadcasts than there were records. But they came on so late and my folks wouldn't let me stay up to listen. But I'd ease up and crack the door and I'd sit there and listen. So I says I'll fix this, and I asked for a radio. So they gave me the radio for Christmas. So I remember I would listen and Earl Hines would come on, I'd search and I'd turn the volume down real low until I found it. Then I would get under the covers with the pillow and all, and listen to it. And every night this went on and they were none the wiser so then after it was over I'd put it back on the table. After it was over that was a time when mothers usually come in and tuck you in, and I'd fake like I'm sleeping. Well, one night, I fell asleep before the broadcast was over. The radio and me and everything is under the pillow and I'm sound asleep. So it woke me up and she pulled the pillow back and I says uh oh, this is it, I'm know I'm going to get it. She called my father in and they laughed. They said look at that. So then after that they started letting me listen, as long as I was in bed, and I could turn it on and listen to it.[5]

Jazz Tales from Jazz Legends

Film, as well as radio, provided a strong draw in the pre-television years. Earning money for an afternoon at the movies provided powerful motivation to a young Jon Hendricks in Depression Era Toledo:

MR: When did you get the first idea of listening to an improvised solo, and doing what you do with it?

JH: Where I got the idea to write what is now known as vocalese, was when I was a kid, it was in the middle of the Depression. And you have no idea how hard times were in the Depression. I mean people talk of hard times now. These are luxury hard times compared to those times. Redd Foxx had something in his act about that. He said, "Times were so hard that one day my father was sitting on the front step and he hollered up and said, 'Martha—the garbage man's coming.' And she said, 'Tell him to leave two cans.'"

MR: Oh, that is hard.

JH: That's right, times were tough and there were, my father and my mother and fifteen children. Twelve boys and three girls in the Depression. So it was very, very difficult. So I didn't have a nickel to buy popcorn, and a dime to go into the movie theater. With all my brothers and sisters my father just couldn't afford to give everybody a dime to get in and a nickel to buy popcorn. So we all had to find some way of finding 15¢ on Saturdays to go to the movies. And so my brothers would go out and get what we called "junk" you know, they would go "junking," which was they'd walk through the alleys. At that time every street had a back part which was the alley, and people would throw away things—papers, old lamps that broke—all these they would pick up in a wagon or a cart and take them to the junk yard. And you'd be surprised how everything is worth something. And this guy would buy the things off them maybe for 25¢. Well, there's a quarter, it means you can take somebody else to the movies, and you've got a nickel for the popcorn. So we used to do that. I used to go to the men's room of the bus station or the train station and when somebody was going to put a nickel into the slot that goes to the lavatory, I'd say, "Wait a minute! Just give me the nickel." And I would crawl down underneath, open the door, and make 15¢ after I did that three times. I would go to the movies and have a nickel for the popcorn. Then I found out something else. People played the juke box. And it cost a nickel. So I learned all that stuff that was on the juke box, and I could hum most of those songs. So I said, "Why don't you learn those songs?" And so I would learn the solos and then I would stand in front of the juke box and then

Motivation and Inspiration

when somebody was going to play I'd say, "Wait a minute, don't put the nickel in yet, what are you going to play?" And they would say, "'Yard Dog Mazurka' by Jimmy Lunceford." I said, "Don't put it in there, give it to me and I'll sing it." [Jon scats]

[musical notation with lyrics: bi-dl ya bum bop bop bop ba doo ddo bop bop bop doo wah bi-dl ya bum bop bop bop ba doo ddo bop bop bop doo wah doo wah doo wah doo wah ba da ba dop bop ba doo doo bop]

JH: And they couldn't resist that. So you know they would give me the nickel and I would say [scats]. I would sing the whole thing—solo and all—and the whole place would be —
MR: Oh that's fantastic. And how old were you then?
JH: I was about thirteen. And I would earn enough money, and then I would go to the movies. And I forgot about that until I wrote "Sing a Song of Basie." And I said, "Hey, yeah, I know how to do this."[6]

Later in the chapter we'll offer another excerpt from Jon concerning "Sing a Song of Basie."

The Cannonball Adderley Quintet has always been my favorite jazz group, due in large part to the tunes penned by Cannon's brother, Nat. Like Jon Hendricks, Nat also drew inspiration from childhood memories that eventually evolved into tunes such as "The Work Song" and "Hummin'." When I asked if "Hummin'" had a backstory, Nat responded:

NA: "Hummin'." Boy. Well, I guess the only way to do it is to tell you the way that it really was. "Hummin'" was written about an old woman who lived on my street when I was a little boy in Tallahassee. Miss Sally was her name. Southern people have strange ways of saying things. But there was Mrs. Coleman lived there, Mrs. Lasser lived up the street, and Mr. Lasser. Miss Sally was about eighty years old but she was "Miss Sally," there was no man there. She was a tall black woman and I describe it—she looked like they look in *Roots* like the ladies looked. She wore that long dress, as long as an evening gown and she wore an apron, and the apron was as long as the dress. Miss Sally must have been about six feet tall. She was a tall, African-looking black woman. Miss Sally sat in this rocking chair on her porch. And her front porch was, of course the houses were boards, little wooden houses. She sat in this rocking chair on the front porch and she had a loose board on that porch. And that's where she had the rocking chair. And Miss Sally would sit there and rock, and like, for example, shell peas. She'd take the peas out the shells, drop the peas in the pot that she was holding in her lap, and the hulls in the apron behind the pot. Now and then she'd move the pot and dump the shells on a piece of paper on the floor and then go back to shelling peas. Meanwhile she would rock. And on that loose board when she'd rock forward, the board would hit—bomp. And when she'd rock backwards the board would hit from the front and rear—bu bomp. So she'd be rocking—bomp, bu bomp—bomp, bu bomp—bomp, bu bomp. All us little boys used to come by. We used to like to, because Miss Sally was a bit eccentric—at least I know now that she was eccentric, we just thought Miss Sally was crazy, but after I went to college I learned that there was such a word as eccentricity. Once she'd keep this stuff going, we'd say, "Miss Sally you want us to fix that board?" Miss Sally say, "Get the hell out." So we'd leave. Now, years, later when I was thinking about that again, I wrote this song. Oh, I left out a part. Miss Sally used to hum little churchy sounding things, [hums], kinda Gospel sounding. Meanwhile, bomp, bu bomp—bomp, bu bomp. So I wrote the song.

NA: A little later on, and this is the addendum to it. I was living in New Jersey and had this big house, and my mother was visiting. And my mother came downstairs one morning, and she'd been listening to the radio at night. My momma said, "Listen—why don't you write a song that's got some meaning, like 'Stardust?'" She said, "You and your brother write them little ittilie boobly songs and they don't have no meaning." I had just done it. I said, "You know that song I got called 'Hummin',' the new one?" She said, "Yeah." I said "You know,

Motivation and Inspiration

Quincy Jones recorded it, Cannonball recorded it, I recorded it?" I said, "You know that song is about old Miss Sally." She said, "What?" I said, "You know the rhythm represents that board hitting—bomp, bu bomp—bomp, bu bomp—and melody is something like an old Gospel sounding thing [hums]." And Momma say, "Yeah," kind of skeptically, "yeah, sure." But that night we were working down in the Village at a place called the Village Gate. Momma came down that night, and we played "Hummin'." Momma, she called me over to the table, "Hey, come here, boy," she said. "You know I listened to that song, and now that you told me what it means," she said, "I could just see that old woman sitting on the porch and the board hitting." And she said, "You know old Miss Sally been dead about fifteen years now, but we all remember that old board hitting." So she said, "Now that I see that, you know, I'm gonna get off your case." That's when I knew Momma was hip. She said, "I'm gonna get off your case and I'm going to say, I agree, your songs have meaning."[7]

Before the era of codified jazz education programs that provide an assigned listening syllabus, radio and LPs provided the listening resource for impressionable young musicians. But seeing a live performer is what often made the largest impression. Buddy Rich in particular had a strong effect on a number of aspiring drummers, including Stanley Kay:

SK: I'd go home and listen to Chick Webb and Jimmy Lunceford and Duke Ellington and Count Basie and Woody [Herman], stay up and listen to the remote broadcasts at night. "From the Park Central Hotel, and now, the King of the Drums, Chick Webb." And he'd do a thing called "Let's Get Together." So I knew all the theme songs. And then [in] Benny Goodman's band, Gene Krupa was the innovator. And I listened to him and I said, "Boy, that's the greatest." And my sister said, "Well, I know somebody that's better than that." And I said, "Who's better than Gene Krupa?" "Buddy Rich," she said. "He's playing at the Hickory House with a little band named Joe Marsala." That was his first band after he left vaudeville. Vaudeville was over when he was about seventeen years old. He was a vaudeville star.

MR: And he tap danced too, didn't he?

SK: He tap danced. Yeah. He was known as Traps the Drum Wonder. And he was the second highest paid child star to Jackie Coogan. He was making about $1,500 a week. But [with] the decline of vaudeville, he had no job. And he worked on the WPA when they had the WPA. And putting on a wig and dancing and stuff like that see? And well anyway, she told me Buddy Rich. So on Sunday afternoon on 52nd Street was a place called the Hickory House. And it was a round bar, it was a steak house. It was owned by a guy named Popkin. And my sister called Buddy and she paid the way for me. And I'm fourteen years old. You could eat there, so at fourteen you're okay, you could go in. And jam sessions were about from three to six o'clock on Sunday in this big round circular bar. And it was Joe Marsala, his wife played harp, Adele Girard, his brother Marty Marsala played trumpet, Artie Shapiro played bass, and Nat Jaffe played piano. And I walk in and I introduced myself. And he's nineteen now, he was five years older than me. So he greeted me, but all the guys used to sit in from all the bands on this jam session. Like bands like Tiny Bradshaw and Andy Kirk's band. And it was now getting towards like five-thirty and I wanted to hear this guy play. Supposed to be this genius, see? And he sat down and played the last thing. It was what we call a flag waver, it was called "Jim Jamp's Stump." And when I heard Jim Jamp, and I heard him play, I said, "That's it." My sister was right. That's the greatest thing I ever heard. And I just idolized him. And I followed him.[8]

Stanley Kay became a manager and cheerleader for Buddy Rich for much of his life, and a mentor to another Rich fan, Sherrie Maricle:

SM: Where I grew up was a town called Endicott, New York, and Binghamton. And that was amazing to grow up there. Slam Stewart, the jazz bass player, lived there, and every big band that there was came through town. Buddy Rich and Woody Herman and Count Basie. I saw all of those bands. And I was lucky to have a teacher that took me. When I was eleven a teacher took me to see Buddy Rich and his Killer Force Orchestra, and that was when I was eleven that I said that was exactly what I wanted to do then was just play the drums. And I never changed, ever, from that.

MR: You anticipated a question. I was going to ask if there was a pivotal moment when you were young, seeing or hearing something.

SM: Well, that definitely set me right off into my direction and I literally never, ever thought of anything else. I remember telling my eighth grade teacher, I know exactly what I'm going to do, and I have to move to New York. I mean really, I remember having this conversation with this guy when I was twelve years old. But prior to that when you were first allowed to take musical instruments, fourth

Motivation and Inspiration

grade or whatever, I went up to the teacher and said, "I want to play the trumpet." "No, girls don't play the trumpet, here's a metal clarinet" and he gave me this thing to squeak and squawk on. I was horrible and he was horrible and I quit. I was like I don't want to play music, this is terrible, this teacher, you know. And then the teacher actually called the house, I think he was a little unstable, called my mother and said, "She is so talented." And I was terrible. I could barely make a sound on this metal clarinet. But he begged for me to be in the school band so I went back. And then somehow I started on the cello and played that for like three years and then one day someone needed someone to hit the bass drum. And I was like, "I'll do it." Any chance to hit something. So I went back and played the bass drum and then kind of just stuck with drums after that. But then when I saw Buddy, that was it.[9]

The popularity of jazz and its virtuosos was not confined to the United States. Music has always been one of America's greatest exports, and jazz in particular has found avid fans on almost every continent. Clarinetist Eiji Kitamura described his fascination with the "King of Swing" in post-World War II Japan.

MR: How did jazz come to you in Japan? Was it through records?

EK: Yes. When I was fourteen years old, a young boy, I had one record, an SP record. My father liked classic music, Mozart, Beethoven and Mendelssohn, and then I found very small SP record, and I have that record. I was very surprised at that music. What kind of music, I saw a record label "Don't Be That Way" by Benny Goodman. But only this. And what kind of music—I didn't know jazz. And then I saw a record label, the fox trot, I mean, do you know? Fox trot.

MR: Oh fox trot. Yes, sure.

EK: But when I was fourteen years old, I didn't know, what means fox trot? And then I understand this music, the fox trot. And then I went in school and I told my schoolmates, I heard a very funny music, fox trot, by Benny Goodman. And they were very surprised. And this was my treasured record.

MR: You just had that one record?

EK: Just one.

MR: Was there a tune on the other side?

EK: Um hum. On the other side, something, Benny Goodman Trio plays something, the other, a very fast tempo number. But I liked "Don't Be That Way" with orchestra. And then when I was sixteen

Jazz Tales from Jazz Legends

years old, this second war ended. Japanese. And I had the Far East Network Radio, and they used to play jazz programs.

MR: You were hearing lots of fox trots, weren't you.

EK: Yes. And then I knew jazz music, and that I should begin some jazz music. And when I was a child I studied classic piano. And my mother likes classic, my father likes classic, and I played only classic piano. And then I wanted to play the clarinet like Benny Goodman.

MR: So were you self-taught on the clarinet then in the beginning?

EK: Yeah. When I was nineteen years old I played the clarinet. And it was very funny. My classmate, he got one clarinet, and he couldn't play the clarinet. Many classmates tried to learn to play it. And then I tried clarinet, to blow [imitates a note]. "Oh Eiji's a genius." And then how to push key. I don't know, I found only two notes [scats]. "Oh Eiji played 'Sentimental Journey.'" [Eiji sings]:

EK: And then my classmates said, "Eiji's a genius." And then I began the clarinet.[10]

The concept of a deity has inspired jazz composers, most notably Duke Ellington and Dave Brubeck. In the latter part of their careers they both turned to the religious oratorio, a classical form in which they could combine the sound of their jazz ensemble with a choir singing material extracted from religious texts. Much like composers in the classical world, Brubeck was able to create significant music with only brief excerpts from these writings.

MR: If you were to start a new piece of your own choosing, is it possible to say where your inspiration might come from?

DB: I was working on one this morning already, and I will try to complete it today. And it's really coming from the war that's going on now in Afghanistan. And the prediction of Christ just before he was crucified. And I had my wife look at it today and she said, "You don't want anybody to sing that, it's too sad." And I said, "Well, I am sad, and this is what I'm doing." She said, "I don't think people will want to hear that." And so I thought it over and I said, "Well, I've written other sad things, they're not all happy, and that didn't bother you." She said, "But this is too sad." It's Luke chapter 23, I think, verse 18

Motivation and Inspiration

and 19. And it's Christ on his way to the cross where he's telling the women of Jerusalem to be fortunate if you don't have children and you're barren.

MR: Regarding your choral work, if you could pick a section of a particular piece that you felt really came together as far as the way the text was set and the orchestration that resounded the best for you, is there a moment, a favorite of yours?

DB: There's moments in almost all of the pieces. For instance we're going to do the "Christmas Cantata" at Fifth Avenue Presbyterian Church in New York. I think this will be the fifteenth year. And that has a happy ending that when I finished the cantata I was in the back of a Volkswagen bus where I had a card table. My wife was driving. We were going up to see our youngest son who was in a music camp in Vermont. And I said to Iola, "I've finished." And she's driving along. She said, "No you haven't. You haven't finished." I said, "Why?" She said, "Because look, we've left out the most important thing about Christmas." And I said, "Well, what is that?" And she said, "God's love made visible." And I said, "Well, that just doesn't fit. I can't hear any way to set that." So she said, "Well, fine, see what you can do because we've got to end the piece with that." So pretty quick I said, "Iola, it's perfect in five." "God's love made visible/He is invincible." So this was summer. And we were offered a ski cabin to stay in near the music camp called Kinhaven. My youngest son went there year after year, he loved it. And so when we got there it was an A-framed ski chalet, kind of small but three stories. Up on the top floor was a piano, which I was glad to have, but all the Christmas decorations from the year before were all up there, all over this room. So I got into the Christmas spirit and finished that in the middle of summer up there.[11]

In true Brubeck fashion, "God's Love Made Visible" was set in 5/4 time, but flows as gracefully as any Christmas classic.

Returning to Jon Hendricks, his vocal treatment of the Basie LP "Count Basie Swings, Joe Williams Sings" required a massive amount of original writing, creating words and sounds for every note the band and soloists played. A highly spiritual man, he described the creative process that became directed from outside himself.

MR: When you did "Sing a Song of Basie," it seems like a tremendous amount of writing went into this.

JH: Yes.

Jazz Tales from Jazz Legends

MR: Did it take a long time?

JH: It took a shorter time to write it than it did to learn it. I can attest to the spirituality of the creative process, and there have been symposia on that, people have talked about that. And I know that when you're in the process of creating something, you become God's pencil, you know? Because you're watching the pencil to see what's coming out. So if you're the one doing it, you wouldn't have to do that. You would know what's coming out. But all during "Sing a Song of Basie" I would be watching the pencil to see what was coming. And it was almost like revealed writing. It just came. And to this day if I do a lyric I do the whole band with the solos and all in one draft. And I go back and maybe I have to change one or two words here, but it just pours out.

MR: It sounds like how Mozart wrote, from what I've read.

JH: Yeah. I think it's revealed. I think that's the way it is.[12]

Saxophonist Bobby Watson remarked that inspiration can be divine, but there will still be work to follow:

BW: I keep a little journal. If I hear something I'll write it down and then I'll get back to it later. You may have a change here or there, but basically, if something comes to you, you write that down. You used to say like your divine inspiration—divine inspiration doesn't come that often. And usually when it does it comes in four bars. Very rarely do you hear a song and it's complete. I must have written a few songs that way, it just comes so fast you can't hardly get it down on paper, the whole song. I can probably count that on one hand. But most of my songs, you know you have to toil over them, and I get maybe four bars of divine inspiration. And with the craft you stretch that into a whole song.[13]

Divine inspiration can be a powerful motivator, as these musicians confirm. But practical matters can be equally strong. A "rich jazz musician" is an excellent example of an oxymoron, and many jazz personalities spent years living from gig to gig. Singer and writer Annie Ross, a member of the vocal jazz trio Lambert, Hendricks & Ross, composed a classic vocalese to the 1949 song "Twisted" by saxophonist Wardell Gray. When released in 1952 as part of "The Farmer's Market" record, it set her career on a fast track:

MR: Tell me how "The Farmer's Market" came about.

Motivation and Inspiration

AR: Well, necessity is the mother of invention. And the necessity was the money. I knew George Wallington's wife, who was the piano player with the Lionel Hampton band when I joined. And she took me down to see a man called Bob Weinstock, who owned Prestige Records, which was a very popular record label for young artists—Miles and people like that—who would be paid and who would sell their songs and be very happy to sell it because it meant money in the hand. "Moody's Mood" had just come out. And he said to me, "Do you know 'Moody's Mood'?" I said yes. He said, "Do you think you could write words to an instrumental like Eddie Jefferson did?" [Eddie having done "Moody's Mood for Love."] So I said, "Yeah." I mean if you'd asked me if I could fly I would have said yes. So he said, "Well, here's a pile of records, go back to your place, pick one, write the words, when you're ready come to me." Well, I was sharing a floor, I had a room in this big building where you shared the kitchen, you shared the bathroom and it was—yich. And so I was there the next morning with "Twisted."

MR: That's amazing.

AR: I hurried up and wrote those words. I got out of that place.

MR: And the tenor player, was it Wardell Gray?

AR: Wardell was the one who wrote the tune, yeah.

MR: How did the initial idea come from that?

AR: From the title. "Twisted." What would that be? And then I looked at myself. When I write I write very fast. I'm very lazy. I really, you know, I should be much more productive than I am. I bide my time.

MR: But when necessity—

AR: Yeah, when necessity calls I really get to work.[14]

Perhaps percussionist Don Alias had the best motivation for choosing a career in music. He spoke about his indirect path and the decision to take the road less traveled:

DA: I never really thought about being a professional musician. I went to school and studied medicine. My mom wanted me to be a doctor. And I went to a certain point and got my degree in biochemistry, but I got bit seriously. Literally. How it happened is that I had this wonderful job working in a research laboratory, cancer, up in Rhode Island, in hematology, it was a great laboratory. And I was also playing at night in Boston. So this trip back and forth, living in Providence and back to Boston, back and forth. And one day I walked into that laboratory and I was dead tired, and I sat down and said what is the thing that makes you the happiest? Come on now. What is it that really makes you happy for a length of time? And I chose to play music.

MR: Well, I'm wondering what the phone call to your mother was like when you decided to switch careers.

DA: Hell. That's the only thing, for want of a better word. Take into consideration the time. It was the '50s and '60s. I'm a black American growing up in a certain kind of environment and the revolution wasn't really going on when I was going to school, I'm talking about '58, '59. It wasn't really prevalent then. There were no revolutionary activities around that time. Parents wanted their kids—I'm talking about Afro-American parents—wanted their kids to be doctors, lawyers, something with some kind of clout to it intellectually. Stuff like that. And needless to say when I told her that I had quit my laboratory job she didn't like that. As a matter of fact it was only recently—when I say recently I'm talking about maybe seven years—that she—I think she liked more the people I was playing with than the playing. I said, "Mom I'm playing with Miles Davis." "Oh, Miles Davis." "Lou Rawls." "Oh, Lou Rawls, oh." She would love all of that. But me being a musician, no, she didn't want that. She was really upset about that.[15]

Numerous interviewees responded to a question regarding advice for aspiring jazz musicians. Phil Woods directed his comments to the issue of passion:

MR: Do you have advice for aspiring jazz musicians that might help them in their careers?

PW: Advice for young jazzmen. No. I figure that if they're going to do it, no matter what I say they're going to do it. It's for those ones in between, those ones that aren't really sure, those are the ones I worry about. I mean, I think jazz is only for those that have no choice. I think if you're a young man and you're entertaining thoughts of becoming a brain surgeon or a jazz tenor man, I'd go with the brain surgery. If you have a choice. If you've got two burning desires, don't pick jazz. I mean, keep playing it. Sometimes I envy the amateur, like all those dentists and doctors who play for kicks. They don't have to worry about making bread at it. They really enjoy making music. And that's really what it's about. Never forget that joy, that first time you made a note and it made you feel good. Musicians kind of forget that stuff. They're sitting in the [orchestra] pit and reading

Motivation and Inspiration

The Wall Street Journal and grumpy, grumpy, grumpy. They forgot that feeling, that burn of the belly the first time they sounded decent. And it's easy to get kind of trapped into just making some bread and trying to exist when the bloom is off the rose. But a young man should consider—you only have one life. When you make a choice, a career decision, it should be well thought out. Not too carefully structured mind you, but I wouldn't rush into anything. I wouldn't rush to go to a jazz school or any university. I always recommend take a year off man. Hitchhike around the world. Take your horn and see if you can play for your supper around the world. See what life is about while you can, before you have a family, before you need bread. Get a couple of thou and just do it, man. Take a chance. Because you might never have a chance to do it, and that's when you can really kind of get inside your head. It's hard to do it when you're surrounded by your peers or family or the pressures of society. Go somewhere where it's all fresh and find out who you are. And then when you decide, you're going to be a much better player for this experience.

MR: Well, I think you just gave some good advice in spite of yourself.
PW: Darn. There goes my image as the curmudgeon.[16]

While these artists cite a range of motivating factors in their lives, they all share the same overwhelming drive to engage in jazz performance and composition. That drive and desire is a necessity for any musician who hopes to sustain a career in this challenging and competitive business.

Chapter 9
Potpourri

In this last chapter I'd like to include some topics which don't warrant an entire chapter, but present common themes that interviews touched on.

The Concept of Swing

The New Grove Dictionary of Jazz is one of the prime sources for facts about jazz and its artists, and begins their definition of "swing" as follows: "Swing—a quality attributed to jazz performance. Although basic to the perception and performance of jazz, swing has resisted concise definition or description."[1]

It's difficult to define the magic of an artistic concept. What makes a work of art stand out is, in the end, undefinable. We can look at the parts and discover some truisms about them. Jazz musicians know that when they see a series of eighth notes, which normally divide a beat into two equal parts, they play the first one longer than the second. This is a clearly definable part of swing. We know that swing music is predominantly in 4/4 time, that it involves a combination of instruments working together, and that it is the basis for a genre of music that employs the same name. Nonetheless we still try to specifically define the concept, and it's been a favorite question of mine in gathering interviews for the Jazz Archive.

Drummers and bassists are most responsible for making things swing. Drummer Ed Shaughnessy stated the following about swing:

MR: Are you able to put what swing is into words?
ES: I finally think I can do it. I struggled with it for a long time. Before I do it I want to say how often swing is used as a noun representing the type of music. They'll say the swing bands of the '30s and '40s, right? And they played swing. We're going to deal with it as "it swings," that's an adjective. Because what I find the problem is sometimes is that youngsters, and even oldsters, they mix up the terms "to swing" and lock it in exclusively to jazz music. Now I think bluegrass music swings like hell. Without drums, right? It swings. Now what is that swinging I'm talking about? It's infectious. The main thing I think that swing means, for me, is that it's an infectious beat that makes you want to move, whether it's to dance or to sit and tap your foot or

to clap your hands, but it makes you want to move in a sense, and in a response to it. It brings something out in you. Maybe it makes you happy. But mostly it makes you want to get with it. Infectious is the best word I can use. That's why I don't like the fact that someone, who is very hard-headed about anything other than jazz, like if I say to them, "You know some of James Brown's funk rhythms would swing you out into bad health." "Well, I don't like rock & roll." I say look man [scats]—I say if you could hear that and you can't move yourself, you are dead, they should embalm you, see? But that's a form of swing. If you hear a bunch of Africans playing [scats] and they're playing that 12/8 stuff like the Watusi people do, and even if you don't see them dancing, if you hear that, it's infectious. It gets you going too. So to me, any music, like bluegrass, or jazz, or funk music, or Watusi music, it's infectious and communicates to you rhythmically, and gets a visceral thing going. That's what I think swing is about. And I don't think it's an exclusive property of jazz. I really don't. However, some people will play jazz and it doesn't swing. That's the part that I think people should understand. To be swinging is a certain feeling. I think the error sometimes is to feel that if you're playing jazz it's necessarily swinging. No, it's not necessarily swinging. It might be a little cerebral, a little abstract, and you don't feel very much of that visceral communication. That's the absence of swing. That doesn't mean other things can't be there. Improvisation can be there. Imagination can be there. And feeling can be there. But I've heard for instance a bass and a drummer, both of whom were very well known, and they don't play good together. They are not compatible. It never settles into a good, unified pulse. So it isn't swinging too good. Infectious is really what swing is about. [Snaps fingers.] When I see audience, and I'm playing and I see some of that, it doesn't have to be everybody, if I see just a smattering of that, I think we're getting it across. And if I see nobody moving, I don't think we're getting it across.[2]

I have the enjoyable task of booking highly respected jazz artists to perform at the college, grouping them together in unrehearsed ensembles. It's interesting to hear the musicians talk in private about how things felt. You might assume that musicians at the top of their game can make things swing at will, no matter who the personnel may be. This is not always the case, and I often overhear talk about which bassist and drummer don't work well together, and which bassist, drummer, and guitar player really lock in and make things swing.

Jazz Tales from Jazz Legends

Swing of course is not just rhythmic—there's a harmonic component to the music that was developed in the mid-1930s. Pianist, actor, and composer Steve Allen addressed this part of the definition of swing:

MR: Can you define for me why one thing swings and the next thing doesn't?

SA: The dominant factor is rhythm I think. Well, people would think of that right out of the barn, but that isn't all there is to it. There are certain ways of voicing instruments, if you're talking now about a big band—fourteen, fifteen, sixteen pieces—there are certain kinds of harmonies sometimes, now it's so common we don't even notice it or comment on it, but sometime in the late '30s you began to hear more chords. Even if it's a simple chord, a C chord let's say, where they added the sixth note of the scale instead of the tonic. [scats]. Let's see, C-E-G, to those three notes they added the A which is the sixth note in the group. And why that sounds hipper, or cooler as they would say today, it's not easy to explain in purely scientific terms, but that's the way it is. Even before it happened with instruments it happened with voices. If you listen to trios or quartets, there were no five group singing groups that I know about in the old days, until the Hi Lo's and groups like that came along, they didn't get that complex with their harmonies. But we all remember the term "barbershop quartet." [sings] "Down by the ol' mill stream." That's nice stuff, but the harmonies are as simple as possible. Only the necessary notes are there. There's no enrichment or adornment. But then about 1937-ish or so a group called the Merrimacks, if you can find any of their old recordings, play them sometime with this comment, you'll see what I'm talking about. They were the first people to add the sixth and to add other harmonic enrichments. Then from the Merrimacks, that opened the window of opportunity, and you had groups like the Pied Pipers, the Mello-Larks. Mel Torme had a great group, the Meltones I think they were called, in which the harmonies were more typical of what was also happening at that time in voicing the reed sections—the saxophone sections— of orchestras. When they only had four notes, they could still put in the sixth and some enrichments, but when they added a fifth saxophone, which now all the big bands had had for years, somehow that enlarged the harmonic possibilities and we associated that kind of harmonic hipness, with big band, with jazz, with swing.[3]

If you want to go to the piano to see what Steve was talking about, simply play a C-E-G and add the A, the sixth tone in the key of C. For a more authentic swing voicing, put the C on top (play E-G-A-C in your right hand from the bottom up). Play a single low C on the bass end. That's a good swing chord.

Women and Jazz

Women are well represented in the Archive, and their views have an added dimension. Several women spoke about the state of jazz today and their stories shared a common theme, especially early on in their careers. Saxophonist Jane Ira Bloom summed up her views on women playing jazz:

MR: Well, there's a movement for women in jazz. Has it ever felt to you like you have been at a disadvantage or at an advantage because you were a woman playing jazz?

JB: No easy answer to that question, that's a big one. There are both sides to the equation. When I began playing in the early '70s, there was a lot of consciousness in the air about women's issues. There were a lot of women's jazz festivals that sprang up that I played at, and I got exposure. Had they not been there I might not have been heard. But they were the one venue that I saw a possibility to play. At that point in time I'd play anyplace, anywhere, anytime. So there was something beneficial about that environment at that time. Disadvantages? It's been my point of view that things haven't changed as much as I had hoped they would in twenty years. When I first started playing I thought things would be a lot better, the playing field would be a lot more equal than I see it today, and mostly in respect to the business environment of jazz. Because there are plenty of women players who are now out there, and they're playing horns and they're playing drums and bass, all the rhythm instruments, all the things that were not considered instruments for women to play in jazz, they're out there playing them now. But the thing that kind of is upsetting is that when I talk to some of these younger women, I'm still hearing some of the same stories I remember listening to twenty years ago about social acceptance and business acceptance. So it has gotten better, but boy, not as quickly and not as much as I had thought.[4]

Bassist and vocalist Nicki Parrott spoke of some of the obstacles she faced, including her immigration to the U.S. from Australia:

MR: I wondered if you feel you have to pay more attention to how you dress.

NP: No. I used to try to dress way more like a guy when I was first starting out in music. Oh yeah. And I was so conscious of not being taken seriously. There was one instance when I got called for a gig and they said, "Is this Nick Parrott?" And I said "Well, actually it's Nicki." "A bass player?" "Yeah, Nicki Parrott." Click. So it was instances where I was really fragile. I was still trying to learn how to play. And I was eighteen or nineteen and I noticed that guys out in Newcastle were getting all these great gigs and it was the first time I was aware that, oh God, I'm a woman in this business. It was like the first time I'd really become aware of this is going to be different for me, in a way. It was like subtle differences. But I've been one of the lucky ones though. I've been a professional musician for basically twenty-two years with an eight-month stint in fashion. These days it doesn't matter, you know—woman, man, black, white, anything. It's just a more difficult time to be a musician. So all of that stuff is gone by the wayside because economically it's a challenge whoever you are. It doesn't matter anymore. That's how I feel now. I feel it's pretty much an even playing field, where there are gigs to be had and you have to work really hard at getting them it seems.

MR: Have you noticed that it's gotten harder in your twenty-two years?

NP: Yes. Because even when I first came here and I was doing gigs on Broadway, there was still a happening studio scene in New York. There were still things going on. I mean I think that time in New York was really great. I got hooked up with a whole corporate party scene at the end of '94, and I got sponsored by this club date organization, sponsored for an 01 visa. So I was actually able to get legal. This would be much harder to do now. It's a different time in a post 9/11 world and the politics are much different now, and it was a much easier time then. You know there were all these gigs and corporate, and all that, and so I got sponsored for an 01 visa.[5]

Marian McPartland also reminisced about her experiences integrating into the American jazz music scene, in this interview from 1997:

MR: Obviously it's been different for you as a woman pianist to fit into what is essentially a man's world in jazz.

MM: Oh, yes.

MR: Was there ever a point where it was an advantage to you? Or has it always been pretty much kind of an uphill struggle?

MM: I don't think it was ever an uphill struggle for me, because I sort of had my indoctrination in working with Jimmy [McPartland], and boy, Jimmy was so supportive and proud of me. And when I started at the Embers as a trio and Ed [Safranski] and Don [Lamond], they couldn't be nicer. I mean very seldom did I have a bad experience. I did have one guy at the Embers for a short time, I can't think of his name—just as well—and I had to fire him, and boy, having to fire somebody—I could probably do it now with great aplomb but luckily I haven't had to. But I never had a real problem there. The only things would be like I remember the first review I had from Leonard Feather was, "She has three strikes against her: she's English, white and a woman." It didn't bother me that much. I don't remember being too upset about that. And if there were things it'd probably be from the audience like, "Oh you play good for a girl," or, "You sound just like a man." I mean you don't hear those things anymore. And there were a lot of women on the scene: Mary Lou Williams, Barbara Carroll, people I'd heard before I got there—Hazel Scott, Lil Harden. I never felt that the women were in such bad shape, I guess. They went ahead and they had consciousness raising and I remember talking to Barbara about this, and she said, "Well, I didn't know it was a thing, we've just been playing and doing our thing right along." And I never had to feel that things were tough. I never did.

MR: I sometimes think it's the people that are observing from outside [who] assume there's a problem that needs to be dealt with.

MM: We're all doing well but I expect there's probably still an air of male chauvinism there. But I don't care. I still like things like having the door opened for me and I don't have trouble with political correctness. If the bass player wants to put his arm around me, that's okay.[6]

Flautist Holly Hofmann received a rude awakening upon experiencing her first cutting contest, early on:

MR: Can you recall one of the worst gigs you ever played?
HH: It wasn't an actual gig. I was being brought in to sit in with players in New York City my first year in New York, by Slide [Hampton], who decided to involve me in a cutting session. That was my worst performing nightmare.
MR: Well, if you don't mind, tell me about that. Because I've often wondered what that would be like. I've never been in a real cutting session. Was it the tunes they called?

Jazz Tales from Jazz Legends

HH: It was the tunes and the tempos. It was a very famous group in New York City who were quite appalled that Slide brought this little flute player in to sit in with them, and they just decided that they were going to see if I could play. Thank God my dad had given me a list of cutting session tunes, like "Cherokee," and you know the ones that they really do it to you on. And they called "Cherokee," and it's one-one-one-one. It's so fast that they can't play it, but it doesn't matter because they want to see if you can play it.

MR: Put you on the spot.

HH: Right. And then the saxophone player, who shall remain nameless, came over and said, "Well, honey, do you think you can play 'Just Friends'?" And I said, "Yes I can." He says, "Okay, B major, [counts extremely fast] one-two, one-two-three-four."

MR: Get out. He did that?

HH: Yeah. And Slide went over and said, "Guys, don't do this, because it's making you look bad." And Slide just said, "You will stay." I wanted to get off the stage. And he said, "You will stand there and you will play because this is the tradition. This is what's been done. This is what Diz did to Miles. This is what has been done to people over the years as long as jazz has been an art form." So he said just to stay with it and do it, and to do the best you can, and I did okay. And you know, "Just Friends" in B major is a real trip. But thank God I was playing by ear.[7]

Challenging Gigs

Holly Hofmann's story brings up the subject of memories of problematic gigs. Vince Giordano, who leads a 1920s-style jazz band, had no trouble recalling an unfortunate gig:

MR: What was the worst gig you've ever played?

VG: Oh that's easy. I wouldn't say my worst gig, one of my worst gigs, let's go like that. We got hired to do a New Year's Eve party out in New Jersey, oh maybe fifteen, eighteen years ago. And I got there in time and the weather was nice, everything was going along fine. The people did not want any kind of swing or acoustic music whatsoever. They just hated it. So after like about twenty minutes comes, "Could you guys take a break?" I said sure. So we all took a break and the DJ took over. The place was mobbed. So here it is, it's New Year's Eve and it's like about ten minutes before twelve, and the maîtré d' comes—you know we're not on, we've been on a break since like nine-twenty. And so the guys are drinking, they're eating, they don't

Potpourri

care. And the party planner says, "Do youze guys know the New Year's Eve song? The DJ doesn't have it." I said, "You mean 'Auld Lang Syne'? Yes we know that." "Well, could you play that, and then take a break?" "Okay," I said, "You have the check, now?" So we played "Auld Lang Syne," a couple of choruses, and back to Joe the DJ. And that was it. And it was one o'clock and guys, I'm sorry, but it was just one of those things that people have certain likes and dislikes and it was one of those nights that we were definitely the wrong band for that party. And that's the way it goes.

MR: At least you got paid.
VG: Exactly.[8]

Saxophonist Charles Davis opined on the necessity of playing to please the audience:

MR: Do you feel that your playing changes from one venue to the next?
CD: Yes, it does, according to what you're dealing with. What motivates one audience doesn't motivate the next audience so you have to keep that in mind.
MR: Did you ever do much rhythm & blues playing in your career?
CD: Well, Clarence Henry was rhythm & blues. I played with quite a few rhythm & blues during the course of my career coming up.
MR: Did you have to do that honking tenor sax thing?
CD: Well, that was a part of growing up. There was a lot of honking. John Coltrane had to honk. A lot of people had to honk. That was a tradition—honking and walking the bar. Sometimes you were forced to do it. Sometimes you were forced to do it at gunpoint in Chicago. People put a gun on you because they knew the solos so you couldn't fool them. They paid that much attention to the records. They'd get the records, everybody knew the solos. So I know this happened to quite a few different people. They wanted to hear what was on the record. If you didn't know it then you had to go home and learn it. You couldn't fool us. People wanted to hear "Flyin' Home," they wanted to hear the solo. If you couldn't play it then you'd get off of that.
MR: They don't teach that in school.
CD: No, no, no, they don't teach you that. And if they want you to walk the bar, they wanted you to walk the bar. You couldn't say that wasn't in your contract. It's time to walk the bar. People wanted to see a show. When it was show time then you had to go out and put on a show, you couldn't sit around and be that cool, saying that's not my

thing. So if it's show time you get up and put on a show.
MR: You want to get paid, you better do it.
CD: Yeah. You may do it and don't get paid. Guys put on a show laying on his back and playing the saxophone behind his back, anything to get through that scene.
MR: Sounds like a tough town.
CD: Yeah. But that was the tradition during that time.[9]

Free Jazz

Vince and Charles were performing styles of jazz that are separated by over four decades, both oriented towards the listening and dancing audience. Free jazz marks the other end of the spectrum and occupies a niche for the truly adventurous musician and listener. Journalists and music fans frequently labeled free jazz as angry, disrespectful of traditional values, and the exclusive domain of the untalented. A number of our interviews offered an alternate view of the creative process involved in performing free jazz and the intent of the creators.

From drummer Rashied Ali, who was interviewed with bassist Henry Grimes:

MR: The free jazz that was happening in the '60s in New York, did you guys sit and talk about music and say, well, if we played this way this could happen, or did it mostly just happen on the bandstand?
RA: We didn't ever really talk about it. We just did it. For me, and the guys I was hanging out with, we didn't sit down and say now we're going to play in or we're going to play out or we going to tie, and play without bars, you know. It was just something that we did. Something that we heard and something that we listened to. It happened spontaneously.
HG: We did a lot of things but it was never talking. It was now let's play this.
RA: It was just something that we all wanted to do, man, because we all knew what bebop was, because we listened to it. We listened to it forever. And, it's just evolution to change. Just the days and the times that we live in was different from the way it was when Bird was living, or the way it was when Satchmo was living. It was a different time. And our music reflected what was happening at that time. And so it was time to play something different because everybody was in a different frame of mind.
MR: Can you be specific about that?
RA: Well, say Rosa Parks got on the bus one day and decided that she

wasn't going to sit in the back of the bus because she was too tired. And say, like a bunch of service guys was on the train and we were all from New York and Pennsylvania and New Jersey, and we got on the train to join a unit in the South. And on the way down South we get off at the train station because everybody wants something to eat, they're hungry and they walk to the door and they see a sign that says "Colored that way, whites only." You'd see signs like that. And they'd just go inside where the white place was and start taking stuff off the shelves and invading stuff and everybody gets detailed or gets in trouble or whatever. That kind of a thing was going on. So the music reflected that. It reflected the hard times. That's why maybe they would say like we were playing angry music or whatever they might say it was, but it really wasn't. It was just reflecting the time of day it was. And I think we sort of outgrew the Bebop Era and wanted to start playing something different from what it was, because we were different people. We were not the same people as those people who lived in that bebop time. And I think that's evolution. Everything changes over time. People live differently. And the music reflects the way you live. That's how I feel.[10]

Pianist Karl Berger has been in the forefront of free jazz since the 1960s and regularly organizes large gatherings of musicians at his Creative Music Workshop. He surprised me by refuting the idea that anything can be played at any time in this music.

MR: Do you think of yourself as a conductor when you're doing this, or do you think of yourself as something else?
KB: I'm conducting.
MR: But what are you hoping to get?
KB: I'm trying to harmonize people in terms of dynamics. There are really two chief elements in music that are the most important and that's dynamics and rhythm or timing. And a conductor can do a lot about that. The same sound is going to work harmonically if it's in a certain dynamic spectrum and it won't work in another. And timing is crucial to that as well. And those two elements a conductor in an improvised situation can have control, and give people an idea where to come out, where to go in, where to blend and how to blend. And blending has a lot to do with dynamics but also with timing. And those two parameters are the most important in music. It doesn't matter what note you play it's how you play it.
MR Can you expand on that?

Jazz Tales from Jazz Legends

KB: Well, every note contains every other note if you know about the overtones. Right? There is no note left out. Once you hit a sound all others will show up in the overtone spectrum. You can't really hear them, but you can hear them in the timbre. So anyone could play any other note to that, but depending where it sits in the overtone range it has to be dynamically softer or stronger you see. And then you will harmonize. So one practice we do for a half hour every time we perform is we play a random chord. Everybody keeps that note in mind that they played. It's random. On cue. Everybody at the same time. So it's totally cacophonic we would call it, right? So now we're going to spend the next twenty minutes, maybe fifteen minutes, repeating this chord until it harmonizes. And only by way of dynamics. And if that doesn't work, which we'll find out after five minutes—a player may switch like within a half-tone. So you think of let's say you play a D. So the D can be flat or the D can be sharp. Right? You would just find the right tuning so to speak. All of a sudden it sounds like you couldn't have written it any better.

MR: So the chord that you arrive at after all this, it could be a very complex chord?

KB: Yeah, but we are also using scales. So we do a lot of that too. So it really alternates between simple and complex also. Like I may use a pentatonic scale. But then you have the 12-tone scale around that as approach notes. But you have a pentatonic core, right? So you create your chords there and then you improvise. And there's no such thing as twelve tones. There is like millions of tones, as I explained to you. And the other part that I'm trying to emphasize is the novelty of every sound. You know there is no sound that can ever be repeated. Because the overtone, the amount of harmonics is in the thousands—or actually it's like an ant in a sense. Would you think that the ants are going to be organized in the same relationship to each other. So there is no sound that you will ever repeat. Everything is new. So once you become aware of that then you're going to become a lot more careful about what you do.

MR: That's such an interesting thing for you to say, about being careful.

KB: Well, it's about more precision. More freedom is not about less precision, it's about more precision. The more precise you get the more free you are, you know. See, the whole thing is people think of a sense of freedom, free jazz, it's about, oh yeah, I can lose all these rules. Actually I'm creating my own rules and they're much more stringent. You have to become self-disciplined. But you are creating a sense of self-discipline and responsibility for each note you play.

How does it harmonize? How does its timing work? You are helping the others to sound good. So it becomes like going to heaven.
MR: It's like going to heaven?
KB: It's like going to heaven. That's what I imagine heaven to be. So we are going to heaven every other week.

New Orleans saxophonist Kidd Jordan performed on a release entitled "Palm of Soul." He had approached one cut as a warm-up and was surprised it was included on the CD.

KJ: I was thinking it was going to be like one of the sessions I usually do, we start playing in one of them knock-out drag-out sessions. When it's free we call it improvised. Some people call it free but it's not as free as you think it is. Because William [Parker] will always lay down some keys, some things, some sounds and then pull it out from under me, and then I've got to go with him and then I get settled again and I have to go somewhere else. Now the first one on there was just a warm-up for me to try the mouthpiece. And they put that on there and named that the first one. They kept that. I was trying to see how the mouthpiece was going to work. They even kept that one.
MR: That brings me to a question. I think it's easy to misread the intention of musicians. If you listen to some of the later Coltrane records you might think that John Coltrane was really angry.
KJ: Some people say he was stark raving mad.
MR: You made a comment regarding this and I'm reading from the [liner notes from "Palm of Soul"], "The album's turbulent passages almost instinctually call to mind the destructive surge of Katrina." That was this person's thought. You said that you acknowledged that but with a chuckle. "I was contending with the powerful forces all right but they were my compatriots. They were the guys I was playing with."
KJ: Exactly. That's right. Katrina didn't have nothing to do with that. I wasn't even thinking about Katrina. That was all over.
MR: So it was a musical response.
KJ: That's right, it was a musical response other than that, that's right.
MR: So when you use the term "knock-out drag-out" you are talking about really wailing.
KJ: That's right, what's going on. Like you say Trane stark raving mad. Trane was just into his thing, I mean that's what he wanted to do.
MR: Where did that inspiration for that kind of playing come from? Do you have any idea?

Jazz Tales from Jazz Legends

KJ: I haven't the slightest idea. Well, Trane heard everything. And he heard that the saxophone, like you heard that tune that he did at the Olatunji Center with he and Pharaoh Sanders, that live date? I mean that was a hell of a date. I mean they were completely out on that. I got a good idea how he put all that together. And I talked to Pharaoh about that and he said, "Man look, that was just a few Hallelujahs." I mean Trane, when you get to that point, and I think he was sick because that might have been one of the last recordings. So I mean they just pulled everything out. And I wish I could have been there just to hear it in that place and hearing it the way it is really, they're really on top of it.[12]

Song Titles

Continuing with Kidd Jordan, the subject of song titles provided enlightenment regarding their relevance to the music:

MR: So where did the titles come from?
KJ: They [the producers] named them.
MR: "Last of the Chicken Wings"?
KJ: We had some chicken wings and we was in the session. Somebody says, "That's the last of the chicken wings." I mean the voiceover. Somebody said, "Last of the chicken wings." So that's how that came about.[13]

In contrast, band leader and banjoist Béla Fleck takes great care when naming his work, and spoke about his songwriting process:

MR: Do you have trouble thinking of titles sometimes?
BF: Yeah. I'm really picky about titles, and usually the crunch is when it's time for the record to come out, that's when the titles have to get settled. So I keep a list of titles now in my computer and I'll look through them. And often I don't find anything that fits the song. I want it to really fit. And again, why it fits the song, I can't tell you, but when it's the right one it clicks in and I go, oh, that feels right.
MR: Now "Sunset Road" sticks in your head. And there's something really evocative about that song, it reminds me of a song like "Harlem Nocturne." Does it strike you that way?
BF: Yeah. I was really happy with it. It popped out. I was recording an album called "Solo Banjo Works" back whenever it was, before the Flecktones. And I was testing the microphones and I just was improvising a little bit and that melody came out and I just kept

playing it over and over again. My older brother was recording it. And he said, "Are you going to get onto what we're going to record?" I said, "Yeah, I just want to capture this because I think this is good." And so I just kept it and put it aside and then I was looking for a bridge for the longest time. And then finally I came up with a bridge. And then the title came from a signpost. We were driving on the bus and I was sitting in the front early in the morning. We were driving through someplace in South Carolina, and I was looking for titles for that first—I might have still been in New Grass Revival possibly, the band before the Flecktones. Because we had made the Flecktones record and I was on tour looking for titles. And I saw that sign go by, "Sunset Road." That one's done.

MR: When you're working on some of those modulations—not modulations, really the cadences in that song, some of them go where you think, and some don't. Do you consciously think about that?

BF: When I'm writing, sure, yeah. Yeah, you want a certain amount of the expected and then a certain amount of unexpected in a good composition I think is to put it really simply. Yeah, I want there to be surprises but I don't want them to be necessarily jarring. Well, sometimes I want them to be jarring. You could lull somebody into a sense of security and then, vamm—switch into a whole different thing. And that can be really exhilarating to listen to. But it depends. Like with that one there's some nice harmonic stuff in the bridge that when I first wrote it I thought it was a bit esoteric but the more we played it over and over and got into it and got to know it actually wasn't very esoteric and it wouldn't even qualify as complex harmony. But it was a surprise from what the verse was.

MR: Is there a story behind "Sinister Minister?"

BF: Not really. We were just looking for a title and I think Howard Levy came up with it and we all thought that was funny. And anytime someone had a title that made us laugh we tried to use it.

MR: Okay. The titles can put a spin on things that may not be your intention.

BF: Yeah. But it seemed to fit the song perfectly. It made the song more than what the song was before it had that title. I don't know how. I don't know why. It worked that way with "Sunset Road" too. And I think "Big Country." Sometimes when you get a really classic title for a song, the song has another connection for the listener. It's not, "Oh what's that song," cut eleven on whatever record, "I like that song whatever that was." It's like, "I like 'Big Country.' I like

Jazz Tales from Jazz Legends

'Sinister Minister.'" It's a connect. So a title is really important. I always wondered whether Béla Fleck and the Flecktones was the best name for the band. It just seemed like the right one at the time and then we were in and it was too late to rethink it. But I think many people think it was some like California jazz, contemporary jazz thing or something, or like some silly—you know, the graphics and the covers, they made it take us less seriously for some people. But it's worked out.[14]

Steve Allen was a prolific songwriter, and offered his view of song titles:

MR: If you sit and write a tune that's meant to be an instrumental, such as the thing you did with Benny Goodman, is it sometimes a chore to think of a title to put on it?

SA: That also is a marvelous question, that's what you do for a living, you ask marvelous questions. I jump back to, I don't know about forty years ago, I once got intrigued by that question, and I wrote to about twenty band leaders, including Benny. This was long before I'd met him. He had some instrumentals, one was called "Benji's Bauble," and another one with the name of one of his daughters. Now I didn't know that those were named after two of his children until he wrote back and said, "Dear Steve, in answer to your question, Benji is one of my sons"—his own name, Benny, Benjamin—and I forgot what the other one had to do with. But anyway he'd used the name of his two children. But I was noticing was that there was really no meaning, nor could there be any meaning to a pure melody. You might somehow think of a message if you hear a march or something of that sort, but that's your own interpretation and a thousand people would have a thousand separate interpretations. You can't say a note means a word or a thought, or if you do you're talking nonsense. So anyway, to get back to your earlier question, of all of the ways there are to write songs I work in, sometimes I just start with a title. One of my hit songs, in fact just last night I was listening to three different recordings of it doing some organization work, it's called "Pretend You Don't See My Heart." It was a big hit by Jerry Vale and it's been sung by Vic Damone and a lot of good singers. It's a very Italian waltz, purposely written in the Italian vein. It was originally recorded as an instrumental but it was always in the Italian groove. Anyway what occurred to me first was the title, that obviously would relate to a broken love affair, and the question, oh what will happen if I run into her or him or whatever. So pretend you don't see her, that would be the solution, just don't get involved anymore, it's too late. Everything's too sad or whatever. So again in that case, starting with the title thought. In other cases, in most cases in fact, I have a melody first which has no meaning whatever, although it does have a mood. There is such a thing as really sad melodies. There are other things which are soaringly romantic melodies, at least to American ears or western European ears. What an Eskimo would think of if he heard "Rhapsody in Blue," well, we'll have to ask him.[15]

Playing with a Master
Drummer Eddie Locke played with a number of jazz legends, including Coleman Hawkins and Roy Eldridge [a/k/a Lil' Jazz]. Eddie was one of the fifty-seven jazz artists who posed for the 1959 *Esquire* magazine photo "A Great Day in Harlem,"[16] and was acutely aware that he was surrounded by the elder jazz masters of the time. He spoke of the relationships with Roy and Coleman and an on-the-gig lesson he never forgot:

EL: Roy Eldridge was my conscience. He was like my—I don't know what to call him. I had a great relationship with him and Coleman, but both of the relationships were very different. And Roy Eldridge was the godfather of my children. It was like my family. You know what I really loved about them? They never, ever B.S.-ed me about what I could do. He'd say, "You're not great but you're okay. You just keep doing what you're doing. You're all right." They didn't put that stuff in your head, like you're the greatest drummer I ever saw, just to say things like that. I think that's one of the worst things that happens to a lot of young musicians today. They make a CD or a record or something, and somebody tells them that they're the greatest thing that's been here, and they don't grow anymore. I'm still growing. I can play better now than I could ten years ago. And I think it came from that. I mean you knew they liked you because you wouldn't have been there. But they never were just like polishing you off all the time, how great you are and all you did. You were there, it's okay. And they treated you nice if you did what you were supposed to be doing. Like as Papa Jo [Jones] said, take care of the bandstand. That's another thing those guys did. When they went up on the bandstand, it was a business for them. And they took care of the bandstand. The music part, everything. And Jo did say, "You've got to know how to get on the stage, you've got to know how to get off the stage." "Don't wear out your welcome," he said. And they could do so much with a little. They never ranted and raved a long time, and that's another thing I learned from them was that's something wonderful to be able to do, to get your little piece done, and don't wear the people out.

MR: Yeah. Two choruses instead of eight.

EL: Instead of eight, yeah, yeah. And do tell the story. Like I said before, I must have been the luckiest—and I thank God for it. I mean I don't go to church all the time but I do thank God for it all the time. Because that was really luck. You've got to be good but you've got to be lucky too.

MR: Roy had quite a competitive spirit, didn't he?

EL: I've never played with anyone that loved to play as much as him. Never. And my greatest story, every time I tell somebody this, they always, they love it, but I'm going to tell this so this will be on film forever. I will never forget, we were playing in a place and there was no one in the place, just like this room we're in now, with the band. We were up there playing. And I was just like that [scats lazily]. And he turned around and he leaned over the drum set at me and he said, "What are you doing?" And I said, "Well, Roy" I says, "there's nobody in here." He looked me right in—I mean he got closer—he said, "I'M HERE!" That was the scariest thing, I mean and the way he said it, you know what I mean? But it made a difference in me. He said, "I'm here! Let's play!" Because that's what he did. I mean I've heard him play some of the greatest music I ever heard, in a room just like this with nobody in it. He loved that horn. That's why at his funeral, when Dizzy said, "Y'all gotta find something else to do now," he said, "because this is the only person that was ever named Jazz." And that's what he was. I've seen him, I mean Jo Jones told me, he said, "One of these days you're going to be playing with him, man, and he's going to rip you right out of that drum seat." I said, now that is really deep. I didn't pay that much attention. But he did. Right up in Toronto one time. Oh God. I had this feature on "Caravan" that we did, and when he got to the bridge one time boy, it was just so dynamic. It was just like I couldn't do it. I couldn't even play. It just took me away, I'm telling you. It was unbelievable. I never felt nothing like that before in my life. His presence when he played was just like unbelievable. I heard him every night. I never played with him—he's the only person I've ever been around like that. It was never a night where sometime during the night I said, "Wow." Do you know what I mean? I mean he would do something that I'd never heard him do before. Like this stuff so dynamic that it would be just like, whoa. That was amazing. He was amazing.[17]

Why Jazz?

Artists don't often describe what they do in words. Defining art forms is inherently difficult, and is usually left to writers and historians. The memorable definitions that are shared here have more to do with the value of jazz rather than the specifics of how it is created. British pianist Keith Ingham was so enamored of the music that he left his own country to pursue it.

MR: Are there any counterparts of American musicians who've gone over to England and learned as much about your music as you have about —

KI: What do you mean, the British music? I mean we never had anything as wonderful as jazz. You see, I think it comes from a melting pot society where you've got all these different strains coming together. That's the whole point. You had Italians here, so you have these wonderful lyric qualities. You have Afro-Americans as they're called now, but you have that rhythmic thing they do they brought that looseness and that sense of swing. You had the Germans here so you have the correctness of intonation and things like that. You have that whole melting pot. And they all brought their music. You have the Russians with all that minor key, soul stuff. It's wonderful. Gershwin is Russian but also very Jewish and that kind of sad, soulful feeling that's in his music is, I think more Jewish than Russian or American. I mean "Porgy and Bess" could almost be a Jewish opera rather than a black opera. But it's wonderful. It's the melting pot that America is that made American music. That's what it is. There's nothing like it in the world. You're so lucky, don't lose it, because it's your great contribution to world culture. I mean it's your Beethoven, your Haydn, your Schubert, your Debussy, your Ravel, your Elgar, your Henry Purcell, or whatever you want. Your Rachmaninoffs, your Stravinskys, it's all there. It's Duke Ellington, it's Fats Waller, it's Henry "Red" Allen, it's Bix, it's Eddie Lang, it's Joe Venuti, it's up there. And God bless it.[18]

Pianist Norman Simmons was attracted to the democracy of the bandstand:

MR: Was there a point growing up in Chicago, where you started to feel that you had the confidence that you could actually make a living in this business?

NS: Well, that's an interesting concept because I've always looked at it in a different way. I guess you might say in the artistic sense, that I didn't consider how I wanted to make a living, I just considered how I wanted to live. And that decision was made when I was in maybe my second year in high school—maybe not the second, maybe the third or maybe the fourth year. Because I had a wonderful English teacher named Mr. Reinstein, and he had us doing a thing on careers. And in high school I was doing pretty good, I mean my biology teacher wanted me to advance in science and my art teacher wanted me to go to art school. Because I coasted through everything. I had good instincts, in other words it wasn't that I was at home doing a lot of homework and stuff like that, but I was out there playing baseball all of the time. The requirements in the art department, if we had to turn in three pictures in a week I did all three of them in one night and turned them in and then played hooky the rest of the time. So it was like that. So when we got to this English class there was significant things about this teacher, in composition—because we had to write—of course the same thing—I'd just sit down, I just wrote my stuff out and he loved it. And it wasn't until the second semester that he decided that we needed to go to the library and pick out a subject and write about it that. I collapsed. Because I did not want to go to the library and I did not want to write about what somebody else was thinking. And it was the end of the semester because he had been carrying me all that semester from the previous semester where he liked all my creative work, and he said, "You know you have not done your work this semester." And he was giving me high marks still. So anyway, when all of the kids, you could hear them outside in the summertime and everybody's getting out of school, I was up there writing. And we had a course in careers and I decided to look at it and say, well now, if I decide to be an artist there's going to be someone over me. If maybe I'm going to be like painting pictures and waiting until I'm dead before I get any recognition from them, or I'm going to work in a situation where someone is going to be telling me what to do. I decided, in being who I was in the black community, I said democracy was mostly represented in the music. This is where individuals accepted each other on another level other than the way the rest of society did. And I decided this is where I wanted to be in that situation. So it was how I wanted to live my life regardless of how much I was going to make."[19]

Potpourri

Late in his life, trombonist Benny Powell became an advocate for the vital role jazz has played in American society:

MR: I wanted to follow up on something that you just mentioned, jazz being the story of your culture and America's culture. There's been a lot of press lately about the conflict of looking at jazz history from a racial standpoint. And just a couple of weeks ago there was a thing in the *Times* from an author who was complaining that the white musicians that he considered innovators—

BP: Have you heard him play?

MR: I have not heard this man play.

BP: Well. Well, he has his opinion. But for me, I wish we'd get over all of that. Acknowledge that everybody had something to do with this. One of the things I think that's never been played enough is Benny Goodman's role in showing a visible democracy. Up until then you'd see pictures of Franklin Delano Roosevelt with Dr. George Washington Carver [or] Eleanor Roosevelt with Marian Anderson, but they weren't doing anything. Benny Goodman with Lionel Hampton, Teddy Wilson, Gene Krupa, was one of the first visible evidence that we could work together in that kind of respect. And I don't think history books have made enough of that. I think if that were the case then we wouldn't still have these arguments, because we would have decided that then, we all made this stuff. Now if you go into the non-racial thing then you're disrespecting my heritage because you see the blues came from people being whipped and beaten and all of that. I know we'd all like to forget about that, but I think it was because of that—I have a contention, no great art is ever created by happy people. It's always adversity that creates art. So when I do my lectures, I start off my lectures with Negro spirituals because they chronicle the experience, which is "Nobody Knows the Trouble I've Seen," and I tell the people about the voice of being cut off. Anyway, it's a deep story behind it, and jazz is being left out. That's one of the things that I have a problem with now. A lot of jazz education that's being taught, the people, or the judges and so forth, are people—well, IAJE [International Association of Jazz Educators] for instance was started by a man from Kansas who was a Stan Kenton fan. And that's great. But the emphasis on a lot of the conferences I've been to, starts jazz off there. And so they kind of leave out Count Basie, Fats Waller, Louis Armstrong, Duke Ellington, and so forth. So I kind of have a problem with that. But whenever

I have a problem with anything, rather than complain about it, I provide another solution. That's why I am teaching. And this guy, I don't know whether I should call his name or not but I guess I shouldn't now that I've made my little smart remarks. I think I'd like to get past all of this. Because when you walk to the microphone, it don't know whether you're blue or black or green, a man, a woman, a midget or whatever. And that's the common denominator. Writers have their place and so forth, but when it comes to explaining music, I say, well, if you know so much about it, take your horn out and let's play.[20]

Finé

In January 2001 I attended the annual IAJE conference in New York City. I struck up a casual conversation with a gentleman in the lobby, only realizing who it was after he handed me his business card. Veteran saxophonist Harold Ousley offered a thoughtful reflection about life; a resonant final chord for our book:

HO: I've had some good experiences. But I feel that in life, I think we all, number one, are here for a purpose. It's not just being here. So there are certain experiences for us to have that help to fulfill us, help us to grow, give us understanding, patience. A lot of the things that we need as individuals. And I believe in karma. I think our karma takes us to those experiences that we need. If it's music that we're trying to excel at, or if it's writing, or whatever it is, we come in contact with people who help us to develop that, who inspire us, or who can give us the information, or whatever, to help to take us to that next level. And so we play an important part in their lives and they play an important part in ours. So we are taken to all of those experiences that we need, that are important for us, to take us to that next experience. So like our being here together, we didn't know each other before. Experience has brought everybody to this point, where we are because of the interest in music, and what we are trying to do next. And it's in one way or another we are helping each other with that program, because it's all about networking.

MR: You've told me things today that I hadn't heard before. So it was fortuitous that we met last night.

HO: Well, this is what propels me in my life—to feel that there is a reason, there is a force, there is something that has created all of this, because it takes intelligence to do this. You know we are sitting here talking but this planet is going through space at a tremendous speed, it's turning over, and then it's circling around and it's not bumping headlong into any other planets, and it's been doing it for a long time. And out of all the stars and planets in the universe that are working, things are working in harmony with each other. Because if not, things couldn't exist. But I feel that we are learning who we are and why we are. And as we get to that point, then we begin to do what we are here to do, to help everything to work together better. I think we've been put here to improve everything on this planet, like caretakers, whatever we can do, whether we're doing it through music or whatever we're doing, if we're helping to add some meaning to other people's lives. Like in music a lot of times people are going through a lot of things in their life, a lot of tension, you know, a lot of things they're uptight about, they go to a musical concert and this helps to, that moment in their life becomes a beautiful moment. And it gives them incentive to go for another day. You know I've had people say, well thank you so much for that. Because we have to have something to take us to that next moment. And when people don't have anything to take them to their next moment, they think about suicide or they drink or whatever. Because that inspiration, that incentive, to live to the next moment, isn't there. So we need to stay inspired, to have a goal, to believe that we can achieve that goal, and to believe that there is help outside, from another source other than ourselves. There is a system, and when we go through a day, we get up and go back to bed, whether we know it or not, we've had assistance in being able to get through that day without something tragic happening. You see what I mean? So I feel that there is a source that can assist us, and the more that we are able to connect with it, a lot of times we avoid paying a lot of dues or we avoid getting into problematic areas. Not that doesn't solve everything because I believe in life there is yin and yang. There is drama in everybody's life. So there are moments that we'd rather not have that can be disappointing, or there may be moments when cash flow is short, or there may be moments when we don't feel well. But we have to be able to go through those moments and stay centered and have that determination to get over this, so that we can get back to that point where we're feeling good and we're feeling energetic and inspired. Then we can go out and work on a plan. And so it's important to have those kind of inner feelings. And I think that's part of the spirit.[21]

Notes

Chapter 1
1. *A Portrait in Song*, directed by Burrill Crohn, Hamilton College, 1996.
2. Joe Williams, interview by Monk Rowe and Burrill Crohn, Clinton, NY, September 8, 1996.
3. Joe Williams, interview by Monk Rowe and Burrill Crohn, Clinton, NY, September 7, 1996.
4. Bill Hughes, interview by Monk Rowe and Burrill Crohn, Clinton, NY, September 7, 1996.
5. Iola Brubeck, interview by Monk Rowe for the Fillius Jazz Archive, Wilton, CT, July 27, 2011.
6. Jillean Williams, interview by Milt Fillius and Monk Rowe for the Fillius Jazz Archive, Clinton, NY, May 20, 1995.
7. Norman Simmons, interview by Monk Rowe and Burrill Crohn, Clinton, NY, September 6, 1996.
8. Joel Dorn, interview by Monk Rowe for the Fillius Jazz Archive, New York, NY, January 13, 2007.
9. Nat Hentoff, "A Great Night in Providence for Jazz and Snow," *Wall Street Journal*, March 30, 2005.
10. John Levy, interview by Monk Rowe and Burrill Crohn, Clinton, NY, September 7, 1996.
11. John Williams, interview by Monk Rowe and Burrill Crohn, Clinton, NY, September 7, 1996.
12. Joe Williams, interview by Monk Rowe and Burrill Crohn, Clinton, NY, September 7, 1996.

Chapter 2
1. John Lamb, interview by Monk Rowe for the Fillius Jazz Archive, Clearwater Beach, FL, March 16, 2001.
2. Louie Bellson, interview by Monk Rowe for the Fillius Jazz Archive, Sarasota, FL, April 12, 1996.
3. Grover Mitchell, interview by Monk Rowe for the Fillius Jazz Archive, Sarasota, FL, April 13, 1996.
4. Clark Terry, interview by Joe Williams and Michael Woods for the Fillius Jazz Archive, Clinton, NY, May 19, 1995.
5. Ibid.
6. Harry "Sweets" Edison, interview by Monk Rowe for the Fillius Jazz Archive, Los Angeles, CA, July 3, 1995.
7. Snooky Young and Gerald Wilson, interview by Monk Rowe for the Fillius Jazz Archive, Los Angeles, CA, January 29, 2000.
8. Jimmy Lewis, interview by Monk Rowe for the Fillius Jazz Archive, New

Notes

York, NY, November 16, 1995.
9. Grover Mitchell, interview by Monk Rowe for the Fillius Jazz Archive, Sarasota, FL, April 13, 1996.
10. Frank Foster Part II, interview by Monk Rowe for the Fillius Jazz Archive, Clinton, NY, April 7, 1998.
11. Benny Powell Part I, interview by Monk Rowe for the Fillius Jazz Archive, New York, NY, July 27, 1995.
12. Benny Powell Part II, interview by Monk Rowe for the Fillius Jazz Archive, New York, NY, January 16, 1999.
13. Butch Miles, interview by Monk Rowe for the Fillius Jazz Archive, Scottsdale, AZ, March 4, 1995.
14. Al Grey, interview by Michael Woods for the Fillius Jazz Archive, Scottsdale, AZ, March 3, 1995.
15. Sonny Igoe, interview by Monk Rowe for the Fillius Jazz Archive, Emerson, NJ, July 31, 2003.
16. Jerry Jerome, interview by Monk Rowe for the Fillius Jazz Archive, Sarasota, FL, April 12, 1996.
17. Dave Pell, interview by Monk Rowe for the Fillius Jazz Archive, Sarasota, FL, April 11, 1996.
18. Eddie Bert, interview by Monk Rowe for the Fillius Jazz Archive, Danbury, CT, November 20, 2011.
19. Conte Candoli, interview by Monk Rowe for the Fillius Jazz Archive, Aspen, CO, October 12, 1997.
20. Tommy Newsom and Ross Tompkins, interview by Monk Rowe for the Fillius Jazz Archive, Los Angeles, CA, September 3, 1995.
21. Ed Shaughnessy Part I, interview by Monk Rowe for the Fillius Jazz Archive, Los Angeles, CA, September 1, 1995.

Chapter 3
1. Eddie Bert, interview by Monk Rowe for the Fillius Jazz Archive, Danbury, CT, November 20, 2001.
2. Sonny Igoe, interview by Monk Rowe for the Fillius Jazz Archive, Emerson, NJ, July 31, 2003.
3. Bucky Pizzarelli Part II, interview by Monk Rowe for the Fillius Jazz Archive, Clinton, NY, May 23, 2003.
4. Jay McShann, interview by Monk Rowe for the Fillius Jazz Archive, Sarasota, FL, April 12, 1996.
5. Jimmy Lewis, interview by Monk Rowe for the Fillius Jazz Archive, New York, NY, November 16, 1995.
6. Kenny Davern Part II, interview by Monk Rowe for the Fillius Jazz Archive, Clearwater Beach, FL, March 16, 2001.
7. Lanny Morgan, interview by Monk Rowe for the Fillius Jazz Archive, Los Angeles, CA, January 14, 1999.
8. Phil Woods, interview by Monk Rowe for the Fillius Jazz Archive, Delaware Water Gap, PA, November 8, 1999.

Jazz Tales from Jazz Legends

9. Billy Mitchell, interview by Monk Rowe for the Fillius Jazz Archive, New York, NY, November 16, 1995.
10. Jerry Dodgion, interview by Monk Rowe for the Fillius Jazz Archive, New York, NY, March 9, 1996.

Chapter 4

1. *The Glenn Miller Story*, directed by Anthony Mann, Universal-International Pictures, 1954.
2. Dick Hyman Part I, interview by Monk Rowe for the Fillius Jazz Archive, Scottsdale, AZ, March 4, 1995.
3. Michael Abene, interview by Monk Rowe for the Fillius Jazz Archive, Toronto, Canada, January 11, 2003.
4. Bill Holman, interview by Monk Rowe for the Fillius Jazz Archive, Los Angeles, CA, January 13, 1999.
5. *Swamp Women*, directed by Roger Corman, Woolner Brothers, Inc., 1955.
6. Bill Holman, interview by Monk Rowe for the Fillius Jazz Archive, Los Angeles, CA, January 13, 1999.
7. Derrick Gardner, interview by Monk Rowe for the Fillius Jazz Archive, Clinton, NY, May 9, 2013.
8. Ray Conniff, interview by Monk Rowe for the Fillius Jazz Archive, San Diego, CA, February 14, 1998.
9. Manny Albam, interview by Monk Rowe for the Fillius Jazz Archive, Tarrytown, NY, October 31, 1998.
10. Ibid.
11. Lew Soloff, interview by Monk Rowe for the Fillius Jazz Archive, Scottsdale, AZ, April 16, 2000.
12. "Gemini" by Jimmy Heath, from "Cannonball Adderley Sextet Live at the Village Vanguard," January 12 & 14, 1962.
13. Orrin Keepnews, interview by Monk Rowe for the Fillius Jazz Archive, San Francisco, CA, August 7, 2002.
14. Dave Rivello, interview by Monk Rowe for the Fillius Jazz Archive, Rochester, NY, January 11, 2012.
15. Ibid.
16. Maria Schneider, interview by Monk Rowe for the Fillius Jazz Archive, New York, NY, January 12, 2001.
17. Ibid.

Chapter 5

1. Doc Cheatham, interview by Monk Rowe and Michael Woods for the Fillius Jazz Archive, New York, NY, July 28, 1995.
2. Richard Wyands, interview by Monk Rowe for the Fillius Jazz Archive, New York, NY, January 7, 2002.
3. Orrin Keepnews, interview by Monk Rowe for the Fillius Jazz Archive, San Francisco, CA, August 7, 2002.
4. Joel Dorn, interview by Monk Rowe for the Fillius Jazz Archive, New York,

Notes

NY, January 13, 2007.
5. Dick Hyman Part I, interview by Monk Rowe for the Fillius Jazz Archive, Scottsdale, AZ, March 4, 1995.
6. Derek Smith, interview by Monk Rowe and Michael Woods for the Fillius Jazz Archive, Royal Caribbean's *Majesty of the Seas*, May 29, 1995.
7. Joe Wilder Part II, interview by Monk Rowe for the Fillius Jazz Archive, Clinton, NY, October 12, 1998.
8. Ibid.
9. Dick Hyman Part I, interview by Monk Rowe for the Fillius Jazz Archive, Scottsdale, AZ, March 4, 1995.
10. Bob Rosengarden, interview by Monk Rowe for the Fillius Jazz Archive, Clinton, NY, October 6, 1996.
11. Panama Francis, interview by Michael Woods for the Fillius Jazz Archive, Los Angeles, CA, September 1, 1995.
12. Ray Sherman, interview by Monk Rowe for the Fillius Jazz Archive, San Diego, CA, February 13, 1998.
13. Paul Smith, interview by Monk Rowe for the Fillius Jazz Archive, Los Angeles, CA, January 14, 1999.
14. Ernie Watts, interview by Monk Rowe for the Fillius Jazz Archive, Toronto, Canada, January 11, 2003.
15. Plas Johnson, interview by Monk Rowe for the Fillius Jazz Archive, Sarasota, FL, April 12, 1996.
16. Bucky Pizzarelli Part II, interview by Monk Rowe for the Fillius Jazz Archive, Clinton, NY, May 23, 2003.
17. Bucky and Ruth Pizzarelli, interview by Monk Rowe for the Fillius Jazz Archive, Saddle River, NJ, January 19, 2015.
18. Ibid.
19. Phil Woods, interview by Monk Rowe for the Fillius Jazz Archive, Delaware Water Gap, PA, November 8, 1999.
20. Derek Smith, 1995.
21. Howie Shear, interview by Monk Rowe for the Fillius Jazz Archive, Dunkirk, NY, October 17, 2014.

Chapter 6
1. "Nigerian" is Clark Terry's substitute for the "n word."
2. Clark Terry, interview by Joe Williams & Michael Woods, for the Fillius Jazz Archive, Clinton, NY, May 19, 1995.
3. *A Great Day in Harlem*, directed by Jean Bach, Home Vision Entertainment, 1994.
4. *Esquire*, January 1959, 98-99.
5. Jean Bach, interview by Monk Rowe for the Fillius Jazz Archive, New York, NY, October 18, 1995.
6. Sonny Igoe, interview by Monk Rowe for the Fillius Jazz Archive, Emerson, NJ, July 31, 2003.
7. Mona Hinton, interview by Milt Fillius & Michael Woods for the Fillius Jazz

Jazz Tales from Jazz Legends

      Archive, Scottsdale, AZ, March 4, 1995.
8. Joe Wilder Part II, interview by Monk Rowe for the Fillius Jazz Archive, Clinton, NY, October 12, 1998.
9. Ruth Brown, interview by Michael Woods for the Fillius Jazz Archive, Scottsdale, AZ, March 4, 1995.
10. Louie Bellson, interview by Monk Rowe for the Fillius Jazz Archive, Sarasota, FL, April 12, 1996.
11. Helen Dance, interview by Monk Rowe for the Fillius Jazz Archive, San Diego, CA, February 12, 1998.
12. Lionel Hampton, interview by Monk Rowe for the Fillius Jazz Archive, New York, NY, October 18, 1995.
13. Jon Hendricks Part I, interview by Monk Rowe for the Fillius Jazz Archive, New York, NY, October 18, 1995.
14. Milt Hinton and David G. Berger, *Bass Line: The Stories and Photographs of Milt Hinton*, Temple University Press, 1988, 165.
15. Jamey Aebersold has published a series of books with accompanying DVDs under the titles *Jazz: Anyone Can Improvise*, Jamey Aebersold Jazz, Inc.
16. Frank Foster Part II, interview by Monk Rowe for the Fillius Jazz Archive, Clinton, NY, April 7, 1998.
17. Jon Hendricks Part II, interview by Monk Rowe for the Fillius Jazz Archive, New York, NY, January 29, 2000.

Chapter 7
1. Marian McPartland, interview by Monk Rowe for the Fillius Jazz Archive, Utica, NY, April 26, 1997.
2. Clark Terry, interview by Joe Williams and Michael Woods for the Fillius Jazz Archive, Clinton, NY, May 19, 1995.
3. Bill Charlap, interview by Monk Rowe for the Fillius Jazz Archive, Scottsdale, AZ, April 16, 2000.
4. Charles McPherson, interview by Monk Rowe for the Fillius Jazz Archive, San Diego, CA, February 12, 1998.
5. Ken Peplowski, interview by Monk Rowe for the Fillius Jazz Archive, Aspen, CO, October 10, 1997.
6. Joe Wilder Part II, interview by Monk Rowe for the Fillius Jazz Archive, Clinton, NY, October 12, 1998.
7. Winard Harper, interview by Monk Rowe for the Fillius Jazz Archive, Utica, NY, October 10, 2014.
8. Dan Barrett, interview by Michael Woods for the Fillius Jazz Archive, Los Angeles, CA, September 3, 1995.
9. Bill Watrous, interview by Monk Rowe for the Fillius Jazz Archive, Clinton, NY, March 26, 1999.
10. Bill Crow, *Jazz Anecdotes* (New York: Oxford University Press, 1990), 95.
11. Bill Watrous, interview by Monk Rowe for the Fillius Jazz Archive, Clinton, NY, March 26, 1999.
12. Randy Sandke, interview by Monk Rowe for the Fillius Jazz Archive, Aspen,

Notes

CO, October 10, 1997.
13. Denny Zeitlin, interview by Monk Rowe for the Fillius Jazz Archive, San Francisco, CA, August 8, 2002.
14. www.cabcalloway.cc/dizzy_gillespie.htm.
15. Gary Smulyan, interview by Monk Rowe for the Fillius Jazz Archive, Utica, NY, October 17, 2010.
16. Ralph LaLama, interview by Monk Rowe for the Fillius Jazz Archive, Utica, NY, May 23, 2010.
17. www.ted.com/talks/stefon_harris_there_are_no_mistakes_on_the_bandstand? language=en.
18 Jon Weber, interview by Monk Rowe for the Fillius Jazz Archive, Clinton, NY, June 2, 2012.
19. Jamey Aebersold has published a series of books with accompanying DVDs under the titles *Jazz: Anyone Can Improvise*, Jamey Aebersold Jazz, Inc.

Chapter 8

1. Keter Betts, interview by Monk Rowe for the Fillius Jazz Archive, Sarasota, FL, April 11, 1996.
2. John Pizzarelli Jr., interview by Monk Rowe for the Fillius Jazz Archive, New York, NY, January 29, 2000.
3. Kenny Davern Part II, interview by Monk Rowe for the Fillius Jazz Archive, Clearwater Beach, FL, March 16, 2001.
4. Ibid.
5. Junior Mance, interview by Monk Rowe and Michael Woods for the Fillius Jazz Archive, New York, NY, July 27, 1995.
6. Jon Hendricks Part I, interview by Monk Rowe for the Fillius Jazz Archive, New York, NY, October 18, 1995.
7. Nat Adderley, interview by Monk Rowe and Michael Woods for the Fillius Jazz Archive, Royal Caribbean's *Majesty of the Seas*, May 29, 1995.
8. Stanley Kay, interview by Monk Rowe for the Fillius Jazz Archive, Clearwater Beach, FL, March 18, 2001.
9. Sherrie Maricle, interview by Monk Rowe for the Fillius Jazz Archive, Clearwater Beach, FL, March 18, 2001.
10. Eiji Kitamura, interview by Monk Rowe for the Fillius Jazz Archive, Los Angeles, CA, January 13, 1999.
11. Dave Brubeck, interview by Monk Rowe for the Fillius Jazz Archive, Wilton, CT, November 21, 2001.
12. Jon Hendricks Part I, interview by Monk Rowe for the Fillius Jazz Archive, New York, NY, October 18, 1995.
13. Bobby Watson, interview by Michael Woods for the Fillius Jazz Archive, Clinton, NY, January 19, 1996.
14. Annie Ross, interview by Monk Rowe for the Fillius Jazz Archive, New York, NY, January 13, 2001.
15. Don Alias, interview by Monk Rowe for the Fillius Jazz Archive, New York, NY, January 6, 2002.

Jazz Tales from Jazz Legends

16. Phil Woods, interview by Monk Rowe for the Fillius Jazz Archive, Delaware Water Gap, PA, November 8, 1999.

Chapter 9
1. Barry Kernfeld, ed., *The New Grove Dictionary of Jazz*, 2nd ed. (New York: Grove, 2002), 3:697.
2. Ed Shaughnessy Part II, interview by Monk Rowe for the Fillius Jazz Archive, Clinton, NY, April 25, 1998.
3. Steve Allen, interview by Monk Rowe for the Fillius Jazz Archive, Los Angeles, CA, January 15, 1999.
4. Jane Ira Bloom, interview by Monk Rowe for the Fillius Jazz Archive, Clinton, NY, March 3, 1998.
5. Nicki Parrott, interview by Monk Rowe for the Fillius Jazz Archive, Utica, NY, November 6, 2010.
6. Marian McPartland, interview by Monk Rowe for the Fillius Jazz Archive, Utica, NY, April 26, 1997.
7. Holly Hofmann, interview by Monk Rowe for the Fillius Jazz Archive, San Diego, CA, February 13, 1998.
8. Vince Giordano, interview by Monk Rowe for the Fillius Jazz Archive, New York, NY, January 11, 2007.
9. Charles Davis, interview by Monk Rowe for the Fillius Jazz Archive, Clinton, NY, August 23, 1997.
10. Rashied Ali and Henry Grimes, interview by Monk Rowe for the Fillius Jazz Archive, Clinton, NY, January 31, 2009.
11. Karl Berger, interview by Monk Rowe for the Fillius Jazz Archive, Woodstock, NY, August 11, 2014.
12. Kidd Jordan, interview by Monk Rowe for the Fillius Jazz Archive, Rome, NY, August 22, 2006.
13. Ibid.
14. Béla Fleck, interview by Monk Rowe for the Fillius Jazz Archive, Clinton, NY, December 7, 2004.
15. Steve Allen, interview by Monk Rowe for the Fillius Jazz Archive, Los Angeles, CA, January 15, 1999.
16. *Esquire*, January 1959, 98-99.
17. Eddie Locke, interview by Monk Rowe for the Fillius Jazz Archive, New York, NY, January 13, 2001.
18. Keith Ingham, interview by Monk Rowe for the Fillius Jazz Archive, Chautauqua, NY, September 12, 1997.
19. Norman Simmons Part II, interview by Monk Rowe for the Fillius Jazz Archive, Clinton, NY, September 27, 2007.
20. Benny Powell Part II, interview by Monk Rowe for the Fillius Jazz Archive, New York, NY, January 16, 1999.
21. Harold Ousley, interview by Monk Rowe for the Fillius Jazz Archive, New York, NY, January 12, 2001.

Glossary

Jazz has its own language. Some of these words and phrases were coined by musicians, while others were conceived by critics and historians to describe what the players do:

Break — a moment in a performance, usually two or four measures, when all the musicians stop except for the soloist.

Blue note — a scale tone purposely played a half-step lower than usual, typically the third, fifth, or seventh. Blues singers first did this, later they were copied by instrumentalists.

Bridge — not all songs have a bridge but most standards do (see Standards). Jazz musicians for years have performed popular songs from the '30s and '40s and they often are written in an A-A-B-A form. The music to each A is the same or similar; the B section (the bridge) offers something new. Also called the "George Washington" or the "channel."

Changes — the chords to a particular song. The changes provide the blueprint for the improvisations. The term "rhythm changes" is shorthand for the chords to the song "I Got Rhythm."

Chart — a written piece of music (the whole arrangement or an individual part).

Chorus — usually refers to the part of the song that has the title. Jazz players also use the term to describe improvising once through the whole song (i.e., each player takes one chorus).

Comp — the guitar, piano, and bass play the changes behind the soloist(s), improvising the rhythms to fit the feel of a particular style. Freddie Green, long time guitarist with the Count Basie Orchestra, had a comping style named after him, a steady chunking strum on each beat.

Cutting contest — two like instruments "battling" each other by trading improvised choruses. More competitive than a jam session, a cutting contest often provided an opportunity to establish a reputation, or sometimes lose one.

Fusion — a jazz genre that incorporates elements of rock, classical, and world music.

Jazz Tales from Jazz Legends

Head arrangement — a band arrangement created in rehearsals or on the spot by the players. It is committed to memory and may later be written down if it is a keeper.

Inside/outside — when an improviser uses notes that correspond to the change (chord) they are playing inside. Going outside is experimenting with notes that may sound wrong, especially to traditionalists or new listeners.

Jam session — an informal gathering of jazz players playing standards and blues, a valuable experience for aspiring musicians.

Laying out — refers to a player in the rhythm section who purposely does not play at all for a length of time (also called "strolling"). The bassist rarely lays out.

Modes — eight-note scales with whole and half steps in varying order. Modal jazz pioneered by Miles Davis and John Coltrane became popular in the 1960s and offered an alternative to the intensity of bebop.

Overdubbing — by the 1960s, technology allowed for instruments and voices to be recorded separately and as many times as desirable. Jazz recordings use this technique sparingly.

Rhythm section — bass, drums, piano, and/or guitar. They provide the background for the soloists and set up the groove. The rhythm section instruments can also solo, and a rhythm section can be a band in itself.

Riffs — short but memorable phrases that can be played behind soloists or function as a melody. The early Basie band was well known for classic riffs that were combined to create a head arrangement.

Standards — songs that jazz musicians are expected to have memorized. These tunes are typically from the '30s and '40s and were written by songwriters that included George Gershwin, Duke Ellington, Jerome Kern, etc. Knowing standards allows musicians who have never previously met to play a whole night together without written music. Newer tunes are constantly added to the list.

Straw boss — the second in command of a swing band. Straw refers to a saxophone reed. The first alto sax was often the designated straw boss, responsible for running rehearsals and keeping the group performing at a high level.

Sweetening — the adding of horns, strings, or background vocals to a

Glossary

prerecorded rhythm section track.

Tag — adding a phrase at the end of the song. The tag is usually cued by the group leader when it's time to go "home" (i.e., to end the piece). The tag is usually the last four measures played extra times.

Vocalese — the technique of composing a lyric and story that utilize a previously recorded instrumental improvisation as the melody.

Voicings — placing the notes of a chord in a specific order from bottom to top, either at the keyboard or in arrangement for individual instruments.

Walking bass — the bass player plays one note for every beat of the music. Essential in swing music. Also referred to as playing "in four," as opposed to "in two" (two bass notes per measure).

Walking the bar — part of providing a show for the patrons. A musician, usually the tenor saxophonist, would pace up and down on the bar while wailing away in an extroverted style.

Hamilton College Honorary Degree Recipients for Jazz

1988	Joe Williams
1991	Milt Hinton
1994	George Shearing
1995	Clark Terry
1996	Harry "Sweets" Edison
1997	Marian McPartland
1998	Bob Wilber
1999	Bob Rosengarden
2000	Kenny Davern
2001	Ralph Sutton
2002	Dick Hyman
2003	Bucky Pizzarelli
2004	Joe Wilder

Interviews by Category

The following list represents the individuals interviewed on videotape on behalf of the Fillius Jazz Archive at Hamilton College. They are listed here by their primary instrument or area of expertise.

Arrangers
Michael Abene
Manny Albam
Ray Conniff
Skitch Henderson
Dave Rivello
Maria Schneider

Banjo
Donn Andre
Béla Fleck

Bass
Keter Betts
Walter Booker
Ray Brown
Ron Carter
Bob Cranshaw
Bill Crow
Ray Drummond
Phil Flanigan
David Finck
Steve Gilmore
Henry Grimes
Bob Haggart
John Heard
Milt Hinton
Chubby Jackson
Kristen Korb
John Lamb
Jay Leonhart
Jack Lesberg
Jimmy Lewis
Bob Magnusson
Earl May
Christian McBride
Michael Moore
Nicki Parrott
Mitchell Player
Rufus Reid
Larry Ridley
Genevieve Rose
Hide Tanaka
Frank Tate
Buster Williams

Clarinet

Evan Christopher
Kenny Davern
Buddy DeFranco
Bobby Gordon
Eiji Kitamura
Abe Most
Joe Muranyi
Ken Peplowski
Allen Vache
Sol Yaged

Drums

Rashied Ali
Don Alias

Jazz Tales from Jazz Legends

Carl Allen
Eddie Alley
Joe Ascione
Louie Bellson
Frank Capp
Greg Caputo
Terri Lyne Carrington
Jimmy Cobb
Danny D'Imperio
Panama Francis
Chico Hamilton
Jake Hanna
Winard Harper
Louis Hayes
Ralph Humphrey
Sonny Igoe
Duffy Jackson
Vince Lateano
Eddie Locke
Sherrie Maricle
Eddie Marshall
Roy McCurdy
Butch Miles
Adam Nussbaum
Bernard Purdie
Alvin Queen
Mickey Roker
Bob Rosengarden
Ed Shaughnessy
Dick Sherman
Hal Smith
Earl Watkins
Jackie Williams
Jimmy Wormworth

Filmmakers

Jean Bach
Carol Bash
Burrill Crohn
Don Wolff

Flute

Holly Hofmann
Kent Jordan
Sam Most
Dave Valentin

Guitar

John Abercrombie
Howard Alden
Billy Bauer
Gene Bertoncini
Carmen Caramanica
James Chirillo
Cal Collins
Herb Ellis
Marty Grosz
Henry Johnson
Lou Pallo
Bucky Pizzarelli
John Pizzarelli Jr.

Patrons

John Budd
Milt Fillius Jr.

Piano

Toshiko Akiyoshi
Steve Allen
Shelly Berg
Karl Berger
Warren Bernhardt
Joanne Brackeen
Dave Brubeck
Ray Bryant
John Bunch
Joe Bushkin
Bill Charlap
Jeannie Cheatham
Bill Dobbins

Interviews by Category

Dave Frishberg
Onaje Allan Gumbs
Herbie Hancock
Roland Hanna
Dick Hyman
Keith Ingham
Jon Jang
Jane Jarvis
Pete Jolly
Dick Katz
Roger Kellaway
Bob Kinkel
Roy Kral
Pete Levin
Harold Mabern
Junior Mance
Gap Mangione
Dave McKenna
Marian McPartland
Jay McShann
Rick Montalbano
Marty Napoleon
Oscar Peterson
George Shearing
Ray Sherman
Norman Simmons
Derek Smith
Paul Smith
Frank Strazzeri
Ralph Sutton
Billy Taylor
Al Tinney
Ross Tompkins
Johnny Varro
Dan Wall
Jon Weber
Gerald Wiggins
Mike Wofford
Richard Wyands
Denny Zeitlin

Producers

George Avakian
Mat Domber
Joel Dorn
Orrin Keepnews

Promoters

Jackie Harris
Phoebe Jacobs
Stanley Kay
John Levy
J. Leo Rayhill
Greg Thomas
George Wein

Saxophone

Eric Alexander
Harry Allen
Tom Baker
Jane Ira Bloom
Nick Brignola
Buddy Collette
Charles Davis
Jerry Dodgion
Frank Foster
Chico Freeman
Al Gallodoro
Jim Galloway
Scott Hamilton
Bob Hardaway
Jimmy Heath
Red Holloway
Bill Holman
Javon Jackson
Jerry Jerome
Plas Johnson
Bruce Johnstone
Kidd Jordan
Sam Kininger

Jazz Tales from Jazz Legends

Ralph LaLama
John LaPorta
Carmen Leggio
Charles McPherson
Don Menza
Bobby Militello
Billy Mitchell
James Moody
Lanny Morgan
David Murray
Tommy Newsom
Harold Ousley
Dave Pell
Houston Person
Flip Phillips
Vi Redd
Jerome Richardson
Scott Robinson
Ray Shiner
Gary Smulyan
Fred Staton
Lew Tabackin
Buddy Tate
Joe Temperly
Norris Turney
Benny Waters
Bobby Watson
Ernie Watts
Frank Wess
Bob Wilber
Steve Wilson
Phil Woods

Spouses

Mona Hinton (Mrs. Milt)
Ruth Lion (Mrs. Alfred)
Ruth Pizzarelli (Mrs. Bucky)
Jillean Williams (Mrs. Joe)

Trombone

Wayne Andre
Arthur Baron
Dan Barrett
Eddie Bert
Jimmy Cheatham
Buster Cooper
John Fedchock
Wycliffe Gordon
Urbie Green
Al Grey
Slide Hampton
Bob Havens
Bill Hughes
George Masso
Phil Mead
Grover Mitchell
Benny Powell
Alan Raph
Roswell Rudd
Bill Watrous
Spiegle Willcox

Trumpet

Nat Adderley
Bill Berry
John Best
Wendell Brunious
Conte Candoli
Pete Candoli
Doc Cheatham
Jim Cullum
Rusty Dedrick
Peter Ecklund
Harry "Sweets" Edison
Derrick Gardner
Bobby Johnson Jr.
Jon-Erik Kellso

Interviews by Category

Clyde Kerr Jr.
Joe Magnarelli
Joey Morant
Sam Noto
Jimmy Owens
Jack Palmer
Ed Polcer
Dave Robinson
Randy Sandke
Bob Schulz
Howie Shear
Jack Sheldon
Lew Soloff
Byron Stripling
Clark Terry
Warren Vache
Joe Wilder
Gerald Wilson
Snooky Young

Tuba

Vince Giordano
Bob Stewart

Vibraphone

Peter Appleyard
Terry Gibbs
Lionel Hampton

Violin

Michi Fuji
Claude "Fiddler" Williams

Vocal

Germaine Bazzle
Ruth Brisbane
Ruth Brown
Jackie Cain
Giacomo Gates
Jon Hendricks
Pug Horton
Etta Jones
Sheila Jordan
Rebecca Kilgore
Tom Lellis
Jane Monheit
Ann Rabson
Dianne Reeves
Annie Ross
Ingrid Sertso
Janis Siegel
Joe Williams
Nancy Wilson
Jimmy Witherspoon

Writers

Iola Brubeck
James Lincoln Collier
Helen Oakley Dance
Stanley Dance
Ira Gitler
Leslie Gourse
Nat Hentoff
Leslie Johnson
Chuck Mancuso
Howard Mandel
Dan Morgenstern
Albert Murray
Phil Schaap
Peter Vacher

Index

Entries in bold are excerpts from Fillius Jazz Archive interviews.

Abene, Mike, **69-70**
Adderley, Cannonball, 22, 98, 144, 151, 153; "Cannonball Adderley Sextet Live at the Village Vanguard," 81-82
Adderley, Nat, 81, **151-53**
Aebersold, Jamey, 123, 135, 143
Albam, Manny, **77-78**
alcohol, 56-57, 66, 183
Ali, Rashied, **170-71**
Alias, Don, **159-60**
All-American Rhythm Section, 33
Allen, Steve, **164, 176-77**
"Alright, OK, You Win," 18
Anderson, Marian, 23, 181
"Anyone Can Improvise," 123, 143
"April in Paris," 39
Arbors Records, 133
Armstrong, Louis (Satchmo), 9, 23, 117, 137, 170, 181
arrangements, 68-86, 100; arrangers' tools, 85; less is more, 73; sweetening, 74, 78, 193; use of computers, 82-83; work for hire, 74. *See also* charts
Atlantic Records, 100
Bach, Jean, 10, **115-16**
barber shop quartet, 164
Barnes, George, 146
Barrett, Dan, **133-34**
Basie, William (Count), 31-42, 54, 64, 70-73, 74, 77, 80, 101, 151, 153, 154, 157, 181; "Count Basie Swings, Joe Williams Sings," 16, 157; bandstand communication, 35; Basie ending, 72; choosing repertoire, 37; dynamics, 35; as a leader, 38-42; New Testament band, 36; Orchestra 10, 15, 17, 28, 70-73, 88, 123; relationship to Joe Williams, 17, 22; "Sing a Song of Basie," 151, 157, 158; small group, 18, 35
Bass Line, 122
Bates, Peg Leg, 30
"Battle Royal," 39
Beatles, The, 79, 145
bebop, 34, 54, 76, 136, 143, 170, 171
Bellson, Louis, 10, 26, **27-28, 120-21**
Berger, Karl, **171-73**
Bert, Eddie, 10, **50-51, 55-56**
Betts, Keter, 94, **144-45**
"Beyond Category," 134
Big Band Era. *See* Swing Era
Big Show of 1951, 30, 120
Bird. *See* Parker, Charlie
Blanton, Jimmy, 25
Blood, Sweat & Tears, 78
Bloom, Jane Ira, **165**
bluegrass, 162
blue notes, 79, 128, 191
blues, 17, 54, 127, 128, 181
"Blues Backstage," 37
"Blues in Hoss' Flat," 37
"Blues Roar," 70
bop. *See* bebop
Borge, Victor, 139
Brass Rail (Chicago), 29, 35
break, 112, 132, 191
Brecker, Michael, 110
bridge, 17, 80, 84, 175, 191
Brookmeyer, Bob, 78, 82, 83, 84, 109
Brown, Lawrence, 28
Brown, Les, 49-50
Brown, Ruth, 10, 103, **119-20**
Brown, Walter, 59

Index

Brubeck, Dave, 19, 144, **156-57**
Brubeck, Iola, 10, **18-19**, 156-57
Brunious, Wendell, 134
Burns, Ralph, 109
"Bye Bye Blues," 145
Byers, Billy, 78
Calloway, Cab, 117, 118, 139, 145
Candoli, Conte, **51-52**
"Caravan," 28, 178
Carney, Harry, 27, 28, 121
Carson, Johnny, 51-52, 91, 105
challenging gigs, 168-70; pleasing the patrons, 168-70
"Chances Are," 104
changes, 17, 131-32, 137, 140, 191
Charlap, Bill, 10, 128, **129**, 132
Charles, Ray, 109
charts, 67, 73, 79, 191
Cheatham, Doc, **96-97**
"Cherokee," 168
"Chicken a la Swing," 147
chorus, 48, 81, 130, 141, 191
Christian, Charlie, 122
Civil Rights Era, 35
Clayton, Buck, 33
Club DeLisa (Chicago), 19
Cohen, Porky, 118
Cohn, Al, 82, 109
Cohn, Sonny, 40
Coker, Henry, 41, 70
Cole, Nat King, 120
Colomby, Bobby, 80
"colored people's time," 101-02
Coltrane, John, 131, 169, 173, 174
"Concerto to End All Concertos," 51
Connick, Harry, 74
Conniff, Ray, **75-77**; "'S' Wonderful," 77; "'S' Marvelous," 77; "'S' Awful Nice," 77
contractors, 103
Cooper, Al, 79
Copani, Mark, 124
Cranshaw, Bob, 21
Creative Music Workshop, 171
Crohn, Burrill, 15, 16

Culley, Wendell, 62, 70
cutting contest, 167, 191; "Cherokee," 168
Dance, Helen, 10, 121
dancing, 37, 51, 55, 59-60, 64, 80, 162-63, 170
Davern, Kenny, **62-64**, 89, 93, 94, **148**
Davis, Charles, **169-70**
Davis, Miles, 139, 168
DeFranco, Buddy, 35
democracy in jazz, 123-24, 180
DeNicola, Tony, 94
Depression Era, 150-51
Dick Cavett Show, 104, 109
divine inspiration, 158
Dodgion, Jerry, **67**
"Don't Go to Strangers," 97, 98
Dorn, Joel, 10, **21, 99-100**
Dorsey, Tommy, 19, 47, 72, 117
Down Beat, 55, 84
drugs, 56-57
dues, 66
dynamics, 35, 48, 72, 171, 172
Eckstine, Billy, 60-61
Edison, Harry (Sweets), 10, 19, **32-33**, 72
eighth notes, 162; swing, 162
Eldridge, Roy, 117, 177-79; competitive spirit, 178
Ellington, Edward (Duke), 10, 23, 24-31, 34, 36, 42, 54, 64, 70, 73, 96, 115, 118, 120, 127, 153, 156, 179, 181; collaboration with Billy Strayhorn, 27-28; hiring sidemen, 24-26; "seagulling," 115; and superstitions, 27
Ellington, Mercer, 26
Esquire, 115
Evans, Bill, 98, 99
Evans, Gil, 82
"Every Day I Have the Blues," 15, 16, 18
"Far East Suite," 26
"Farmer's Market," 158

Jazz Tales from Jazz Legends

Feather, Leonard, 167
"Feel the Spirit," 23
Ferguson, Maynard, 64, 69, 70
Fillius Jazz Archive, 9, 12-13, 15, 21, 24, 31, 55, 88-95, 127, 162
Fillius, Milt, Jr., 11-12, **19**, 21, 93
Fillius, Nikki, 94
"First Time Ever I Saw Your Face," 109
"First Time: The Count Meets the Duke," 39
Flack, Roberta, 109
Flanagan, Ralph, 62
Fleck, Béla, **174-76**
"Fly Me to the Moon," 70-73
Forrest, Jimmy, 41
Foster, Frank, 10, 22, **36-38**, 70, 71, 74, 75, 82, 101, **123-24**
4-beat, 34, 193
Fowlkes, Charlie, 38, 41
Francis, David (Panama), **105-06**
free jazz, 135-36, 170-74; intent of performer, 171-74; precision in, 172; randomness, 172; rules, 172
Fuller, Curtis, 41
Gardner, Derrick, **74-75**
"Gemini," 81
"Georgia on My Mind," 109
Getz, Stan, 49, 110
"ghosting," 56
Gillespie, John (Dizzy), 41, 76, 131, 135, 139, 168, 178
Giordano, Vince, **168-69**
Gleason, Jackie, 122
"God's Love Made Visible," 157
Goodman, Benny, 9, 10, 35, 42-46, 48, 55, 91, 116, 121-22, 153, 155, 156, 176, 181; and integration, 121-22, 181; the ray 45; and song titles, 176
Grammy awards, 80, 84, 109, 110
Gray, Wardell, 35, 158-59
Great Day in Harlem, A, (film) 115; (photo) 177
Green, Freddie, 30, 31, 33, 34, 35, 72

Grey, Al, 10, **41-42**, 70
Grimes, Henry, **170**
Guess Who, The, 78
Haggart, Bob, 104
Hair, 62
Hall, Al, 145
Halligan, Dick, 79
Hamilton College, 11-13, 15, 64, 88, 90, 92-95, 123; Fallcoming jazz, 12; Fillius Events Barn 12; honorary degrees in jazz, 11-12, 194
Hamilton, Jimmy, 29
Hampton, Lionel, 10, 35, **121**, 122, 159, 181
Hampton, Slide, 167
"Harlem Lullaby," 149
Harper, Winard, **132-33**
Harris, Stefon, 142, 143
"Havin' a Good Time," 21
Hawkins, Coleman, 177
head arrangements, 32, 192
Hear Me Talkin' To Ya: The Story of Jazz as Told by the Men Who Made It, 9
Heath, Jimmy, 81
Hefti, Neal, 31
Henderson, Skitch, 51, 91
Hendricks, Jon, 121, **122**, **124-25**, **150-51**, **157-58**
Hentoff, Nat, 9, 21
Herman, Woody, 35, 56, 64, 73, 116, 153, 154
Hinton, Milt, 11-12, 100, 111, 117, 122, 144-45
Hinton, Mona, **117-118**
Hodges, Johnny, 25, 28
Hofmann, Holly, **167-68**
Holman, Bill, **73**, **74**, 82, 83
"Honeysuckle Rose," 146
hotels. *See* travel
Howard, Bart, 70
"How Much is That Doggie in the Window," 108
Hubbard, Elbert, 23
Hughes, Bill, 10, **18**

Index

"Hummin'," 151-52
Husing, Ted, 148
Hyena Records, 21
Hyland, Brian, 109
Hyman, Dick, 10, **68-69**, **100**, **103-04**; whistling, 104
Igoe, Sonny, **42-46**, 54, **56-57**, 59, **116-17**
Igoe, Tommy, 57
"I Got Rhythm," 47, 48, 191
improvisation, 48, 100, 126-143, 150, 168, 171, 172, 174; comparison to language, 128-30, 132; "get off," 127-28, 136; intuition, 131; phrasing, 129; playing by ear, 68, 127-28, 140, 168; as problem solving, 143; psychology of, 138-39; structure, 126, 136; tension and release, 141-42; thought process, 132-33, 134, 136-37; transitioning, 132-33; wrong notes, 131, 135, 139-143
Ingham, Keith, **179**
inside/outside, 135-36, 170, 173, 174, 192
inspiration. *See* motivation
"In the Mood," 54
Institute of Jazz Studies at Rutgers, 9
"Intermission Riff," 50
International Association of Jazz Educators, 181, 182
"Itsy, Bitsy, Teeny, Weeny, Yellow Polka Dot Bikini," 109
Jacksons, The, 107
James, Harry, 76
jam session, 19, 42, 135, 191
Japan, jazz in, 155
jazz education, 54, 124, 126-27, 128, 130, 131, 133, 135, 143, 153, 161, 181
"Jazz Life," 134
Jazzmen, 9
jazz parties, 12, 112
Jerome, Jerry, 10, **46-48**
Joel, Billy, 110, 146

Johnson, Gus, 35
Johnson, Plas, 107, **108**
Jones, Etta, 97
Jones, Jo, 31, 33, 34, 177, 178
Jones, Quincy, 70-72, 153
Jones, Thad, 22, 70
Jordan, Kidd, **173-74**; Hurricane Katrina, 173; "Palm of Soul," 173
Joseph Drown Foundation, 12
"Jumpin' at the Woodside," 33
"Just Friends," 168
"Just the Way You Are," 110
Kansas City, 31
Kay, Stanley, **153-54**
Keepnews, Orrin, 10, **81-82**, **98-99**
Kenton, Stan, 50-51, 73, 116, 181
King manuscript paper, 82
Kingdom of Swing, The, 9
King of Swing, 42
Kitamura, Eiji, **155-56**
Krupa, Gene, 35, 45, 117, 153, 181
"L'il Darlin'," 32
LaLama, Ralph, **141-42**
Lamb, John, 10, **24-26**
Lambert, Hendricks & Ross, 124, 158
Lateef, Yusef, 81
Lee, Peggy, 73
Levy, John, 16, 20, **22**
Lewis, Ed, 33
Lewis, Jimmy, 10, **35**, **60-62**
Lipsius, Fred, 79-81
Lloyds of London, 78
Locke, Eddie, **177-79**
Lunceford, Jimmy, 34, 151, 153
Mance, Junior, 21, **149**
Mancini, Henry, 108
Manne, Shelly, 43, 50, 51, 116
Maricle, Sherrie, **154-55**
Mathis, Johnny, 104
McCann, Les, 100
McPartland, Jimmy, 167
McPartland, Marian, 10, 91, **127**, **166-67**
McPherson, Charles, **129-30**

Jazz Tales from Jazz Legends

McRae, Carmen, 77
McShann, Jay, 10, **59-60**
melting pot society, 123, 179
"Memphis Blues," 148
mentors, 22, 32-33, 41-42, 177-79, 182
Metronome, 47
Miles, Butch, 10, **40-41**
Miller, Glenn, 46-48, 54, 68, 117, 144; *The Glenn Miller Story*, 46, 68
Millinder, Lucky, 118
Mitchell, Billy, **67**
Mitchell, Grover, 15, 22, **28-29**, 35, **36**
modes, 134, 137, 172, 192
Monk, Thelonious, 98
Monroe, Vaughan, 57, 58
Monterey Jazz Festival, 28
"Moody's Mood for Love," 159
Moore, Michael, 93
Morgan, Joe, 29
Morgan, Lanny, 64, **65-66**
Morgenstern, Dan, 9-10
"Moritat," 104
Morrison, Peck, 25
Moten, Benny, 32
motivation, 144-161; financial considerations, 159, 161; passion as, 159-61
Mr. Edd, 55, 56
Mulligan, Gerry, 77
Murrell, Chris, 16
Musicians Union, 26, 98, 99, 110; pay scale, 26, 99, 110
National Endowment for the Arts, 9
Negro spirituals, 23, 181
networks and musicians, 36; ABC, 36; Black Entertainment Network, 115; CBS, 36; NBC, 36, 51, 104, 105; segregation in hiring, 36
Neve, The (San Francisco), 28
New Grove Dictionary of Jazz, 162
Newman, Joe, 41, 70
Newsom, Tommy, **52-53**
New York Times, 181

Oliver, King, 9
"One O'clock Jump," 32, 39
Original Dixieland Jazz Band, 96
Ousley, Harold, **182-83**
"Out the Window," 32
overdubbing, 97, 192
Page, Patti, 108
Page, Walter (Big 'Un), 31, 33, 34
Parker, Charlie (Bird), 59, 76, 121, 170
Parrott, Nicki, 165, **166**
Pastor, Tony, 49
Patterson and Jackson, 30, 120
Paul, Gene, 21
Payne, Sonny, 40, 41, 71, 72
Pell, Dave, **49-50**
Peplowski, Ken, **131-32**
Peterson, Oscar, 12
"Pink Panther," 108
Pizzarelli, Bucky, **57-59**, 91, 94, **108-10**, 145
Pizzarelli, John, 59, **145-48**
Pizzarelli, Ruth, 109, **110**
Plater, Bobby, 41
Portrait in Song, A, 15, 16
Powell, Benny, 10, **38-40**, **181-82**
Prestige Records, 97, 98, 159
Preston, Billy, 108
"Primrose Lane," 106
Procope, Russell, 28, 121
race relations, 113-125, 181-82; segregated venues, 116, 118-19
radio, 148, 149, 153, 156
Rainey, Ma, 96
Ramone, Phil, 110
"Real Ambassadors, The," 18
Reinhardt, Django, 146
relief band, 49
revealed writing, 158
"Rhapsody in Blue," 177
rhythm & blues, 106, 108, 119, 169
rhythm section, 13, 69, 80, 134, 192
rhythm *See* time
Rich, Buddy, 52, 64, 153-54; "Traps the Drum Wonder," 153
Richardson, Jerome, 19, 97, 98, 99;

Index

"Roamin' with Richardson," 97
Riddle, Nelson, 78
riff, 32, 192
Rivello, Dave, **82-84**
Roach, Max, 132
rock & roll, 53, 64, 66, 78, 100, 105, 106-07, 110, 163; triplets, 106-07
Roker, Mickey, 21
Rollins, Sonny, 110
Rose, Genevieve, 124
Rosengarden, Bob, 91, 93, 100, **104-05**, 109, 111
Ross, Annie, 158, **159**
Royal, Marshall, 38, 42
royalties, 98
Rushing, Jimmy, 17
Russell, Pee Wee, 148
Sanders, Pharaoh, 174
Sandke, Randy, 92, **137-38**
Satchmo. *See*, Armstrong, Louis
scat singing, 17, 151
Schneider, Maria, 10, 82, 83, **84-85**
Sebesky, Don, 70, 78
segregation. *See* race relations
"Sentimental Journey," 156
Severinsen, Doc, 51-53, 91, 105, 108
Shapiro, Nat, 9
Shaughnessy, Ed, 52, **53**, **162-63**
Shaw, Artie, 75-76
Shear, Howie, **111-112**
Shearing, George, 12
Sherman, Ray, **106**
"Shiny Stockings," 37, 38
Shoobe, Lou, 36
Short, Bobby, 116
sidemen, 18, 23, 24-54, 55, 69; as arrangers, 69; switching bands, 29
Simmons, Norman, **19, 21**, **179-80**
Simon, George, 46
Sims, Zoot, 49
Sinatra, Frank, 19, 59, 70
singers. *See* vocalists
Singleton, Zutty, 116
"Sing Sing Sing," 54
"Sinister Minister," 175

16-bar blues, 136
Smith, Derek, 10, 93, 100, **101**, **111**
Smith, Paul, **106-07**
Smithsonian Institute, 9
Smithsonian Jazz Masterworks Orchestra, 74
Smulyan, Gary, 139, **140-41**
Snow, Phoebe, 110
Soloff, Lew, **79**, 80, 123
song form, 17
"Spinning Wheel," 79-80
Stamm, Marvin 78
"Stardust," 152
"Stompin' at the Savoy," 26
straw boss, 38, 42, 192
Strayhorn, Billy, 26-28, 121
Streisand, Barbra, 107
"String of Pearls," 48
studio work, 36, 96-112, 122; segregation in, 36, 122; technology, 111-12
"Sunset Road," 174
Swamp Women, 74
Swing Era, 42, 46, 54, 55, 78, 100, 111, 126
Swing that Music, 9
swing, 33, 34, 162-165, 179; harmonic component, 164-65; infectious nature of, 162-63; 2-beat versus 4-beat, 33
"Swinging the Blues," 32
tag, 72, 193
"Take the A Train," 27, 39, 54, 126
Tatum, Art, 116-7
"Teach Me Tonight," 18
tempo. *See* time
Temptations, The, 108
Terry, Clark, 10, 12, **29-31**, **31-32**, 35, 36, 91, **113-15**, 121, **127-128** 134; leaving Basie for Ellington, 29-31
32-bar song form, 71, 136
"This Little Light of Mine," 23
Thomas, David Clayton, 79, 80
time, 31, 32, 35, 55, 71, 76-77, 123,

205

Jazz Tales from Jazz Legends

136, 168, 171
titles for instrumental songs, 174-77; connection for the listener, 175; importance of, 175-76; meaning of, 176
Tompkins, Ross, **52-53**
Tonight Show band, 51-53, 91, 104, 107
Torme, Mel, 164
Toscannini, Arturo, 105
travel, 55-67, 113, 115, 116-17, 118, 120; hotels, 115, 117, 118, 120; Pullman cars, 118
12-bar blues, 16
2-beat, 34, 193
"Twisted," 158-59
"Undecided," 48
Vaughn, Sarah, 30, 107, 120
vocalese, 150-51, 158, 193
vocalists, 55, 62, 73, 97; as musicians, 17
voicings, 27, 77, 82, 164-65, 193
walking bass, 34, 193
walking the bar, 169-70, 193
Wall Street Journal, 21, 161
Waller, Fats, 181
Waters, Ethel, 23
Watrous, Bill, 78, **134-36**
Watson, Bobby, **158**
Watts, Ernie, **107-08**
"We'll Understand it Better By and By," 23
Webb, Chick, 153
Weber, Jon, **142-43**
Webster, Ben, 21
Wess, Frank, 10, 38, 41, 72, 92, 93, 101
"White Christmas," 103
White, Barry, 108
Wilder, Joe, 10, 93, **101-03**, **118-19**, **132**, 134
Wiley, Lee, 116
Wilkins, Ernie, 16
Williams, Claude (Fiddler), 31, 124
Williams, Cootie, 26
Williams, Jillean, **19**, 21, 71, 89

Williams, Joe, 9-13, 15-23, **29-31**, **32**, 70, 88, 89, **113-14**; comparison to Jimmy Rushing, **17**; sharing the mic, **16**; solo career, 19; tenure with Basie, 17, 19
Williams, John, 10, **22**
Wilson, Gerald, **33-34**
Wilson, Nancy, 22
Wilson, Teddy, 35, 121, 181
women in jazz, 165-69; discriminatory issues in hiring, 165-66
"Wonderful Wonderful," 104
Wooding, Sam, 96
Woods, Michael, **41**, 127
Woods, Phil, **66-67**, **110-11**, **160-61**
World War II, 12, 54, 156
Wright, Ray, 78
Wyands, Richard, 10, **97-98**, 107
"Yard Dog Mazurka," 151
"You Stepped Out of a Dream," 70
Young, Lester, 33, 35
Young, Snooky, 10, **33-34**, 42, 52, 70, 91
Zappa, Frank, 142
Zawinul, Joe, 81
Zeitlin, Denny, 10, **138-39**

Acknowledgements

Hamilton College extends its gratitude to all the individuals who contributed to the Fillius Jazz Archive by granting interviews and generously sharing memories and stories.

There are always a number of significant behind-the-scenes players who contribute to the success of a scholarly or creative endeavor. Christian Goodwille is the director of Special Collections at Hamilton College and it was his suggestion to mark the Archive's twentieth anniversary with the writing of this book. Randy and Mary Anne Ericson skillfully edited the manuscript and assembled the final product. Marianita Peaslee employed her always exquisite vision and skill in the creation of the cover and preparation of the photographs. Jim Britell studied early book drafts and was an excellent sounding board.

A special thank you and acknowledgement goes to Romy Britell, my personal transcriptionist, editor, organizer, collaborator, and wife. She has been an integral part of this project from the start, painstakingly transcribing the interviews and organizing them in a fashion that enabled me to locate and cite the smallest details from over three hundred sessions, as if they were committed to my memory. She has taken my too-frequent ramblings about these artists and molded them into a cogent text, while managing to maintain my enthusiasm that came from conversing with childhood heroes.

A number of people in the Hamilton community have contributed to the success of the Fillius Jazz Archive since its inception in 1995, and they have my gratitude. Tim Hicks, of our Audio-Visual Department, deserves accolades for capturing the videos and shepherding nine road cases worth of film and audio gear during our many interview trips across the country. Gene Tobin, who was president of the college during the formation of the Archive, was a strong supporter. David Smallen, Peter MacDonald, Lisa McFall, and Gisella Stalloch of Library and Information Technology Services, have been instrumental in ushering the Archive resource into the twenty-first century. The staff from Communications & Development, including Janie Bassett, Ben Madonia, and Dean Abelon, provided invaluable guidance over the years. From the Music Department, Sam Pellman, Michael Woods, and Rob Hopkins lent assistance during the initial Archive start-up. Jillean Williams entrusted the legacy of Joe Williams to Hamilton, and enriched the Archive with donations of

Jazz Tales from Jazz Legends

memorabilia from his career.

The Archive would not exist without Milt and Nikki Fillius and the funding of the Joseph Drown Foundation of Los Angeles. Milt often said to me, only partly in jest, "I gave you the job I wanted." He had the highest regard for his favorite musicians and he would not allow anyone to be involved in this endeavor who did not genuinely share that respect and passion. Milt and his wife Nikki enriched my life and that of my family, and enabled the tales of these jazz legends to live on.

About the author:

Monk Rowe has been an instructor of saxophone at Hamilton College and the Joe Williams Director of the Fillius Jazz Archive since 1995. In this role, he has personally conducted videotaped interviews with over three hundred jazz personalities across the country. Monk is an active pianist and saxophonist and has composed and arranged music for numerous ensembles, including the Fredonia Alumni Jazz Ensemble and the Utica Symphony. He is active in the field of aesthetic education and frequently conducts interactive workshops on blues and improvised music.

Monk Rowe. Photo by Nancy L. Ford.

Information about the Fillius Jazz Archive may be accessed at http://www.hamilton.edu/jazzarchive

Interview transcripts and audio as well as the Milt Fillius photography collection may be accessed at http://elib.hamilton.edu/jazz-archive